Educating Students With Autism Spectrum Disorders

Sara Miller McCune founded SAGE Publishing in 1965 to support the dissemination of usable knowledge and educate a global community. SAGE publishes more than 1000 journals and over 800 new books each year, spanning a wide range of subject areas. Our growing selection of library products includes archives, data, case studies and video. SAGE remains majority owned by our founder and after her lifetime will become owned by a charitable trust that secures the company's continued independence.

Los Angeles | London | New Delhi | Singapore | Washington DC | Melbourne

Educating Students With Autism Spectrum Disorders

Partnering With Families for Positive Outcomes

Robin LaBarbera
Biola University

Los Angeles | London | New Delhi
Singapore | Washington DC | Melbourne

FOR INFORMATION:

SAGE Publications, Inc.
2455 Teller Road
Thousand Oaks, California 91320
E-mail: order@sagepub.com

SAGE Publications Ltd.
1 Oliver's Yard
55 City Road
London EC1Y 1SP
United Kingdom

SAGE Publications India Pvt. Ltd.
B 1/I 1 Mohan Cooperative Industrial Area
Mathura Road, New Delhi 110 044
India

SAGE Publications Asia-Pacific Pte. Ltd.
3 Church Street
#10-04 Samsung Hub
Singapore 049483

Acquisitions Editor : Karen Omer
Editorial Assistant: Sarah Dillard
Content Development Editor: Jennifer Jovin
Production Editor: Kimaya Khashnobish
Copy Editor: Jared Leighton
Typesetter: C&M Digitals (P) Ltd.
Proofreader: Susan Shon
Indexer: Jeanne R. Busemeyer
Cover Designer: Janet Kiesel
Marketing Manager: Jillian Oelsen

Copyright © 2019 by SAGE Publications, Inc.

Printed in the United States of America

Library of Congress Cataloging-in-Publication Data

Names: LaBarbera, Robin, author.

Title: Educating students with autism spectrum disorders: partnering with families for positive outcomes / Robin LaBarbera, Biola University.

Description: Thousand Oaks, California: SAGE Publications, Inc., [2019] | Includes bibliographical references and index.

Identifiers: LCCN 2017025532 | ISBN 9781506338866 (pbk. : acid-free paper)

Subjects: LCSH: Autistic children—Education—Case studies. | Special education teachers—Training of—Case studies. | Special education—Parent participation—Case studies.

Classification: LCC LC4717 .L33 2018 | DDC 371.94—dc23
LC record available at https://lccn.loc.gov/2017025532

This book is printed on acid-free paper.

18 19 20 21 22 10 9 8 7 6 5 4 3 2 1

Contents

Preface

This is a book designed to give voice to the parent perspective in educating students with autism spectrum disorders. There are a number of textbooks written for teachers that provide an understanding of educating students with ASD, but few offer strategies for partnering with parents in the planning and implementation of interventions that support a child's development through the day, even after the school day has ended. This book will be invaluable for preservice and inservice teachers who seek a deeper understanding of autism and, beyond that, how to extend student learning from the classroom to the natural environment. This book is written to fill the void left by much of the educational literature currently on the market.

This book gives a voice to families, based on recent quantitative and qualitative research conducted by the author. Such a focus on collaborating with the rapidly growing group of children with ASD and their families cannot be found among the books currently available. Unlike anything currently on the market, *Educating Students With Autism Spectrum Disorders: Partnering With Families for Positive Outcomes* brings together the most relevant features of existing literature on autism and collaboration, and it enhances the discussion to form a cohesive text that also gives voice to parents. As we seek ways to best serve students and their families, we must seek to understand the family's perspective of raising a child with ASD.

Overall, the focus of *Educating Students With Autism Spectrum Disorders: Partnering With Families for Positive Outcomes* is on practical strategies for educating children with autism spectrum disorders in the classroom, with additional features describing how to partner with families in the implementation of many of the strategies discussed in the text. A partnership where teachers and parents work toward shared goals is important, where both parties can work together to plan learning activities that can occur at school and at home to support a child's development throughout the day.

A quote from Karl Menninger provides the inspiration for the text. Menninger said, "Listening is a magnetic and strange thing, a creative force. The friends who listen to us are the ones we move toward. When we are listened to, it creates us, makes us unfold and expand." This text was created with the belief that when educators and parents listen to one another, valuing their experiences and perspectives, we are better able to facilitate greater student academic and behavioral outcomes through our collaborative efforts.

ORGANIZATION OF THE TEXT

The book is organized around professional teaching standards for preservice and inservice special educators. Current and future teachers who work with students with ASD in special or general-education environments will find the progression of information useful for addressing their students' unique strengths and needs.

First, we provide an overview of ASD that discusses the major criteria for an ASD diagnosis, common features of ASD, and the importance of working with families to educate students with ASD. Chapter 2 details what families who have children with ASD want most from a school–family partnership, and Chapter 3 addresses potential barriers to parent–teacher collaboration and how to facilitate positive interactions and strengthen those relationships. Chapter 4 describes the components of complete assessment and evaluation of students with ASD and how to make educationally relevant instructional decisions for students that help them reach their full potential. The strategies provided in the remaining chapters provide sufficient detail for educators to support appropriate decision-making to promote behavioral and academic changes from early childhood through the transition to adulthood for individuals with ASD. Overall, the text provides a comprehensive review of the major issues encountered in educating students with ASD, with particular emphasis on connecting these concepts to partnering with families for positive outcomes.

FEATURES OF THE TEXT

Strategies for partnering with families. In every chapter, readers will find a section devoted to partnering with families, a key feature of this text. Collaborating with the family members of your students is one of your primary responsibilities as a special educator. Legally, parents are considered a part of the IEP team and concerns of the parent must be considered in IEP decision-making. Beyond the legal requirements, research advocates that when parents operate as partners in the special education process, there are benefits to students' academic and social progress. This book provides practical ways that educators can partner with families to extend learning beyond the school day into home and community life.

Case studies. Each chapter will feature a case study, developed from interviews with parents and educators related to the collaborative efforts of the school. The unique feature of this book provides parent narratives about what they want educators to know about ASD. Each chapter will also have reflection questions related to the case study, called "What Would You Do?" This case study and reflection format is designed to help readers apply their understanding of the chapter's contents to a situation they may encounter in their professional settings.

"Family Voices" and "Theory Into Practice" boxes. Each chapter includes several "Family Voices" boxes, presenting ideas from the perspective of parents raising children with autism about the particular content of the chapter. Included in each chapter is also a series of "T.I.P.s (Theory Into Practice)," promoting self-reflection and an opportunity to apply chapter knowledge to real-world applications. Each chapter ends with relevant chapter reflection questions to generate lively conversations in university teacher preparation courses or as prompts for online discussion forums.

Inclusion strategies. In many states, the state agencies that govern teacher preparation and the standards for the teaching profession are moving toward greater inclusion. Because of this, each chapter also includes a section devoted to teachers in inclusive environments so that they can carry out many of the strategies detailed in the chapter. The goal is that no matter where students with ASD are being served, whether in special or general-education classrooms, teachers are armed with strategies to meet their needs and help them reach their fullest potential.

INSTRUCTOR RESOURCES

It's easy to log on to SAGE's password-protected Instructor Teaching Site at study.sagepub.com/labarbera for complete and protected access to all text-specific Instructor Resources for *Educating Students with Autism Spectrum Disorders: Partnering with Families for Positive Outcomes*. Simply provide your institutional information for verification and within 72 hours you'll be able to use your login information for any SAGE title!

Password-protected Instructor Resources include the following:

- A Microsoft® Word test bank containing multiple choice, true/false, short answer, and essay questions for each chapter. The test bank provides you with a diverse range of pre-written options as well as the opportunity for editing any question and/or inserting your own personalized questions to assess students' progress and understanding.

- Editable, chapter-specific Microsoft® PowerPoint® slides that offer you complete flexibility in easily creating a multimedia presentation for your course.

- EXCLUSIVE! Access to certain full-text SAGE journal articles that have been carefully selected for each chapter. Each article supports and expands on the concepts presented in the chapter. Combine cutting-edge academic journal scholarship with the topics in your course for a robust classroom experience.

- Video and multimedia links that appeal to students with different learning styles.

About the Author

Dr. Robin LaBarbera is a professor at Biola University's School of Education, where she is the director of the special education credential program, which she helped found. She has published numerous articles in the field of special education, she coauthored a curriculum for students' English language development, and she has presented at conferences and teacher development workshops around the world, in countries such as Papua New Guinea, Uganda, South Africa, Vietnam, Lebanon, and India.

Dr. LaBarbera serves on several boards of directors for school programs for students with learning differences, for charter schools, and for a foundation that helps strengthen urban ministry organizations. She is a reviewer for the California Commission on Teacher Credentialing, and she is a peer reviewer for several academic journals and a book publisher.

Her proudest role is that of an advocate for individuals with learning differences and their families. She feels fortunate to have met these families and the professionals in the schools worldwide who strive to meet the unique needs of their students.

Acknowledgments

I would like to thank the individuals who helped in the development of this book. First, I thank my husband, Carl LaBarbera, for journeying with me as we climbed Mt. Kilimanjaro, won a dance competition in Dancing for Our Stars, and traveled to India to present at a medical conference while this text was being conceptualized and written and, most of all, for never complaining while the laundry piled up and I neglected family meals. I am grateful for my dean at Biola University, Dr. June Hetzel, for allowing space in my leadership and teaching schedule for writing. I also wish to thank my extraordinary assistant, Kimberly Van Lant, who helped me compile the book's glossary, took the lead on many administrative projects, and never flinched when I "freaked out" in the face of impending deadlines.

A special thanks goes to the artists whose work is featured in the online content associated with this book. I had the privilege of being introduced to some amazing artists who showed me what it is like to enter the creative world of individuals with autism. The story behind each piece of artwork was a true inspiration, and they have forever changed me.

Finally, to the parents of children with autism who provided content for the "Family Voices" boxes in each chapter, you have my utmost gratitude for sharing your insights. Your voices will hopefully impact thousands of teachers to come, which will ultimately impact the lives of the students we serve. I am honored that you have opened your hearts to me.

I would like to also thank the numerous reviewers who have provided invaluable feedback in the development of this book.

Maria Linda Agnew, *Holy Family University*
Karen Arcangelo, *Keystone College*
Jonna L. Bobzien, *Old Dominion University*
Miriam C. Boesch, *University of North Texas*
Susan DeLuke, *The College of Saint Rose*
Nanette Edeiken-Cooperman, *Saint Joseph's University*
Heidi J. Graff, *George Mason University*
Jill C. Hamlin, *Averett University*
Victoria J. Hatch, *Kwantlen Polytechnic University*
Patricia R. Huskin, *Texas A & M University, Kingsville*
Ginger L. Kelso, *Stephen F. Austin State University*
S. Kay Kuder, *Rowan University*
Colleen Lelli, *Cabrini College*
Fan-Yu Lin, *Robert Morris University*
Robert J. Loyd, *Armstrong State University*
Jennifer McFarland-Whisman, *Marshall University*
MaryAnn Shaw, *Saint Francis University*
Carol Strax, *Dominican College*
Jerry Whitworth, *Texas Woman's University*

An Overview of Autism Spectrum Disorders

CASE STUDY

Mrs. Avery has a few students in her preschool classroom that she suspects are showing early signs of autism spectrum disorders (ASD). Generally, she looks for evidence that her students exhibit effective communication and sharing enjoyment, making social connections, and seeking social opportunity through play, and when she sees anything suspicious, she likes to refer the child for further evaluation.

One of Mrs. Avery's students, Dylan, demonstrates some concerning behaviors. One particular concern for Mrs. Avery is that she's noticed Dylan has some slight motor delays. For example, Dylan appears to have trouble throwing or catching a ball with accuracy at recess, he seems "clumsy" on the playground and in class, and he has an awkward pencil grip when working on class assignments. Dylan's caregiver reported that during his first six months of life, he vocalized and responded socially to others by smiling and cooing. Mrs. Avery has observed Dylan engaging his classmates in play, showing meaningful pretend play, sharing enjoyment by smiling at people, and interacting with others with ease. She also sees Dylan looking in response to bids to share attention; he appears to be socially engaged and uses eye gaze, vocalizations, and gestures to communicate. Dylan's parents have recently expressed concern to Mrs. Avery about his awkward physical movements.

Mrs. Avery has another student in her class, Erin, who has excellent language skills. She uses words in conversation that are at or above her age level, and all she wants to talk about is dogs. In class, she plays with a stuffed dog exclusively, or sometimes, she plays with plastic farm

LEARNER OBJECTIVES

After reading this chapter, the learner should be able to do the following:

- Discuss causal theories associated with autism spectrum disorders.

- Describe the major criteria necessary for an ASD diagnosis.

- Discuss common features associated with ASD but not necessarily required for a diagnosis.

- Explain the rationale for instructing students with ASD and discuss the least restrictive environment.

- Discuss the importance of working with families to educate students with ASD.

animals, especially the dog, and she likes to line them all up in a row. Erin does not engage with her peers during play, preferring to spend time alone with her toy animals. Erin seems to know everything there is to know about dogs—she can name different breeds and tell you how much to feed them, whether they are puppies or adults, and how often to walk them or let them sleep. When Erin does not get time to play with the stuffed dog or plastic animals, she gets upset, and she cries or screams. The teacher read in the file that Erin had poor eye contact during her 1-year well-baby visit with the pediatrician. Erin also seems to lag behind her classmates in penmanship, and she gets easily frustrated and sometimes has an "outburst" in response to the frustration. Mrs. Avery has also seen Erin flap her hands when she is excited or enjoys something such as when Mrs. Avery blows bubbles, and she has noticed that Erin does not respond to other adults' or children's bids to share attention.

Based on her understanding of the early signs of ASD, Mrs. Avery is considering referring one of her students for further testing.

....

INTRODUCTION

Students with autism spectrum disorders make up one of the largest populations of students receiving special education services in the United States (U.S. Department of Education, National Center for Education Statistics, 2013). ASD is one of the fastest growing childhood disorders in the United States and is one of the most commonly diagnosed disabilities in schools today (CDC, 2015). One in 68 children are identified with ASD, according to a 2010 study reported by the Centers for Disease Control (CDC, 2015). It is more common among boys (1 in 42) than in girls (1 in 189) (CDC, 2015). Newer government estimates indicate that about 1 in 45 children in the United States has an autism spectrum disorder. The report is based on parent interview data collected during the National Health Interview Survey for the years 2011 to 2014 (CDC, 2015).

Children diagnosed with ASD may display, in varying degrees, social communication difficulties and restricted, repetitive patterns of behavior, interests, or activities (American Psychiatric Association, 2013). A diagnosis of ASD, according to the APA, occurs when a child has a severe qualitative impairment in reciprocal social interaction and communication skills and a restricted range of activities and interests (APA, 2013). These key diagnostic criteria must be present for an individual to receive a diagnosis of ASD. ASD is a *spectrum*, which refers to the wide range of symptoms, skills, and levels of impairment that children with ASD have (National Institute of Mental Health, 2015). Some children are mildly impaired by their symptoms while others express more severe impairments.

What we understand about ASD continually progresses. Scientists are actively discovering potential causes, appropriate assessments, and relevant intervention strategies. The purpose of this chapter is to provide the reader with a basic understanding of ASD, given what we know currently. It is our intention to provide information to readers, whether new to the field or whether you've taught children with ASD for years, to assist you in meeting the needs of students with ASD in the best way possible. It is our hope that as your knowledge base increases, you will be better equipped to help children with ASD reach their full potential.

Family Voices 1.1

"Trying to describe Jack's autism to someone who doesn't know him is like trying to describe the bluest ocean to a person who doesn't see. It is deep and sparkling and brilliant and alive. It is slippery and quiet, but it can also be deafening. It likes to make waves. It's not something you can hold in the palm of your hand, and yet, all at once, it surrounds you. It can take your breath away."

Source: Author Carrie Cariello, in, "As a parent of a child with autism, this is what I want you to know about my family," in the Independent news, available at: http://www.independent.co.uk/voices/comment/as-a-parent-of-a-child-with-autism-this-is-what-i-want-you-to-know-about-my-family-10081619.html

---

POTENTIAL CAUSES OF AUTISM

Scientists have yet to determine the exact causes of ASD, but researchers suggest that both genetics and the environment may play a role. Researchers have identified some genes associated with ASD, and imaging studies have found differences in the developmental regions of the brain in some individuals with ASD. Scientists are learning that ASD could be the result of disruptions in brain growth very early in development. Environmental factors may also play a role, although scientists have identified no specific environmental cause. Initial beliefs that childhood vaccines are to blame for ASD have since been disproved by multiple studies showing no increased risk of ASD in children who received vaccines. Research is ongoing, in attempts to identify other potential environmental causes.

GENETIC INFLUENCES

There is some genetic component to autism, according to research, meaning it tends to run in families. If one sibling in a family has ASD, the other siblings have 35 times the normal risk of also developing the disorder (NIMH, 2015). Scientists are actively researching genetic factors and are starting to identify particular genes that may increase the risk for ASD. We also know that some people who receive an ASD diagnosis have no reported family history, which suggests that random gene mutations are likely to affect risk (NIMH, 2015).

Other lines of research provide evidence of genetic influences on autism. One group of researchers suggested that more than half of all cases of autism are traced to a gene-disabling mutation found in the child but neither parent (Iossifov et al., 2015). Iossifov and colleagues conducted DNA analysis of over 1,800 families affected by autism, and they identified a gene mutation that occurs in the mother's egg, the father's sperm, or in early embryo development to suggest that genetics provide meaningful answers to the question of genetic influence (Iossifov et al., 2015). Another group of researchers also found that autism symptoms share a strong genetic correlation, based on their analysis of data from 568 twin pairs with at least one affected by autism (Frazier et al., 2014).

ENVIRONMENTAL INFLUENCES

Genetic factors alone do not account for all instances of ASD. Toxins or other environmental factors may also be associated with ASD, and these things are being investigated. Environmental factors are factors outside the body that can affect health, such as the air we breathe, the water we drink, the foods we eat, or the medicines we take. The surroundings of the child while in the womb or the mother's health while pregnant are other environmental factors. Environmental factors that can increase the risk of ASD include the family history of medical conditions, the age of parents, exposure to environmental toxins, or complications during pregnancy or birth. It is most likely no single environmental factor is responsible for ASD (NIMH, 2015).

VACCINATION CONTROVERSY

A great deal of controversy surrounds the potential risk of vaccines. Health professionals recommend that children receive necessary vaccines early in life to protect against infectious diseases like measles (NIMH, 2015). Children receive many vaccines during the first two years of life, around the same time that ASD symptoms often become noticeable, making vaccines a likely culprit in parents' opinion. In fact, some years back, a study was published that suggested a direct link between the measles, mumps, and rubella (MMR) vaccine and ASD, confirming many long-held suspicions. Numerous studies have since disproved the link between vaccines and ASD.

Recently, in a study conducted with over 95,000 children and published in the prestigious *Journal of the American Medical Association*, researchers established that the MMR vaccine is most definitely not a contributor to ASD in children of any age (Jain et al., 2015). A very interesting component of their study (Jain et al., 2015) considered children who had an older sibling with an autism spectrum disorder. Because so many parents in the study held to the belief that vaccines caused their oldest child's ASD, they refused to vaccinate their younger children. Children who do not get the MMR vaccines are just as likely to receive an ASD diagnosis (Jain et al., 2015), again proving no link between vaccines and ASD diagnosis.

Bryan King (2015), professor of psychiatry at the University of Washington, made this remark in the *Pediatric News* in response to the Jain et al. study:

The findings of Jain et al., taken together with those of approximately a dozen other studies, clearly show that the age of onset of ASD does not differ between vaccinated and unvaccinated children, the severity or course of ASD does not differ between vaccinated and unvaccinated children, and now the risk of ASD recurrence in families does not differ between vaccinated and unvaccinated children. This and other studies allow us to move forward with a more focused and productive search for temporal and environmental factors that contribute to autism risk. (p. 21)

Numerous researchers have sought to determine whether a link between vaccines and autism exists, and since 2010, not one of those studies has confirmed such an association (NIMH, 2015). King (2015) concluded that the results of these studies "should allay families' concerns that the MMR vaccine may be harmful to their children" (p. 21).

T.I.P. – Theory Into Practice 1.1

VACCINATION CONTROVERSY: TAKE A STAND

1. Search the Internet for discussions that debate the link between vaccines and ASD.

2. Write a summary of your findings that provides evidence to support the belief that vaccines cause ASD.

3. Write an opposing argument that refutes those claims.

4. Provide a rationale for why you believe either side to be the correct position.

EARLY SIGNS OF AUTISM

Emerging research has identified behaviors during infancy that may signal a possible ASD diagnosis. For example, children who receive a later diagnosis of ASD may, during infancy, demonstrate early deficits in eye contact, responding to their name, social smile, joint attention, or tolerance of touch, according to Pineda, Melchior, Oberle, Inder, and Rogers (2015). Poor quality of physical movement can be evident as well. Some researchers have even explored social interactions in infants, such as cuddling, irritability, crying, gaze aversion, and response to human interaction (Pineda et al., 2015).

Patterns of development might also generate some concern for parents. Delayed development of communication abilities, such as the use of gestures and speech, may lead parents to suspect developmental differences. Delays in toilet training might be evident, or the child may appear to have acute sensitivity to sensory experiences (e.g., sudden noises or various tactile sensations). Some children may display these characteristics early on, as young as eighteen months, but some children might not exhibit concerning behaviors until well into their second year. Still others can achieve typical developmental milestones, displaying no conspicuous signs of delay, and then, over a very short period, they stop gaining new language and social skills or begin to lose what they had. Early signs will be discussed in more detail in Chapter 13 on early childhood education.

DIAGNOSTIC CRITERIA

The APA (2013) has published the criteria necessary for receiving an ASD diagnosis.

The current diagnostic criteria include persistent difficulties in social communication and social interaction across multiple contexts and restricted, repetitive patterns of behavior.

SOCIAL COMMUNICATION INTERACTION

Impairments in this category include deficits in social-emotional reciprocity, nonverbal communication behaviors used in social interaction, and developing, maintaining, and understanding relationships. By social impairment, we mean more than just having a sense of shyness or inclination toward introversion. Impairments in this area, as well as others included in the diagnostic criteria, must be present in the early developmental period, they should cause significant impairment in important areas of daily functioning, and they should be beyond what is expected for children at that developmental level.

Social-emotional reciprocity. A significant issue for children with ASD is limited social reciprocity, which refers to the back-and-forth flow of social interaction. The American Psychiatric Association's (2013) *Diagnostic and Statistical Manual*, Fifth Edition (*DSM-5*) defines this category of deficits to include difficulties with back-and-forth conversation, reduced sharing of interests and emotions, and a failure to initiate or respond to social interactions.

Young children will show an interest in interacting with others and exchanging smiles, which eventually builds to being able to share in a conversational exchange as they grow to develop language. Children who have impairments in social reciprocity prefer to avoid social games and participate more in solitary activities; they may not notice another person's lack of interest in the focus or topic of conversation, or they might fail to notice another person's distress when it occurs. All of these deficits can contribute to an unsuccessful social exchange.

Nonverbal communicative behaviors. Individuals with ASD are reported to have difficulty interpreting nonverbal communication from others, such as those conveyed through body language, facial expressions, and gestures during social interactions. Nonverbal listener behaviors that convey an *interest* in the speaker include the body, head, or both being oriented toward the speaker, looking at the speaker's eyes or mouth, periodic smiling, raised eyebrows, head nodding, and even vocalizations such as "mmm hmm." Behaviors that seem to show *disinterest* include diverting eye contact away from the speaker, leaning one's head on one's hand, making audible sighs, yawning, or raising eyebrows without a smile. Individuals with ASD can have difficulty understanding what such nonverbal signals mean.

Relationships. The *DSM-5* defines difficulties in this area of developing, maintaining, and understanding relationships to include difficulties adjusting one's behavior to suit different social contexts, difficulties sharing in imaginative play, difficulties making friends, and an apparent absence of interest in peers. On the spectrum of difficulties in relating to people, you might see one child who avoids social interactions, and you might see another who can tolerate social interaction with encouragement and can initiate social contact.

What comes naturally to some children, without conscious thought on the part of the child, may need to be taught specifically to students with ASD. Interventions that have received the most support in the research literature are those that deliver instruction, models, or prompts related to social interactions followed by tangible or social reinforcements delivered for correct responses and error corrections following an incorrect response (Plavnick, Kaid, & MacFarland, 2015). Video-based instruction using an Apple iPad to show video clips of social interactions is a strategy teachers have used with positive results, for example. Social skills groups are also a popular instructional strategy, where individuals with ASD meet several times per week to learn and practice social behaviors with one another and with instructors.

A commonly held misconception is that individuals with ASD do not want to socialize with others. In reality, we often hear that these children or adults do have a desire for friends, but unwritten social codes that are readily understood by others seem indecipherable to them. It is true that they can seem uncomfortable in social settings and have difficulty making friends, but it may not be true that they have no desire to engage in social interactions.

RESTRICTED OR REPETITIVE PATTERNS OF BEHAVIOR, INTERESTS, AND ACTIVITIES

For a diagnosis of ASD according to the APA (2013), difficulties should be found in at least two of the following: (a) stereotyped or repetitive motor movements, use of objects, or speech; (b) insistence on sameness, inflexible adherence to routines; (c) highly restricted, fixated interests that are abnormal in intensity or focus; or (d) hyper- or hypo-reactivity to sensory input or unusual interest in sensory aspects of the environment.

Repetitive motor movements. Behaviors often associated with ASD, such as hand flapping, finger flicking, rocking, and spinning objects or self, are called *stereotypic behaviors*. Stereotypic behaviors are one of the core features of ASD and are one of the most frequent behaviors seen in individuals with ASD (Beighley et al., 2014). "All persons with autism, by its definition, will have some stereotypic behaviors at some time, and they may increase or decrease in frequency and/or intensity based on age and situation" (Boutot & Myles, 2011, p. 23).

Stereotypy comes in many forms. Most common manifestations include hand flapping, shaking objects, and repeating vocal sounds. Other forms of stereotypy can include opening and closing the mouth, grimacing, head tilting, head shaking, shoulder shrugging, tensing the body, stamping feet, spinning, and covering one's ears. Repetitive vocal responses or unusual vocalizations in individuals with ASD are called *vocal stereotypy*. Although exact numbers are unknown, in one study, parents reported that 85% of children with ASD emitted atypical, repetitive vocalizations or speech (Mayes & Calhoun, 2011).

Insistence on sameness. Individuals with ASD tend to prefer things to be the same, or they prefer to be in a predictable environment. Change from one activity to the next, or transitioning from one setting to another (e.g., moving from classroom to outdoor recess) may cause distress. Individuals with ASD may feel overwhelmed when faced with unpredictable events and, as a result, will exhibit behaviors that appear to others as "meltdowns," or they will withdraw from others or run away. Children with ASD prefer absolute consistency in their environment and their routines, and any slight change can be very disturbing. Any change in the normal routine, such as an unplanned stop at the market on the way home from school, could be very upsetting for children with ASD.

Restricted or fixated interests. Hyperfocus on a topic of interest is also a hallmark of ASD. These interests are often not shared with others of similar age (like playing with SpongeBob figures at age 12) or are unusual at any age (e.g., washing machines or construction equipment). A fifth grader, for example, may choose to read only books or talk about machines for months. Many times, these preoccupations can take precedence over social interaction, or they may become the dominant topic of conversation when interacting with others. Sometimes, they have a tendency to talk endlessly about their topic of interest, and they have trouble recognizing when others have lost interest in the topic of discussion.

Children might have a preoccupation with parts of objects rather than the function of the object itself. A child might be interested in spinning the wheels of a toy truck, for example, rather than pretending to drive the truck around the room. Along the spectrum, another child might show a fascination with a particular category of objects and with accumulating as many of the interesting items as possible. For example, a child might collect unusual stones, packets of sweetener, felt-tip markers, or the like. Other children on the spectrum may develop an interest in a particular topic or concept. Common examples include transportation (trains, trucks, etc.), animals, or electronics.

Sensory input. In this category of impairments, children with ASD might have an apparent indifference to pain or temperature, an adverse response to specific sounds or textures, excessive smelling or touching of objects, or a visual fascination with lights or movement (APA, 2013). Many individuals on the autism spectrum can be painfully sensitive to certain sensations, like sights, smells, sounds, or textures.

Family Voices 1.2

"Your classroom is probably a very uncomfortable place for my son. The lights . . . the ticking clock . . . other students chatting and moving around . . . all this hurts his eyes and ears. When these things overwhelm him—which is often—he will act out."

Some individuals with ASD are hypersensitive to sound, smells, or bright lights. The hum of an air conditioner, fan, a pencil sharpener, or the chatting of peers nearby can be a disturbing or painful experience that they seek to avoid, for example. For some children, sounds from a vacuum cleaner, a ringing telephone, an airplane overhead, or a car driving by can cause them to cover their ears and scream. An aversion to certain smells can be problematic as well, as are sensitivities to taste (resist certain textures of food, flavors, or brands). Some people are highly sensitive to bright lights, and they might react strongly to exposure to certain lights in the classroom.

Core Areas of Deficit	
Deficit Area	**Common Behaviors**
Social Communication	• Difficulty learning to interpret what others are thinking and feeling • Make little eye contact • Tend to look, listen, or respond less to people in their environment • Difficulty maintaining personal space, seeming to physically intrude on others • Lacking tact or appearing rude • Difficulty making or keeping friends • Appearing naïve, or easily taken advantage of • Difficulty understanding others' nonverbal communication (e.g., facial expressions, body language, or tone of voice) • Difficulty understanding jokes (often because of the literal nature of their thinking)
Restrictive, Repetitive, and Stereotyped Behavior, Interests, and Activities	• Expresses a strong need for routine or "sameness" • Expresses desire for repetition • Intense preoccupation with own unique interests • Asks repetitive questions • Displays repetitive motor movements, such as hand flapping, pacing, flicking fingers in front of eyes, or covering ears • Difficulty handling transition and change • Apparent indifference to pain or temperature • Adverse response to certain sensations, such as sights, smells, sounds, or textures • Visual fascination with lights or movement

OTHER FEATURES ASSOCIATED WITH ASD

In addition to the core features discussed previously, some studies have reported a number of associated features that are not necessarily required for a diagnosis but are often present in individuals with ASD. Here, we discuss cognitive and motor differences, emotional vulnerability, gastrointestinal problems, and language skills.

COGNITIVE DIFFERENCES

Signs of intellectual disability are also present in some individuals with ASD (NIMH, 2015). Moreover, just as in other areas of deficit on the autism spectrum, there is great variability in the intellectual performance of individuals with ASD. Individuals with ASD can demonstrate differences in verbal and nonverbal reasoning abilities, perceptional reasoning abilities, working memory, and processing speed. Children with ASD can also have differences in reading and math, as well as social cognition abilities (the ability to aware of the feelings of others). Generalizing skills, or the ability to apply concepts to real-life contexts, can also be impacted by ASD.

In reading, children with ASD may show weakened comprehension skills. Their ability to recount facts and details may be evident, yet using those facts to perform abstract reasoning tasks presents more of a challenge. One difficult area for students with ASD is the ability to comprehend text. While some children with ASD demonstrate the ability to decode text at a level above their current IQ, often outperforming their same-age peers in decoding skills, many children with ASD are outperformed by their peers in comprehension abilities (Nguyen, Leytham, Whitby, & Gelfer, 2015).

Inherent difficulties with understanding others' point of view or perspective likely contribute to the challenge of reading comprehension. For example, the curriculum in first grade expects children to understand characters' feelings in a text and relate those feelings to their own. Students with ASD struggle to understand that people have thoughts that differ from their own, or understand others' perspectives, and thus may have difficulties comprehending this part of the text. Individuals with ASD might also have trouble with comprehension due to their weak central coherence (the ability to combine details together to form a whole idea or concept) or challenges with executive functioning (the ability to plan, organize, monitor progress, and complete tasks) (Nguyen et al., 2015). Central coherence and executive functioning are skills necessary for comprehending text.

MOTOR SKILLS

In addition to social, communication, and behavioral deficits, many individuals with ASD have deficits in motor functioning. Such children will have difficulty with balance, manual dexterity, poor handwriting, and poor motor coordination, or they may walk with an awkward gait or walk on their toes. They might display unusual body postures (e.g., stiffness) or facial expressions (e.g., grimacing). Delayed motor milestones are not uncommon in children with an ASD diagnosis. Parents may observe a delay in learning to sit up, to crawl, and to walk or challenges with holding a spoon or small toy.

Impairments in fine motor skills impact a variety of areas for children with ASD, from the classroom to the home environments. For instance, difficulties cutting with scissors and poor penmanship are commonly observed by teachers regarding their students with ASD. Studies have established that children with autism have weaker grip strength than other children, which, in turn, can influence a variety of childhood tasks, such as handwriting

(Alaniz, Galit, Necesito, & Rosario, 2015). Limited grip strength can be problematic at home as well. For instance, any self-care skills, such as manipulating fasteners, tying shoes, or opening packages require fine motor control (Alaniz et al., 2015) and present a challenge for individuals with ASD. Other daily living skills that are impacted by fine motor skills include bathing, dressing, eating, and toileting.

EMOTIONAL VULNERABILITY

Emotions can be challenging for individuals with ASD to interpret. Not only can they be less likely to interpret and understand verbal or nonverbal expression in others, but they also have difficulty understanding or managing their own emotions. When faced with stress or even sensory overload, children with ASD are at greater risk for tantrums or rages that look like "meltdowns" to other observers.

Stress, obsessive worry, anxiety, self-injury (banging head, picking skin, or biting nails excessively, for example), and low self-esteem are commonly associated with ASD. Individuals with ASD may make frequent negative comments about themselves and have symptoms of depression. Depression is common among individuals with ASD. Typical symptoms of depression, such as irritability, sadness, crying, sleep disturbance, and appetite disturbance, can be present. Depression can also be accompanied by an increase in preoccupations and rituals and greater frequency of aggressive outbursts.

GASTROINTESTINAL PROBLEMS

The NIMH (2015) reports that parents say their children with ASD often have gastrointestinal or digestion problems, including stomach pains, constipation or diarrhea, acid reflux, vomiting, and bloating. Food allergies may also be evident in children with ASD. One study suggested that children with ASD might not have gastrointestinal (GI) problems but instead have behaviors that create GI symptoms. The researchers proposed, for example, that a child who insists on eating only certain foods might not get enough fiber or fluids, which leads to constipation. Some parents will put their child on a special diet in their attempts to control ASD or the associated GI symptoms. It may be true that some children can benefit from limiting certain foods, but there is no convincing evidence that these special diets reduce the symptoms of ASD, according to the NIMH (2015).

LANGUAGE SKILLS

Some individuals with ASD have relatively good verbal skills, with only a slight language delay, and they will demonstrate impaired social skills while others may not speak at all or have limited communication and interaction abilities. Still other individuals might use language in unusual ways, speaking only single words or repeating the same phrases over and over. Some might continually repeat what others say (called *echolalia*). The most severe expression of symptoms in the area of communication skills is the silent child who has a vocabulary limited to sounds and not of words. This child may even be able to comprehend language but does not easily express him or herself. Parents might even observe their child's attempts to speak, but the child appears not to be able to connect through vocalizations.

A child who has limited speech may attempt to use other methods to communicate wants or needs. For example, Adele uses a system of symbols as alternative/augmentative communication, and she can point to the picture of a toilet when she needs to use the restroom. If that form of communication is unsuccessful, Adele is forced to resort to less effective means of communicating her needs. Adele was on the playground one afternoon and did not have access to the picture of a toilet to indicate her needs. Because she was unable to express her needs to a teacher, Adele tried tugging on the teacher's hand, but when the teacher could not interpret Adele's needs, Adele began screaming and running away. The teacher shouted to Adele to stop running and return to the playground. This teacher, who was unaware of Adele's needs to use the toilet, interpreted her behavior as defiance and issued consequences that she felt appropriate. Adele was unable to use her alternative method of communicating, which was pointing at pictures, and therefore resorted to another strategy of running toward the toilet despite the teacher's requests to return.

The speaking abilities of some children with ASD may be in place, but they may require some external prompts. For example, when a child immediately echoes the utterance of someone or when he/she can see an object and say the name of the object or when a child uses sentences borrowed from a TV show or another speaker, the child might be using external prompts. Still other children with ASD can initiate original speech but have significant difficulties with pragmatic aspects of language. This child might use an unusual prosody or a tendency to be very pedantic, often making literal interpretations of a person's comments.

T.I.P. – Theory Into Practice 1.3

AUTISM CHARACTERISTICS OBSERVATION

1. Make a checklist of the diagnostic criteria and associated behaviors of ASD discussed in this chapter.

2. Conduct an informal observation of someone you know who has received an ASD diagnosis. Give yourself about 30 minutes to 1 hour to observe the child, at school or at home.

3. Check off each of the behaviors you notice the child exhibiting during the observation time.

4. Write a brief summary of your experience.

INSTRUCTIONAL PRACTICES

One of the most commonly used instructional methods to address the learning needs of students with ASD is Applied Behavior Analysis (ABA). ABA will be discussed in detail in Chapter 5, which is devoted to this method. We will also consider functional behavior analysis (Chapter 6) and positive behavior supports (Chapter 7), environmental supports (Chapter 8), strategies for supporting social skills development (Chapter 9), and strategies for teaching communication (Chapter 10). Chapters 11 and 12 will also be devoted to teaching academic and functional skills to students with ASD. After a discussion of using assistive technology, we will introduce the idea of ASD and sensory processing and the related accommodations and adaptations educators can employ. Finally, strategies for working with children with ASD in early childhood settings (Chapter 13) and transitions to adulthood will be discussed (Chapter 14). All of the strategies at which we will look more closely are research-based and are designed to meet the needs of individuals with ASD.

INCLUSIVE CLASSROOM ENVIRONMENTS

The Individuals with Disabilities Education Act (IDEA, 2004) states that students with disabilities are entitled to experience the "least restrictive environment." School districts are required by IDEA to educate students with disabilities in classrooms with nondisabled peers to the maximum extent appropriate, supported with the aides and services that may be necessary to make this possible. Not every student with ASD must to be in a general-education classroom, however. The members of the IEP team will consider all of the issues and make the decision for each individual student with ASD.

The decision for students with ASD to participate in the general-education environment is referred to as inclusion. Inclusion does not mean that students are just "placed" in the general-education classroom and forgotten. It means that a variety of supports will be provided to create a successful learning environment and experience for everyone involved. Inclusion can be very successful for many children with ASD. Being educated alongside typically developing children can improve the functioning of children with ASD, including their social functioning. Children with ASD who are educated in the inclusive classroom are likely to engage in more social interactions than they would in other environments.

There is some controversy surrounding "inclusion" that should be mentioned here. Researchers and advocates agree that students with disabilities can learn well in inclusive environments alongside their peers, and there is evidence that students with disabilities tend to perform better in inclusive environments (Fruth & Woods, 2015). Despite the evidence, not all team members agree that inclusion is the best option. "Increasing the performance of students with disabilities and differences requires a restructuring of the practice and approach of education," which some team members may shy away from (Fruth & Woods, 2015, p. 352). A concern of many educators is the possible adverse effects of the presence of students with disabilities in the general-education classroom (Fruth & Woods, 2015). Fruth and Woods (2015) advocate that we work toward "dispelling such myths and opening up optimal educational experiences for all students based on practical evidence" (p. 354).

Family Voices 1.3

"Dear General Ed Teacher: I'm sorry—truly sorry—you don't have the training you need to teach my daughter. I know you have 30 students in your class, all with different abilities, and you'll have to give extra time to my daughter, and you don't know how to help. I'm sorry for when she acts out or has a meltdown in your class, and I'm sorry that I don't have all the answers."

Given the IDEA mandate for considering the inclusion for students with special needs, throughout this book we will provide inclusion tips to accompany the instructional *best practices* for students with ASD. The tips provided in subsequent chapters are designed to help you better understand and manage the learning and behavioral characteristics that are unique to students with ASD.

TIPS FOR WORKING WITH FAMILIES

When there has been an ASD diagnosis, it becomes important that teachers and parents work together for the child's best academic and social outcomes. Working with parents of children with ASD can be an important component of helping the child achieve his or her full potential. Parents know their child better than anyone else, and they can provide vital information to help their child succeed in school, and the well-trained teacher can provide strategies for parents to continue classroom learning into the home environment.

An important first step is to get to know the family well. When teachers and parents establish a meeting, it is helpful for the teacher to listen intently and allow the parents to talk about their child. When a parent feels comfortable sharing about their child, it creates the foundation for teachers to share issues that may arise in the classroom later. It is also important for teachers to be familiar with the IEP and to be able to communicate any educational terminology in ways that are easily understood by parents. Try your best to make parents feel comfortable now, and you will be better able to partner with parents in the future.

Family Voices 1.4

"I really, really, really want to communicate with you. I know you are busy, but please tell me about my son's day—every day. If it was a great day, tell me why; if he had a rough day, tell me about it, and let's spend time talking about how to deal with it in the best way. Together we can come up with solutions so that the next day is just a little better."

SUMMARY STATEMENTS

- Children diagnosed with ASD may display, in varying degrees, social communication difficulties and restrictive, repetitive patterns of behavior, interests, or activities.

- Scientists have yet to determine the exact causes of ASD, but researchers suggest that both genetics and the environment play important roles.

- School districts are required by IDEA to educate students with disabilities in classrooms with nondisabled peers to the maximum extent appropriate, supported with the aides and services that may be necessary to make this possible

- Parents and teachers who work together can form the successful partnership the child with ASD needs to reach his or her full potential.

WHAT WOULD YOU DO?

Look back at the case study about Mrs. Avery presented at the beginning of the chapter. Based on what you have read in this chapter and the knowledge you have gained from your professor's presentations or classroom activities, how would you respond to the following questions?

1. Which of the two children, Dylan or Erin, show some of the early signs of ASD?

2. What additional behaviors would you look for, if you were Mrs. Avery, to gain a more complete picture of the children's behaviors?

3. If you were Mrs. Avery, would you refer one of these students for further evaluation?

4. What next steps would you consider taking?

5. How might you respond to a parent who believes that childhood vaccinations were the cause of her child's unusual behaviors?

6. Do you think any of these children could be educated in the least restrictive environment with success?

CHAPTER REFLECTION QUESTIONS

1. Why is ASD considered a *spectrum*?

2. What are some possible causes of autism? Why are some of them controversial?

3. Describe the core deficits necessary to establish an ASD diagnosis.

4. Why might reading comprehension be troublesome for an individual with ASD?

5. What are some ideas about why individuals with ASD engage in repetitive behaviors?

6. Explain the rationale for educating students with ASD in the least restrictive environment.

RECOMMENDED RESOURCES

Autism Diagnostic Observation Schedule: The Autism Diagnostic Observation Schedule—Generic (ADOS-G) is an assessment of communication, social interaction, and play for individuals suspected of having ASD. Available at http://www.google.com/#hl=en&source=hp&q=Autism+Diagnostic+Observation+Schedule&aq=f&aqi=&oq=&fp=400a82fa82571428

Centers for Disease Control and Prevention. *Screening and diagnosis*. Available at http://www.cdc.gov/ncbddd/autism/screening.html

National Institute of Neurological Disorders and Stroke. Autism Spectrum Disorder Fact Sheet. Available at http://www.ninds.nih.gov/disorders/autism/detail_autism.htm

REFERENCES

Alaniz, J. L., Galit, E., Necesito, C. I., & Rosario, E. R. (2015). Hand strength, handwriting, and functional skills in children with autism. *American Journal of Occupational Therapy, 69*(4), 6904220030p1. doi:10.5014/ajot.2015.016022

American Psychiatric Association. (2013). *Diagnostic and statistical manual of mental disorders*, 5th ed. (*DSM-5*). Arlington, VA: American Psychiatric Publishing.

Beighley, J. S., Matson, J. L., Rieske, R. D., Cervantes, P. E., Goldin, R., & Jang, J. (2014). Differences in stereotypic behavior in adults diagnosed with autism spectrum disorders using the *DSM-IV-TR* and the *DSM-5*. *Journal of Developmental and Physical Disabilities, 26*, 193–202.

Boutot, E. A., & Myles, B. S. (2011). *Autism spectrum disorders: Foundations, characteristics, and effective strategies*. Upper Saddle River, NJ: Pearson Education.

Centers for Disease Control and Prevention (CDC). (2015). *Autism spectrum disorders (ASD), data and statistics*. Retrieved October 27, 2015, from http://www.cdc.gov/ncbddd/autism/data.html

Frazier, T. W., Thompson, L., Youngstrom, E. A., Law, P., Hardan, A. Y., Eng, C., & Morris, N. (2014). A twin study of heritable and shared environmental contributions to autism. *Journal of Autism and Developmental Disorders, 44*, 2013–2025.

Fruth, J. D., & Woods, M. N. (2015). Academic performance of students without disabilities in the inclusive environment. *Education, 135*(3), 351–361.

Individuals with Disabilities Education Act (IDEA). (2004). Retrieved December 27, 2015, from http://idea.ed.gov/explore/view/p/, root,statute,I,B,612,a,5,

Iossifov, I., Levy, D., Allen, J., Ye, K., Ronemus, M., Lee, Y., . . . Wigler, M. (2015). Low load for disruptive mutations in autism genes and their biased transmission. *Proceedings of the National Academy of Sciences*. Retrieved from http://www.pnas.org/content/112/41/E5600.full.pdf

Jain, A., Marshall, J., Buikema, A., Bancroft, T., Kelly, J., & Newschaffer, C. (2015). Autism occurrence by MMR vaccine status among US children with older siblings with and without autism. *Journal of the American Medical Association, 313*(15), 1534–1540.

King, B. H. (2015, May). Researchers can now change focus. *Pediatric News*, 21.

Mayes, S. D., & Calhoun, S. L. (2011). Impact of IQ, age, SES, gender, and race on autistic symptoms. *Research in Autism Spectrum Disorders, 5*, 749–757.

National Institute of Mental Health (NIMH). (2015). *Autism spectrum disorder*. Retrieved October 12, 2015, from http://www.nimh.nih.gov/health/topics/autism-spectrum-disorders-asd/index.shtml

Nguyen, N. N., Leytham, P., Whitby, P. S., & Gelfer, J. I. (2015). Reading comprehension and autism in the primary general education classroom. *Reading Teacher, 69*(1), 71–76.

Pineda, R., Melchior, K., Oberle, S., Inder, T., & Rogers, C. (2015). Assessment of autism symptoms during the neonatal period: Is there early evidence of autism risk? *American Journal of Occupational Therapy, 69*(4), 1–11.

Plavnick, J. B., Kaid, T., & MacFarland, M. C. (2015). Effects of a school-based social skills training program for adolescents with autism spectrum disorder and intellectual disability. *Journal of Autism and Developmental Disorders, 45*, 2674–2690.

U.S. Department of Education, National Center for Education Statistics. (2013). *Digest of Education Statistics, 2012*. Retrieved from http://nces.ed.gov/fastfacts/display.asp?id=64

Understanding Family Perspectives

2

CASE STUDY

Mrs. Logan is a new special education teacher in your district. She is excited to work with children who have ASD, and she feels she will bond well with the families she will serve. Prior to the first day of school, she sent a letter to parents introducing herself and inviting parents to meet after school to discuss strategies for collaborating to best meet the various needs of her students. Mrs. Logan thought it best to be brief in her letter, so she simply provided a few sentences about herself and one last comment, "Feel free to stop by after school sometime to discuss how we can collaborate."

At the end of that first day of school, not one family member stopped by her office for a meeting. Mrs. Logan was quite surprised that no one responded to her invitation. Several weeks went by, and still no one expressed an interest in collaborating with her in educating children with ASD. Mrs. Logan remembered learning in her teacher preparation program about the importance of partnering with families of children with ASD, and she wholeheartedly supported the rationale for doing so. She was keenly aware of how collaboration with family members helps support children's development, both academically and socially, and was anxious to get started with those important partnerships.

As time went on, she grew disenchanted with the notion of school-family collaboration. The families' apparent unwillingness to partner with her cultivated a growing frustration. She knew collaboration was beneficial for her students, but for some reason, her students' parents didn't seem to support such a partnership.

....

LEARNER OBJECTIVES

After reading this chapter, the learner should be able to do the following:

- Provide rationale for partnering with families to educate children with ASD.

- Describe what families want in a school–family partnership and the related implications for establishing such partnerships.

- Describe the family's experience of stress associated with raising a child with ASD.

- Examine how culture influences family perspectives and describe how educators can participate in culturally responsive collaboration.

"Listening is a magnetic and strange thing, a creative force. The friends who listen to us are the ones we move toward. When we are listened to, it creates us, makes us unfold and expand."
—KARL A. MENNINGER

INTRODUCTION

The Importance of Family Partnerships

Partnerships are important for several reasons. The Individuals with Disabilities Education Improvement Act (IDEA, 2006) mandates parent–professional collaboration. Interpersonal collaboration is "a style for direct interaction between at least two co-equal parties voluntarily engaged in shared decision-making as they work toward a common goal" (Friend & Cook, 2010). That common goal is to help our students reach their highest potential.

Collaborating with the family members of your students is one of your primary responsibilities as a special educator. Legally, parents are considered a part of the IEP team, and concerns of the parent must be considered in IEP decision-making. Beyond the legal requirements, research advocates that when parents operate as partners in the special education process, there are benefits to students' academic and social progress (Bacon & Causton-Theoharis, 2013; Dabkowski, 2004; Friend & Borsuck, 2009).

IMPORTANCE OF PARTNERING WITH FAMILIES OF STUDENTS WITH ASD

The importance of parent participation in the education of children with autism spectrum disorders (ASD) is well documented, with research linking parent involvement to positive outcomes such as improved academic and social skills (Benson, Karlof & Siperstein, 2008; Moes & Frea, 2002), as well as enhanced family well-being (Koegel, Bimbela, & Schriebman 1996; Renty & Roeyers, 2005). It is widely acknowledged that parent involvement in the education of children with ASD is considered a critical *best practice* (Benson et al., 2008; Moes & Frea, 2002; National Research Council, 2001). There is a considerable body of research promoting the benefits of parent involvement in the education of students with autism.

Parental involvement may be important for students on the autism spectrum due to the nature of the disability and the core deficits in language acquisition and social competency. The severity of the disability can affect the child's ability to communicate, which, in turn, necessitates collaboration between parents and teachers in children's educational planning and implementation (Bachner, Carmel, Lubetzky, Heiman, & Galil, 2006). Because students with autism might have difficulty expressing themselves verbally, it is critical that primary caregivers and teachers keep an open channel of communication to promote students' best interests (Hebel & Persitz, 2014; Stoner et al., 2005). One parent in Stoner et al.'s research lamented that she could never know enough about what was going on at school because although she could ask her child, "he is not going to tell me. Not specifically. And that is the frustrating part for me" (Stoner et al., 2005, p. 46).

Additionally, parents are often well educated about ASD and their child, and they are therefore able to serve as a great resource to schools. Parents of children with ASD often engage in an intense process of self-education when their child receives a diagnosis. It is quite likely that parents have acquired such extensive knowledge about ASD that they can be on near-equal footing with the education professionals in terms of their knowledge base (Benson et al., 2008). Schools would do well to capitalize on such rich resources and engage in sharing information between partners for maximum benefits to children's academic and social development.

Family Voices 2.1

"Consider us the expert on our child. We are valuable members of the educational team. Make time to invite us to be involved in problem solving and decision-making on a regular basis."

The focus of this book is on the responsibilities of professionals to facilitate and ensure collaborative partnerships in the education of students who have ASD. This chapter offers insights from parents' perspectives about what is working and not working related to the education of children with autism. A school–family relationship that is based on mutual understanding of each other's perspectives and realities provides the foundation for meaningful collaboration. It is of primary importance that teachers and school staff have an understanding of the family's perspective—what they experience in living with a child with ASD, what additional sources of stress they encounter, and what they want from a school–family partnership.

YOUR ROLE AS AN EDUCATOR IN PARTNERING WITH FAMILIES

Special education literature discusses at great length what parents want in a school–family partnership; the extent to which we, as educators, meet those needs has a significant influence on whether the partnership is successful. Parents place value on receiving information from educators, family-focused perspectives, cultural responsiveness, and equal opportunities to participate in decision-making. They want professionals to show genuine respect for their children, have the training and skills necessary to successfully support their children's appropriate behaviors, continually search for new knowledge and resources to update their skills, be willing to go the extra mile for their children to address their needs, and be committed to the whole family (Park & Turnbull, 2002). Families also value active parent–teacher communication, a full understanding of their child's abilities, and embracing a family-centered perspective (Hebel & Persitz, 2014). Parents want to feel that they are listened to, valued, and respected (Paige-Smith & Rix, 2006).

DEMONSTRATE RESPECT FOR CHILDREN

Families in Park and Turnbull's (2002) research said that they trust professionals who show genuine respect for children and treat them with dignity. Treating children with dignity, according to the families in Park and Turnbull (2002), means that professionals recognize and value children's humanity rather than focusing only on their problem behavior or other challenges. They behave in ways that are not degrading to children. They see the positive side of children, and they choose to focus on the child's strengths and preferences.

Park and Turnbull (2002) described professionals who maintained positive attitudes toward children as capable of "(a) identifying and valuing unique things about the child, (b) believing in the child's capability to learn, and (c) having a vision for the child's future accomplishments" (p. 119). For participants in Blue-Banning, Summers, Frankland, Nelson, and Beegle's (2004) research, respect meant valuing the child as a person rather than as a diagnosis or a disability label. One parent commented, "If they perceive someone as being less than human then they are going to treat that someone as an object. I want my son to feel like he belongs to the human race, like there's a place for him, like he fits in" (Blue-Banning et al., 2004, p. 179).

MAINTAIN A FAMILY-CENTERED PERSPECTIVE

Family-centered practices are characterized by placing an emphasis on family strengths, encouraging family choice in decision-making (Blue-Banning et al., 2004), and willingness to go the extra mile in their commitment to the whole family (Park & Turnbull, 2002). Educators who "go the extra mile" tend to do more than is required, and they sacrifice their personal time to improve children's development (Park & Turnbull, 2002). Educators who limit their services to a restricted view of time and responsibility, never going beyond the required workday to assist families, leave families disappointed (Park & Turnbull, 2002). Researchers have learned that school personnel should go above and beyond the call of duty, by reaching out to the family outside the scope of school hours, by spending time outside of class with the child, by addressing the child's emotional needs where possible, and by providing personal contact information (Burke, 2012).

A commitment to the whole family, according to Park and Turnbull (2002), means that professionals naturally established and maintained relationships with families, learned about the child's home life, became acquainted with other family members, came to know the needs of the whole family, and responded to those needs as much as they could. Professionals who are flexible, regard their work as "more than a job," regard the child and family as "more than a case," encourage the child and family, and who are accessible to the child and family demonstrate their commitment to partnering with the whole family (Blue-Banning et al., 2004).

COMMUNICATE WITH FAMILIES

An important first step in establishing good communication is to be a good listener. We cannot underestimate the power of listening. Educators might believe that it is important to provide information to families, and they are not wrong. However, taking the time to hear and truly understand the family's perspective is critical. To prevent communication breakdowns, a special educator should practice empathetic listening. *Merriam-Webster* defines empathy as "the feeling that you understand and share another person's experiences and emotions; the ability to share someone else's feelings." It is "the action of understanding, being aware of, being sensitive to, and vicariously experiencing the feelings, thoughts, and experience of another of either the past or present without having the feelings, thoughts, and experience fully communicated in an objectively explicit manner" ("Empathy," n.d.). Families of children with ASD want to know they are heard, first and foremost.

Families also want to receive information. Some have made recommendations that the school system provide families with training programs to improve their understanding of special education issues and take the initiative to encourage parental involvement. Families may be quite knowledgeable about the ASD characteristics their child manifests and may even be keenly aware of various intervention strategies, but it is also important for schools to provide ongoing information that may supplement or enhance what they have learned. Moreover, professionals should not wait to be asked before providing information, as some families could be reluctant to approach educators for any number of personal reasons.

The information that educators share with families should provide a balance of the child's strengths and weaknesses, rather than a strict focus on the deficits they observe. Some parents have felt dissatisfied with how schools sometimes focus on addressing students only by their deficits. For example, parents in Bacon and Causton-Theoharis's

(2013) research grew weary of hearing phrases such as, "This is what he did wrong today." Focusing on deficits as the dominant discussion pattern tends to build walls rather than bridges in partnerships.

T.I.P. – Theory Into Practice 2.2

WEEKLY COMMUNICATION

One way you can communicate with families is to send weekly progress reports to which parents can respond. A sample note home is below:

Date: _____

Student's Name: _____
_____

Overall rating of the day/week (please check):

☐ Poor   ☐ Fair   ☐ Good   ☐ Excellent

Things that went well in class this day/week:

1. _____
   _____

2. _____
   _____

3. _____
   _____

Things that could have gone better:

1. _____
   _____

2. _____
   _____

3. _____
   _____

Teacher's Signature: _____
_____

Parent's suggestions and advice about things that could have gone better:

_____
_____
_____
_____
_____
_____
_____
_____
_____

Parent's Signature: _____
_____

Take initiative. Parents want school professionals to initiate communication efforts. Parents in Stoner et al. (2005) and in other reports (Staples & Diliberto, 2010) placed high value on frequent open and honest communication. They expressed their desire to stay informed about their child's achievements or to be made aware of any problems that teachers encounter so they could be more involved in finding solutions (Stoner et al., 2005). Professionals should not wait for parents to ask before providing the information that parents want (Sheehey & Sheehey, 2007).

Parent involvement tends to increase in response to teacher initiatives to involve them (Rodriguez, Blatz, & Elbaum, 2014). In fact, research shows that the most significant predictor of special education involvement is specific teacher invitations (Fishman & Nickerson, 2015; Rodriquez et al., 2014). The most influential practice to encourage parent participation in meetings and contributions to educational planning is specific and direct communication from the teacher (Fishman & Nickerson, 2015). Given the desire parents have to participate in their child's education, it is a good idea for professionals to engage in purposeful recruitment of parents' involvement and collaboration.

Communicate through multiple means. To maintain a positive school–parent partnership, multiple communications that occur in multiple settings over an extended period are necessary (deFur, 2012). A few simple ways to provide communication to parents include yearly conferences, weekly folders of student work, parent report card pick up, and regularly sent out newsletters (Burke, 2012). Another strategy might include a daily communication journal. Each entry includes a brief summary of the student's performance for the day, as well as any possible IEP progress (Staples & Diliberto, 2010). Weekly communication can include newsletters, and monthly communications, such as telephone or personal communications, can show support for school–family collaboration.

Communication with families is a centerpiece of meaningful school–family collaboration. Create opportunities to share information with families and to receive information as well. Some ideas are to schedule regular meetings over coffee, communicate with teachers through daily notebook entries, or communicate through e-mail. Be respectful to avoid a "one size fits all families" approach; rather, tailor the avenues of communication to meet each family's need (Stuart, Flis, & Renaldi, 2006).

T.I.P. – Theory Into Practice 2.3

IDEAS FOR COMMUNICATING WITH FAMILIES

1. Weekly folder of student work
2. Weekly or monthly newsletters
3. Daily communication on journal/ notebook to exchange back and forth
4. Telephone call
5. E-mail notes
6. Online website families can access
7. Coffee with the teacher opportunities
8. Parent surveys
9. Invite them to share their perspective prior to an IEP meeting
10. Provide parent training sessions
11. "This is what I did well today" notes sent home to parents
12. Schedule family's frequent visits to the classroom for informal observations

INVOLVE THE FAMILY IN DEVELOPING GOALS AND INTERVENTIONS

Families are more motivated to partner with professionals who implement families' perspectives when developing IEPs (Hebel & Persitz, 2014). They view being consulted and "listened to" as essential elements of any educational plan (Paige-Smith & Rix, 2006). Parental satisfaction with the intervention plan is dependent upon the family's feelings being listened to (Paige-Smith & Rix, 2006). Many times, parents are motivated to participate in IEP meetings and decision-making but feel that school personnel do not demonstrate their efforts to listen or value parental input (Burke, 2012). Parents are more willing to engage in the school's efforts to educate children with ASD when they are made to feel their input is valued.

Facilitating effective family–school partnerships requires that we be family-centered or family-driven. Being family-driven refers to approaches to interventions in which goals are established in true partnership with families, combined with the understanding that the family has expert knowledge, gained from experience or training, and they are therefore entitled and expected to contribute the effective interventions for their children in partnership with trained educators who also possess great knowledge about strategies for academic and social development (Bacon & Causton-Theoharis, 2013; Osher & Osher, 2002). When educators include families in decision-making, (rather than simply *telling* them what they must do, and recognizing that when a family understands and agrees with the intervention plan, they are better able to carry out the responsibilities assigned to them) it is beneficial to our students (Osher & Osher, 2002).

Empowering parents means equipping them with the knowledge and skills that will help optimize their child's academic and social development. Researchers recommend that schools work to meet the need for parental self-education by providing training and information concerning related services to parents (Stoner et al., 2005). It is equally important for service professionals to foster ongoing communication with parents, to recognize and value their expertise, and to provide support to parents (Hughes, Valle-Riestra, & Arguelles, 2008; Renty & Roeyers, 2005; Sawyer, 2015; Stoner et al., 2005).

BUILD TRUST

Schools should also communicate to parents that they are trusted. Trust refers to having confidence in another person's word, judgment, and actions and believing that the trusted person will act in the best interest of the person who trusts him or her (Turnbull & Turnbull, 2015). A sense of distrust is a considerable barrier influencing parents' interactions with school personnel. Participants in Stoner et al.'s (2005) study placed high value on establishing trust. Moreover, a lack of open, honest communication between home and school fostered mistrust in Stoner et al.'s (2005) research.

Building trust with parents involves taking children's and parent's best interest to heart. It means being reliable and making sure parents can depend on you to come through for them consistently. Demonstrate competence, showing your ability to perform the tasks required by your position. Remain honest, showing integrity and speaking truthfully to others. Finally, be open, and welcome communication, sharing necessary information with the people it affects (Tschannen-Moran, 2004). Parents need to know that you are qualified, fair, dependable, and have their child's best interests at heart (Bryk & Schneider, 2004).

T.I.P. – Theory Into Practice 2.4

HOW TO BUILD TRUST

1. Communicate with families—relationships improve when you nurture them. Volunteer information. Don't wait to be asked to give up information that is important to them.

2. Be honest—if you tell the truth, even when it's to say you don't know something about ASD, parents will trust you. Always be honest. Don't claim to know everything about everything. Say, "I don't know" when you really don't know.

3. Show respect—respect the family's time by never being late to a meeting and by demonstrating effective listening skills during the meeting. Start and end meetings on time.

4. Ask open-ended questions—learn more about parents and be interested in their answers. Open-ended questions give parents the opportunity to tell you about themselves and their child. Ask more questions based on the answers you get.

(Continued)

(Continued)

5. Have your parents' best interest in mind—parents know when you are looking out for them and for their child and when you are looking out for yourself.

6. Listen attentively—show the other person that you've listened carefully. Paraphrase what was said; giving the information back to the parents in your own words is a great way to show you were listening and to demonstrate your understanding.

7. Don't be defensive—when parents have a question or concern about something, take the time to listen to everything they have to say before you react. Many times it comes down to miscommunication or misconceptions. Don't be afraid to clear up any issues, but do it with a tone that is calm and professional. Listening is just as powerful as explaining your side. Sometimes the frustration is not with you. . . . Parents simply just need to vent.

8. Take time to explain—when families are confused, be patient, and take time to help them understand, whether it is about an intervention strategy you are suggesting or an activity you are asking parents to implement at home.

9. Take responsibility—when something does not go as planned and it's your fault, take responsibility right away, and focus on the next steps. Families will trust a teacher who owns up to her or his mistakes.

10. Take what is being said seriously—don't dismiss another person's comments or challenges as being small or less serious than your own issues. Just listen. Whatever families are going through or dealing with is serious to them, and you should treat it as such.

11. Empathize—acknowledge the feelings behind what is being said, and show empathy. Families will trust you more when they feel that you understand them.

12. Be accessible—when families know they can gain access to you, it builds trust.

13. Stay up to date—remain updated on current best practices for educating students with ASD; with current events in the news, even if they're controversial; and with new ideas for collaborating with families. Always work to improve your skills and competencies to work with students who have ASD.

14. Go ABCD (above and beyond the call of duty)—take time to get to know parents and their child, make phone calls home, spend time outside of class with families and their child, and so forth. Let them know you truly care about them.

Family Voices 2.3

"Teachers don't think to include me as much as I would like. Teachers don't have as much education about ASD as I do. Many teachers hold the view that parents should 'just be parents' instead of empowering them to be meaningful partners in the educational process."

DEVELOP YOUR OWN CULTURAL AWARENESS

Professionals serving children with autism and their families must be sensitive to cultural differences. Parents come into partnerships with varied cultural beliefs, understandings, perceptions, and ways of interacting, and those varied backgrounds and experiences must be understood and respected by school personnel if we wish to form effective partnerships. DeFur (2012) asserts that service providers who wish to develop a trusting relationship with families must respect one another, avoid being judgmental, and engage in cultural responsiveness. Also be aware that cultural differences may impose communication barriers and impede the development of parental collaboration with service providers (Hebel & Persitz, 2014). We must work toward building bridges rather than widening the barriers between partners.

Some of the potential cultural differences that will be explored in this section include (1) differing ways of interpreting disabilities; (2) variations in societal perceptions; (3) ways in which families rely on different sources of family support; (4) differing beliefs about the causes of disabilities; and (5) differing viewpoints about the best strategies for intervention.

Interpretation of disability. Culture plays a role in the way parents interpret their child's disability. Parents of different cultures may have differing views of normalcy and different views of the causes and labels related to disabilities, or they may not have a clear understanding of how their child's disability affects his or her learning. Labels such as autism might not exist in the parents' native culture (Dyches, Wilder, Sudweeks, Obiakor, & Algozzine, 2004; Tincani, Travers, & Boutot, 2009). Some behaviors associated with a disability may be misinterpreted as a willful lack of cooperation rather than a genuine impairment in some cultures (Mandell & Novak, 2005; Tincani et al., 2009). "Unfortunately, educators may be inclined to dismiss differing views toward disability as evidence that families are 'in denial' about their child's condition" (Tincani et al., 2009, p. 85).

Interpretations of social behavior can differ among cultures. For example, in some Nigerian families, as is the case in some other cultures, giving direct eye contact is considered rude and therefore unexpected (Perepa, 2014). When teachers continue teaching children from culturally diverse communities to give eye contact, they are, in fact, violating the family's cultural norms. In some Asian cultures, children may avoid eye contact with adults and respond to a teacher's questions by being silent, out of respect for the adults (Perepa, 2014). "If teachers are unaware of such differences they could be mislabeling the children or teaching them culturally inappropriate skills" (Perepa, 2014, p. 315).

Societal perceptions. Cultural traditions, values, and beliefs can shape the way a society views disability. People from many backgrounds perceive autism as a source of disappointment, annoyance, shame, or worse. The stigma attached to a disability may look different depending on cultural background. For some cultural groups, having a child with a disability may carry implications of shame about one's failure as a parent. For example, having a child with a disability in Korea means that the parents have failed to establish their credibility as effective parents (Kim, 2012). Parents, especially mothers, are often blamed for their child's disability in Korean culture, and it is perceived as a shameful family situation. Some cultures maintain the belief that "bad" mothers who are depressed and withdrawn caused the child to become autistic, rather than considering the possibility that dealing with the hardships of having an autistic child may have facilitated the mother's depression (Grinker, 2007). Many times, a parent's competence is called into question.

In some cultures, the family's name is dishonored when they have a child with a disability (Grinker, 2007). In those families, siblings will often avoid talking about their autistic sibling to friends and strangers to prevent "losing face" or receiving pity (Kwang Hwang & Charnley 2010). Parents may deal with the stigma surrounding autism by choosing to take their autistic child out of the house as little as possible and ultimately remain isolated from society (Kwang Hwang & Charnley, 2010). A great deal of shame and loneliness are associated with a family's inability to escape the cultural belief system, as they feel forced to keep a "secret" life at home (Kwang Hwang & Charnley, 2010). The stigma associated with autism in some cultures is so intense that many families will remain isolated and thereby avoid a diagnosis.

Treatments. A family's culture shapes their beliefs regarding the best course of treatment or intervention. For example, some families might believe that autism is a curable condition and may therefore follow a course of treatment designed to cure the disorder, or they may pursue other nontraditional forms of intervention (Mandell & Novak, 2005). A family that believes their child's autism is the result of biological variables may seek medical treatments specific to that cause while those who believe the cause was environmental may seek behaviorally based interventions (Ravindran & Myers, 2012). Some parents are convinced that if they find the right intervention and use it faithfully, their child will be cured of the condition (Ravindran & Myers, 2012). We must be sensitive to the beliefs of the cultures represented by our students.

T.I.P. – Theory Into Practice 2.5

CULTURAL AWARENESS "ROLE-PLAY"

1. Get several class members to form a team.

2. As a team, select a cultural group, one that is not represented by any member of your team, that you would like to research.

3. Research the various cultural characteristics and their attitudes and beliefs about ASD or disabilities in general.

4. Develop a role-play scenario that demonstrates how you would handle the situation if it arose. Emphasize how various cultural factors influence your interactions in the role-play.

5. Select from the ideas that follow, or come up with your own scenario.

6. Demonstrate your role-play to your classmates.

7. As your classmates watch the presentation, ask them to identify and discuss the various cultural characteristics demonstrated in the role-play.

Role-Play Ideas

1. Imagine you are in an IEP meeting, and the teacher's role is to translate professional terminology into everyday language.

2. Imagine that the teacher has several concerns about a child in the class and has requested a conference to discuss the concerns. The teacher has sent numerous notes home and has left several phone messages, but the parent has not responded to requests to meet.

3. Imagine that you are in a parent–teacher conference, and the family member becomes very emotional in response to something the teacher said.

4. Imagine you are in a parent–teacher conference, and the teacher's role is to explain a particular treatment approach or educational intervention to be implemented.

UNDERSTAND THE STRESS ASSOCIATED WITH RAISING A CHILD WITH ASD

It is important to highlight some of the issues facing parents of children with disabilities such as autism and become aware of the ideas and strategies we can use to support parents through those challenging times. Parents may feel shock, denial, disappointment, fear, sadness, grief, guilt, disbelief, anger, and many other emotions related to their experiences (Dukes & Smith, 2007; Haley, Hammond, Ingalls, & Marin, 2013), or they may feel none of these. We should seek to understand this range of emotions and offer any assistance possible as we work alongside them.

There are times in the lives of families with disabilities that can cause anxiety or stress. The diagnosis of a disability is a stressful event for parents (Dukes & Smith, 2007; Fiedler, Simpson, & Clark, 2007) and may even result in the experience of grief (Haley et al., 2013). As they live with the reality of caring for a child with autism, parents might feel the stress of coping with daily life (Dukes & Smith, 2007). The reality of bringing up a child with special needs can also put tremendous strain on parents and their relationship with one another. Research shows that a higher proportion of marriages fail due to the pressures they experience in raising a child with special needs (Dukes & Smith, 2007; Fiedler et al., 2007). Another concern of parents is that their child will experience peer rejection and failure to develop friendships (Fiedler et al., 2007).

Practitioners may not be in a position to help parents deal directly with their feelings; simply being welcoming and supportive to their children is often a great help to parents, "and there is a huge sense of relief when they realize that they are not alone. They have someone who is interested in their child's needs and how they can be met and [is] willing to work alongside them to help their child reach their potential"

(Dukes & Smith, 2007, p. 100). Regardless of the degree to which families respond and adjust to the stress, it is important that educators demonstrate awareness, understanding, and compassion toward families and strive toward teamwork.

Family Voices 2.4

"Stress is something I'm all too familiar with. But isn't every parent? Bathing, homework, meals, carpools . . . all the stressful things about being a parent are no different for any of us. Having a son with autism just adds another layer to the stress . . . but I wouldn't trade it for anything. My son is an amazing human being with multiple talents and creativity, just like yours."

UNDERSTAND THE SOURCES OF STRESS

It is clear that having a child with ASD can be associated with stress. "Once a child is diagnosed with ASD, challenges for the family continue to build and parental stress rises as parents strive to adapt to meeting the needs not only of their child diagnosed with ASD but also for the positive functioning of their family" (Hall & Graff, 2010, p. 189). The sources of stress that have been identified in the literature to be discussed in the following paragraphs will be grouped into three categories: managing the behaviors associated with ASD, a perceived lack of professional support, and public perceptions of ASD.

Managing behaviors associated with ASD. Challenging behaviors associated with autism are perhaps the most pervasive and enduring source of stress for families. Behavior problems such as noncompliance, conduct problems, and maladaptive social behavior have been linked to parenting stress in the literature (Lecavlier, Leone, & Wiltz, 2006; White, McMorris, Weiss, & Lunsky, 2012). Family stress is often linked to the social and communication deficits and problem behaviors associated with ASD (Jellett, Wood, Giallo, & Seymour, 2015; Johnson, Frenn, Feetham, & Simpson, 2011; Hayes & Watson, 2013; McStay, Trembath, & Dissanayake, 2014; Rao & Beidel, 2009). When their children have limited communication skills, mothers of children with autism tend to report higher stress levels (Pisula, 2011).

A key source of stress for parents of children with ASD is their child's behavior. Maladaptive behaviors, such as physical aggression and screaming, for example, are behaviors that parents may find stressful to manage. Parents may feel helpless when their child's responses to their attempts at calming him down are often unpredictable and incomprehensible (Pisula, 2011). In turn, parents who feel unable to make changes in their child's behavior might feel as if they are in a constant state of crisis (Mount & Dillon, 2014).

Perceived lack of professional support. Parents of children with autism may perceive a lack of professional support. For example, parents have been especially frustrated with the delayed and drawn-out diagnosis process because children with autism may be assessed by more than four professionals before finally receiving a diagnosis (Pisula, 2011). Parents in Mount and Dillon (2014) reported their frustration related to the limited support or advice around coping strategies that were offered at diagnosis. Events leading up to and following a diagnosis of ASD can be overwhelming to families.

Insufficient knowledge of symptoms and a general lack of education among professionals are also cited as a source of stress for parents (Pisula, 2011). Parents expect professionals to have up-to-date knowledge of ASD and to direct the family in decision-making, but this is often not the case. Unfortunately, the accessibility of autism-specific services and professional support is unsatisfactory to a number of parents (Pisula, 2011). As a result, parents can feel they are "left alone to coordinate, advocate for, and make decisions about treatment," and "they are overburdened with duties, sometimes feeling incompetent and anxious about whether they have made the right choice of intervention for their child" (Pisula, 2011, p. 91).

Public perceptions of ASD. Not only do parents of children with autism have to cope with the challenging behaviors associated with their child's ASD and the unsatisfactory experiences with professionals, but they must also bear the stigma society attaches to people with autism. Since the mid-20th century, parents have been blamed for causing their child's autism (Neely-Barnes, Hall, Roberts, & Graff, 2011). As awareness of autism has increased throughout the years, we would expect increasing acceptance and less blaming for causing the child's condition, yet parents still report the experiences of blame from extended family members and the public (Neely-Barnes et al., 2011). Regularly, we hear from parents in the literature of their experiences with being seen as "bad parents" (Neely-Barnes et al., 2011).

Often people interpret the behaviors associated with ASD as a sign of poor parenting or failure to discipline properly. Parents report feeling stigmatized and isolated as a result of people's misjudgments about the child's behavior (Mount & Dillon, 2014). Neely-Barnes et al. (2011) also considered that "constant stares and comments by people in public contribute to the higher levels of stress and depression experienced by parents" (p. 223), concluding that "further education of the general public is needed."

UNDERSTAND THE IMPACT OF STRESS ON THE FAMILY

Parental well-being. Parents of children with ASDs report higher levels of stress than parents of children without disabilities, and they are at increased risk for experiencing anxiety, depression, poorer quality of life, and fatigue. Compared with mothers of children who do not have disabilities, mothers of children with ASD reported higher levels of negative affect, significantly more days when they felt fatigued, more days with work intrusions, more time caring for their children, more time doing household chores, and less time on leisure activities (Smith et al., 2009). They also reported having more arguments and twice as many days with stress at home (Smith et al., 2009).

Researchers have suggested that attending to behavior problems associated with ASD increases the likelihood that parents would report depressive symptoms such as low mood and lack of enthusiasm and initiative (Jellett et al., 2015; Johnson et al., 2011). Others, such as Bromley, Hare, Davison, and Emerson (2004) and Rao and Beidel (2009), have shown that 50% of mothers of children with ASD reported immense psychological distress and that they experienced loss of their own social activities and disregard for their own autonomy and their career. Based on the multitude of stressors that parents of children with ASD report, the negative impact on parental well-being is of little surprise.

Family functioning. Family functioning refers to the extent to which families communicate, manage daily life, and foster positive relationships (Jellett et al., 2015; Johnson et al., 2011). Evidence suggests that when there is a child with ASD, family functioning is often affected. There is greater strain on the family system, less participation in recreational activities, less connectedness, and a higher incidence of anxiety, as family life centers on the affected child (Jellett et al., 2015). Childcare demands, feelings of not being a skilled parent, and lack of social support can significantly affect parental and family functioning (McStay et al., 2014; Rao & Beidel, 2009; Warfield, Chiri, Leutz, & Timberlake, 2014).

Parents also discuss the large amounts of time they must give to their child with ASD, leaving little time and energy for other siblings. A mother in Hall and Graff (2010) described the effect of autism on their family by saying that autism "takes over everything—your whole family . . . our entire family becomes consumed with it" (p. 195). Parents in Mount and Dillon (2014) reported their endless efforts to ensure that other siblings receive adequate parental attention and their constant need to justify the actions of their child with ASD to siblings. The stress associated with caring for a child with autism can have a negative impact on the child, the parent, and the entire family (Hutton & Caron, 2005).

Awareness of the contributors to the stress that families can experience may ultimately lead to targeted interventions that can support families and facilitate family functioning (Hayes & Watson, 2013; Jellett et al., 2015). Educators may also be in a better position to foster parent involvement when they can demonstrate acknowledgment of the demands of raising a child with ASD, the factors that contribute to their stress, and the effect of that stress on the family.

Tips for Partnering With Families

1. Know why establishing partnerships is important.

2. Demonstrate respect for children.

3. Maintain a family-centered perspective.

4. Take the initiative to communicate with families, regularly and through multiple means.

5. Listen with empathy.

6. Involve the family in developing goals and interventions.

7. Promote equality in decision-making.

8. Develop cultural awareness.

9. Understand the stress of raising a child with ASD. Know the potential causes and impact of that stress on families.

SUMMARY STATEMENTS

- Increased awareness of family perspectives is an important step in developing meaningful collaborative partnerships for the education of students with ASD.

- Educator dispositions that help facilitate meaningful school–family collaboration include demonstrating genuine respect for children, maintaining a family-centered perspective, and responding to the needs of the child with professional competence.

- It is critical for schools to engage in ongoing communication with families, promote equality in the decision-making process, and to develop cultural awareness in order to form more effective partnerships with the families they serve.

- Managing the behaviors associated with ASD, a perceived lack of professional support, and public perceptions of ASD are the most common sources of stress reported by families who are raising a child with ASD.

WHAT WOULD YOU DO?

Look back at the case study about Mrs. Logan presented at the beginning of the chapter. Based on what you have read in this chapter and your own experiences, how would you respond to the following questions?

1. What are your first reactions to this situation? Has Mrs. Logan done anything wrong, or has she failed to do something that might be more inviting to parents?

2. If you were Mrs. Logan's principal, what advice would you give her? Give examples of the support you would offer her.

3. Other than the information provided in this case study, what additional information would you seek about the families of Mrs. Logan's students? How would that information help determine the kinds of support you could offer or the ways you would mentor her to facilitate parent involvement?

4. Assume that you identify a need for more *family-centered* practices. What are some strategies for parent involvement that you might help her put into place?

CHAPTER REFLECTION QUESTIONS

1. How does your understanding of the sources and effects of stress on a family that is raising a child with ASD impact how you will approach families in your efforts to collaborate?

2. How do educator dispositions affect family involvement in the education of students with ASD?

3. What can school professionals do proactively to facilitate meaningful school–family collaboration?

4. What are some ways in which cultural differences can create barriers to collaboration?

RECOMMENDED RESOURCES

Communicating With Families

- Pinterest. *Parent/teacher communication.* https://www.pinterest.com/TheBigAWord/autism-parentstudentteacher-communication/

- New Horizons. *How educators and support professionals can help families.* http://education.jhu.edu/PD/newhorizons/Exceptional%20Learners/Autism/Articles/How%20Educators%20and%20Support%20Professionals%20Can%20Help%20Families/

Cultural Awareness & Sensitivity

- http://courses.unt.edu/Ennis-Cole/articles/File2.pdf

- https://www.pdx.edu/multicultural-topics-communication-sciences-disorders/autism-spectrum-disorder-cultural-implications-and-considerations

- http://www.worksupport.com/documents/culturallysensative.pdf

Family Stress

- https://www.autismspeaks.org/news/news-item/ian-research-report-family-stress-%E2%80%94-part-1

- http://iancommunity.org/cs/articles/parental_depression

- http://www.child-autism-parent-cafe.com/stress-on-families.html

REFERENCES

Bachner, Y., Carmel, S., Lubetzky, H., Heiman, N., & Galil, A. (2006). Parent–therapist communication and satisfaction with the services of a child development center: A comparison between Israeli parents: Jews and Bedouins. *Health Communication, 19*(3), 221–229.

Bacon, J. K., & Causton-Theoharis, J. (2013). It should be teamwork: A critical investigation of school practices and parent advocacy in special education. *International Journal of Inclusive Education, 17*, 682–699.

Benson, P., Karlof, K. L., & Siperstein, G. N. (2008). Maternal involvement in the education of young children with autism spectrum disorders. *Autism, 12*(1), 47–63.

Blue-Banning, J., Summers, J. A., Frankland, H. C., Nelson, L. L., & Beegle, G. (2004). Dimensions of family and professional partnerships: Constructive guidelines for collaboration. *TEACHING Exceptional Children, 70*(2), 167–184.

Bromley, J., Hare, D. J., Davison, K., & Emerson, E. (2004). Mothers supporting children with autistic spectrum disorders: Social support, mental health status and satisfaction with services. *Autism, 8*(4), 409–423.

Bryk, A., & Schneider, B. (2004). *Trust in schools: A core resource for improvement.* New York, NY: The Russell Sage Foundation.

Burke, M. M. (2012). Examining family involvement in regular and special education: Lessons to be learned for both sides. *International Review of Research in Developmental Disabilities, 43*, 187–218.

Dabkowski, D. (2004). Encouraging active parent participation in IEP team meetings.

TEACHING Exceptional Children, 26, 34–39.

deFur, S. (2012). Parents as collaborators: Building partnerships with school- and community-based providers. *TEACHING Exceptional Children, 44*(3), 58–67.

Dukes, C., & Smith, M. (2007). *Working with parents of children with special education needs.* London, England: Paul Chapman Publishing.

Dyches, T. T., Wilder, L. K., Sudweeks, R. R., Obiakor, F. E., & Algozzine, B. (2004). Multicultural issues in autism. *Journal of Autism and Developmental Disorders, 34,* 211–222.

Empathy. (n.d.). *Merriam-Webster.* Retrieved from https://www.merriam-webster.com/dictionary/empathy

Fiedler, C. R., Simpson, R. L., & Clark, D. M. (2007). *Parents and families of children with disabilities: Effective school-based support services.* Upper Saddle River, NJ: Pearson Education.

Fishman, C. E., & Nickerson, A. B. (2015). Motivations for involvement: A preliminary investigation of parents of students with disabilities. *Journal of Child and Family Studies, 24,* 523–535.

Friend, M., & Borsuck, W. (2009). *Including students with special needs: A practical guide for classroom teachers* (5th ed.). Upper Saddle River, NJ: Pearson Education.

Friend, M., & Cook, L. (2010). *Interactions: Collaboration skills for school professionals.* Upper Saddle River, NJ: Pearson Education.

Grinker, R. (2007). *Unstrange minds: Remapping the world of autism.* New York, NY: Basic Books.

Haley, M., Hammond, H., Ingalls, L., & Marin, M. R. (2013). Parental reactions to the special education individual education program process: Looking through the lens of grief. *Improving Schools, 16*(3), 232–243.

Hall, H. R., & Graff, C. (2010). Parenting challenges in families of children with autism: A pilot study. *Issues in Comprehensive Pediatric Nursing, 33,* 187–204.

Hayes, S. A., & Watson, S. L. (2013). The impact of parenting stress: A meta-analysis of studies comparing the experience of parenting stress in parents of children with and without autism spectrum disorder. *Journal of Autism and Developmental Disorders, 43,* 629–642.

Hebel, O., & Persitz, S. (2014). Parental involvement in the individual education program for Israeli students with disabilities. *Internal Journal of Special Education, 29*(3), 58–68.

Hughes, M. T., Valle-Riestra, D. M., & Arguelles, M. E. (2008). The voices of Latino families raising children with special needs. *Journal of Latinos and Education, 7,* 241–257.

Hutton, A. M., & Caron, S. L. (2005). Experiences of families with children with autism in rural New England. *Focus on Autism and Other Developmental Disabilities, 20,* 180–189.

Individuals With Disabilities Education Act (IDEA), 20 U.S.C. §§ 1400 et seq. (2006 & Supp. V. 2011).

Jellett, R., Wood, C. E., Giallo, R., & Seymour, M. (2015). Family functioning and behavior problems in children with autism spectrum disorders: The mediating role of parent mental health. *Clinical Psychologist, 19,* 39–48.

Johnson, J., Frenn, M., Feetham, S., & Simpson, P. (2011). Autism spectrum disorder: Parenting stress, family functioning and health-related quality of life. *Families, Systems, & Health, 29,* 232–252.

Kim, H. (2012). Autism across cultures: Rethinking autism. *Disability & Society, 27,* 535–545.

Koegel, R. L., Bimbela, A., & Schriebman, L. (1996). Collateral effects of parents training on family interactions. *Journal of Autism and Developmental Disorders, 26*(3), 347–359.

Kwang Hwang, S., & Charnley, H. (2010). Making the familiar strange and making the strange familiar: Understanding Korean children's experiences of living with an autistic sibling. *Disability and Society, 25*(5), 579–592.

Lecavalier, L., Leone, S., & Wiltz, J. (2006). The impact of behavior problems on caregiver stress in young people with autism spectrum disorders. *Journal of Intellectual Disability Research, 50*, 172–183.

Mandell, D. S., & Novak, M. (2005). The role of culture in families' treatment decisions for children with autism spectrum disorders. *Mental Retardation and Developmental Disabilities Research Reviews, 11*, 110–115.

McStay, R. L., Trembath, D., & Dissanayake, C. (2014). Stress and family quality of life in parents of children with autism spectrum disorder: Parent gender and the double ABCX model. *Journal of Autism and Developmental Disorders, 44*, 3101–3118.

Moes, D. R., & Frea, W. D. (2002). Contextualized behavioral support in early intervention for children with autism and their families. *Journal of Autism and Developmental Disorders, 32*(6), 519–533.

Mount, N., & Dillon, G. (2014). Parents' experiences of living with an adolescent diagnosed with an autism spectrum disorder. *Educational and Child Psychology, 31*, 72–81.

National Research Council. (2001). *Educating children with autism*. Washington, DC: National Academy Press. Retrieved from http://www.nap.edu/catalog/10017.html

Neely-Barnes, S. L., Hall, H. R., Roberts, R., & Graff, J. C. (2011). Parenting a child with an autism spectrum disorder: Public perceptions and parental conceptualizations. *Journal of Family Social Work, 14*, 208–225.

Osher, T. W., & Osher, D. M. (2002). The paradigm shift to true collaboration with families. *Journal of Child and Family Studies, 11*(1), 47–60.

Paige-Smith, A., & Rix, J. (2006). Parents' perceptions and children's experiences of early intervention—inclusive practice? *Journal of Research in Special Education Needs, 6*, 92–98.

Park, J., & Turnbull, A. P. (2002). Quality indicators of professionals who work with children with problem behavior. *Journal of Positive Behavior Interventions, 4*, 118–122.

Perepa, P. (2014). Cultural basis of social 'deficits' in autism spectrum disorders. *European Journal of Special Needs Education, 29*, 313–326.

Pisula, E. (2011). Parenting stress in mothers and fathers of children with autism spectrum disorders. In M. Mohammadi (Ed.), *A comprehensive book on autism spectrum disorders* (pp. 87–106). Rijeka, Croatia: InTech Europe. Retrieved from http://www.intechopen.com/books/a-comprehensive-book-on-autismspectrum-disorders/parenting-stress-in-mothers-and-fathers-of-children-with-autism-spectrum-disorders

Rao, P. A., & Beidel, D. (2009). The impact of children with high-functioning autism on parental stress, sibling adjustment, and family functioning. *Behavior Modification, 33*, 437–451.

Ravindran, N., & Myers, B. (2012). Cultural influences on perceptions of health, illness, and disability: A review and focus on autism. *Journal of Child and Family Studies, 21*, 311–219.

Renty, J., & Roeyers, H. (2005). Satisfaction with formal support and education for children with autism spectrum disorder: The voices of the parents. *Health & Development, 32*, 371–385.

Rodriquez, R. J., Blatz, E. T., & Elbaum, B. (2014). Parents' view of schools' involvement efforts. *TEACHING Exceptional Children, 81*(1), 79–85.

Sawyer, M. (2015). BRIDGES: Connecting with families to facilitate and enhance involvement. *TEACHING Exceptional Children, 47*, 172–179.

Sheehey, P. H., & Sheehey, P. E. (2007). Elements for successful parent–professional collaboration: The fundamental things apply as time goes by. *TEACHING Exceptional Children Plus, 4*(2), Article 3. Retrieved from http://escholarship.bc.edu/education/tecplus/vol4/iss2/art3

Smith, L. E., Hong, J., Seltzer, M. M., Greenberg, J. S., Almeida, D. M., & Bishop, S. L. (2009). Daily experiences among mothers of adolescents and adults with autism spectrum disorder. *Journal of Autism and Developmental Disabilities, 40*, 167–168.

Staples, K. E., & Diliberto, J. A. (2010). Guidelines for successful parent involvement: Working with parents of students with disabilities. *TEACHING Exceptional Children, 42*(6), 58–63.

Stoner, J. B., Bock, S. J., Thompson, J. R., Angell, M. E., Heyl, B. S., & Crowley, E. P. (2005). Welcome to our world: Parent perceptions of interactions between parents of young children with ASD and education professionals. *Focus on Autism and Other Developmental Disabilities, 20*, 39–51.

Stuart, S. K., Flis, L. D., & Rinaldi, C. (2006). Connecting with families: Parents speak up about preschool services for their children with autism spectrum disorders. *TEACHING Exceptional Children, 39*(1), 46–51.

Tincani, M., Travers, J., & Boutot, A. (2009). Race, culture, and autism spectrum disorder: Understanding the role of diversity in successful educational interventions. *Research & Practice for Persons With Severe Disabilities, 34*, 81–90.

Tschannen-Moran, M. (2004). *Trust matters: Leadership for successful schools*. San Francisco, CA: Jossey-Bass.

Turnbull, R., & Turnbull, A. (2015). Looking backward and framing the future for parents' aspirations for their children with disabilities. *Remedial and Special Education, 36*, 52–57.

Warfield, M. E., Chiri, G., Leutz, W. N., & Timberlake, M. (2014). Family well-being in a participant-directed autism waiver program: The role of relational coordination. *Journal of Intellectual Disability Research, 38*, 1091–1104.

White, S. E., McMorris, C., Weiss, J. A., & Lunsky, Y. (2012). The experience of crisis in families of individuals with autism spectrum disorder across the lifespan. *Journal of Child Family Studies, 21*, 457–465.

Identifying and Responding to Challenges to School–Family Collaboration

"When I was a Special Education teacher, I sometimes became frustrated with parents who could not come to meetings or follow up with homework. But when I took off my Special Education teacher glasses and put on my parent point of view, I had a better understanding of their challenges and struggles."

—A PARENT IN TODD, BEAMER, AND GOODREAU (2014, P. 288)

CASE STUDY

Henry is a fifth-grade student at Mountain View Academy in Mr. Acosta's special education class. Henry has a diagnosis of ASD and has attended Mountain View for all five years of his elementary school life. Henry typically exhibits many challenging behaviors associated with ASD, including throwing pencils at staff, attempted running from the classroom, loud noises during instructional time, hitting others during transitions, and refusing to do his math classwork. Recently, Henry's behaviors have begun to escalate. He ran from the classroom screaming after assaulting a classmate who attempted to cut in front of Henry in line, and staff had to physically restrain him. When school staff tried to contact Nina about the incident, she did not answer her telephone.

Mr. Acosta tries very hard to create a community of parent involvement in his class. He sends regular newsletters to the families of his students to keep them informed. He has had specialized training to work with children who have ASD, and he likes to provide regular information to families to share his knowledge. His favorite way of

LEARNER OBJECTIVES

After reading this chapter, the learner should be able to do the following:

- Explain several reasons why parent–teacher collaboration might be difficult to achieve.

- List ways that educators can gain an understanding of different cultures.

- Define *communication*, assess one's communication style, and explain how differences in communication styles and preferences can hinder school–family collaboration.

- Describe how individual parent and family factors can influence a family's motivation to collaborate with schools.

communicating with parents is to hold monthly information sessions that parents can attend, which he calls "Acosta University." At these information sessions, Mr. Acosta likes to act as if he's the "professor," providing lectures to any parent or staff member who attends. Few parents attend "Acosta University," and he is not sure why.

Nina spends hours each week searching the Internet for the latest way to deal with Henry's behavior at home. She works the night shift at the hospital, and sometimes during the late night hours while patients are sleeping, she has the opportunity to read and find answers to her questions about ASD. While she reads, she takes copious notes in a journal she calls "Helping Henry." Nina has learned a lot about ASD and ways to teach new behaviors that are more appropriate. Recently she's learned something very interesting that she would like to share with Mr. Acosta and that she would love for him to implement to improve Henry's behavior. She would love to share what she's learned with Henry's teacher, Mr. Acosta, but in her opinion, he seems uninterested. Since she works all night and tries to find opportunities to sleep during the day, she has limited availability to meet with Mr. Acosta when he asks for a conference during school hours. A face-to-face conference seems impossible given their opposing schedules.

The staff at Mountain View would love for Nina, Henry's mother, to be more involved in Henry's education by coming to school conferences, helping with homework, or participating in other school activities, but she is rarely able to come. Just after a recent staff development day titled, "Creative Strategies for Facilitating Parent Involvement," outside, two teachers had a discussion about Nina. "She just doesn't seem interested in being involved," one teacher lamented. "If she truly cared about Henry's education, she'd find a way to get here." The other teacher responded with, "I have lots of parents who come to school to help. I don't see why anyone should have to find creative ways to get her interested in coming."

Other school staff have complained about how rarely Nina comes to the school, and they imagine that something must be going on at home to cause Henry's challenging behaviors. Several staff members have contacted Nina through telephone messages and notes sent home to explain Henry's poor behavior, but they have received no response. Nina rarely returns the phone calls. Nina said recently to a friend, "Can't the school ever give me good news? Why do I feel like staff thinks Henry is defective in some way? It's always, 'Henry did this or that bad thing.' Is there anything good to say?"

Nina told her friend, who works in the cafeteria at the school, that she feels unwelcome at the school. She said, "I don't want the royal treatment or anything, but I wish Henry's teacher would show a little respect. He's just not very welcoming. Why would I want to collaborate with him? Besides, it's his job to educate my child . . . not mine! How am I supposed to get to the school, anyway? That junker car of mine would never make it all the way there."

....

INTRODUCTION

This is a book about collaborating with parents for the benefit of our students with ASD, and therefore, we highlight strategies for working with parents in every chapter of this text. No book about school–family collaboration would be complete without addressing how collaborators can respond to challenges to the interactive relationship. What are the barriers to parental involvement, and how can we respond in ways that facilitate parental engagement and strengthen relationships? What do we do when collaboration doesn't come so easily? Learning to work effectively with family members is critical for effective collaboration, and that is why this chapter addresses potential challenges to school–family partnerships and how we can respond to them in ways that facilitate positive interactions. Viewing parents as partners who have much to offer professionals is foundational for developing meaningful collaboration.

Other chapters in this text have devoted significant attention to discussing our responsibility as educators to collaborate with families (IDEA 2004; Friend & Cook, 2010) and the benefits of collaboration to students' academic and social progress (Bacon & Causton-Theoharis, 2013; Dabkowski, 2004; Friend & Borsuck, 2009). We've established that our role as special educators is to partner with families, and what deserves our attention in this chapter is an examination of potential barriers to collaboration and what to do when collaborative efforts have been challenged.

We've set the stage for establishing meaningful collaboration, and now we turn to a discussion of the challenges to collaboration and how we can work to overcome those challenges so that our students with autism benefit to the greatest extent possible. It makes sense to devote our efforts toward developing school–family collaboration so that student achievement is maximized. We believe it is important for educators to possess the skills that support successful collaboration, which includes an understanding of the factors that can impede collaborative efforts, as well as strategies for overcoming some of those challenges and building trust in the special education setting. This chapter provides a tool for dealing with common struggles in our relationships with parents of students with special needs.

BARRIERS TO COLLABORATION AND PARENT PARTICIPATION

Collaboration is defined as working or acting together (Sheehey & Sheehey, 2007). Although parents and professions no doubt maintain sincere respect for one another and genuinely want a meaningful collaborative relationship, they sometimes have difficulty establishing a level of collaboration that benefits children with disabilities (Sheehey & Sheehey, 2007). Sheehey and Sheehey (2007) believe this is due primarily to parents and professionals who see collaboration from two different vantage points.

Professionals' thinking may be grounded in theory acquired from years of personnel preparation and accumulated experiences. Parents' thinking may be grounded in personal experiences with their child and the information they have been able to glean from professionals, other parents, the Internet, and the media (Sheehey & Sheehey, 2007, p. 3) about their child's different abilities. Many times, efforts to collaborate are extremely positive while others can seem to end in catastrophic failure (Sheehey & Sheehey, 2007). Let us look at some potential barriers to successful collaboration that might result in less-than-successful collaborative efforts.

Barriers to School–Family Partnerships

1. Cultural and linguistic diversity.
   - ☑ Language barriers
   - ☑ Parents' underlying values
   - ☑ Assumptions and perceptions of school personnel

2. Communication style differences.
   - ☑ Sources of knowledge
   - ☑ Direction
   - ☑ Giving and receiving information

3. Individual parent and family factors.
   - ☑ Current life contexts
   - ☑ Blame
   - ☑ Beliefs about involvement
   - ☑ Perceptions of inequality
   - ☑ Mistrust
   - ☑ Dissatisfaction
   - ☑ Anger

4. Educators.
   - ☑ Use of formal vocabulary, acronyms, and academic jargon
   - ☑ Lack of sensitivity toward cultural differences
   - ☑ Self-perceived position of authority
   - ☑ Deficit view of families
   - ☑ Lack of respect for parent knowledge
   - ☑ Use of "top down," one-direction communication
   - ☑ Use of negative communication about student's performance
   - ☑ Blaming families for their child's behavior
   - ☑ Narrow conception of the role parents should play in collaboration
   - ☑ Failing to deal with conflict when it arises and focusing on the person rather than the problem

CULTURAL AND LINGUISTIC DIVERSITY

Understanding Cultural and Linguistic Diversity

Family involvement in their child's education can range from very active to passive, depending on their culture and the school climate. "If the school environment is open, helpful, and friendly, and there is frequent, clear, two-way communication, then parents are more likely to participate" (Lasky & Karge, 2011, p. 29). There are a number of reasons why parents may be reluctant to participate, including language barriers, interpersonal values, and the attitudes and perceptions of school personnel that prohibits active involvement in educational decision-making.

Language barriers. Sometimes a language barrier impedes collaborative efforts. This may include parents' lack of English skills and the small number of school staff who are able to speak the language of the parents (Lasky & Karge, 2011). A language barrier can also be created by the formal vocabulary and grammar structure that is often used by schools or the use of acronyms and academic jargon, which may make communications less clear to parents. "Although the individual words may be familiar to parents, the content is not readily understandable" (Lasky & Karge, 2011, p. 30). Some concerns about unqualified, untrained translators, who may have "slanted views" of immigrant parents have also been expressed in research (Jung, 2011). The level of English proficiency could serve as a significant disadvantage for linguistically diverse parents in their efforts to communicate with school professionals. The importance of providing qualified and knowledgeable translators should not be underestimated (Jung, 2011).

Parents' underlying values. It may be the case that interpersonal values held by parents dictate taking a more passive role in their child's education (Jung, 2011). Their cultural beliefs may place value in avoiding direct interactions with school professionals throughout the educational process, preferring a more compliant, agreeable stance. In some cultures, school professionals are viewed as the authority. Parents may not be "accustomed to the process of discussing their children's education with school professionals and they believe that school professionals' suggestions are final and inevitable decisions from the beginning of the IEP process, even when parents' opinions are completely divergent from those of the school professionals" (Jung, 2011, p. 23). When educators are viewed as the educational authority, parents can perceive their role is to conform to the recommendations of school professionals (Jung, 2011).

Assumptions and perceptions of school personnel. There are many assumptions by school personnel that can hinder effective parent–school collaboration with cultural and linguistic minority families. For example, schools might hold a deficit view represented by the belief that students fail in schools because their families are characteristically flawed. These assumptions can lead educators to think that certain cultures do not value education and are therefore unwilling to support the school's educational efforts (Lasky & Karge, 2011). Research demonstrates that many families of diverse cultures are very interested in being involved, and in fact, they view education as critical for success in life (Lasky & Karge, 2011). Educators should be proactive to understand the differences that each family brings to the collaborative relationship.

Educators may discourage parental involvement by knowingly or unknowingly withholding certain information. Jung (2011) asserts that very often parents have limited knowledge of their legal rights in the IEP process and that school professionals seem to evade responsibility and allow parents to remain unaware of their rights. This stance may discourage parents from having an influential role in the educational decision-making process, sometimes resulting in severe damage to the collaborative relationship.

> If parents set out to increase their role, surface their opinions, and become more persistent during their child's IEP process, the more adamant the attitudes of school professionals become as they exhibit insensitive, aggressive, and impatient attitudes toward the parents. Consequently, the majority of parents are psychologically and emotionally disturbed by the feelings of isolation, frustration, resentment, and anger. (Jung, 2011, p. 23)

Sometimes, the assumptions of school professionals provide considerable obstacles that hamper effective parental involvement.

RESPONDING TO CULTURAL AND LINGUISTIC DIVERSITY

Working with families who are culturally diverse requires objectivity and sensitivity to any differences. Make efforts to know the backgrounds, experiences, cultures, customs, and communication styles of your students and their families. Raise your diversity awareness. Learning about the customs and backgrounds represented in the families with whom you interact can assist you to be better prepared to welcome all families into your classroom and increase the likelihood of meaningful collaboration (Cramer, 2006). Learn as much as you can about the perceptions of family members from diverse backgrounds. "We can then adapt our outreach methods to dovetail with some of their needs and concerns. We should learn to ask questions and not to presume that we already have answers" (Cramer, 2006, p. 261).

To interact effectively with families of diverse cultures and backgrounds, we must gain an understanding of specific cultures, learn about their families, and learn to value people of different cultures (Cramer, 2006). We should seek to understand that parents choose their level of involvement, and that choice may be a reflection of cultural values (Sheehey & Sheehey, 2007).

Family Voices 3.1

"Cultural differences? In my culture, making eye contact with others is considered a sign of disrespect when children interact with adults. Please don't make my child look you in the eye to show you he is listening. Don't insist that he disrespect you. He's trying very hard not to be disrespectful of adults."

COMMUNICATION DIFFERENCES

Understanding Communication Differences

Promoting positive and proactive school–family communication is not only desirable but also essential to the education of students with disabilities (Koro-Ljungberg, Bussing, Wilder, & Gary, 2011). Sometimes there are barriers to effective parent–teacher communication, and we must consider ways to move from conflict to collaboration. Communicating with family members effectively involves both the giving and receiving of information: "Teachers need to both give information to and get information from family members; this dialogue becomes the basis for educating students" (Cramer, 2006, p. 269).

Sources of knowledge. School–family communication can be influenced by a variety of factors. For example, communication patterns and preferences may exist, with each party having different philosophies regarding who is the source of knowledge, as well as who should initiate communication. Some teachers believe that parents have firsthand knowledge of their child's educational needs, and these teachers are eager to learn from parents through personal conversations, phone conversations, school visits, or written communication. These teachers prefer to be the receivers of information (Koro-Ljungberg et al., 2011). Other teachers prefer to be the senders of information, attempting to enable parents to understand why a certain teaching strategy is implemented or how parents could assist teachers to meet academic learning objectives. Parents are invited to participate in classroom activities, teachers plan classroom presentations, and parents are informed about how they can assist their children in different school activities in this model (Koro-Ljungberg et al., 2011). Moreover, some teachers hold parents responsible for initiating communications with the school or teachers while others feel they are responsible for initiating communications with families.

Parents can be well versed in ASD and special education practices, and they can be a rich source of information that often matches the level of that which educators possess. They have undertaken efforts to educate themselves through their own experiences, from doctors, from disability organizations, or through Internet searches (Trainor, 2010). Many times, teachers are reluctant to accept this "capital" that parents bring to the collaborative relationship. "Having lots of capital does not necessarily mean having lots of power. Parents across groups had experiences in which their equal status with teachers was challenged and their efforts to advocate were ignored" (Trainor, 2010, p. 45). We should be open to receiving the valuable firsthand expertise that parents have gained and promote equal opportunity in decision-making.

Family Voices 3.2

"I have done so much research about what works for my son. Countless hours of reading and viewing videos and talking to other parents and teachers. Can I be of help to you by sharing some things I've learned?"

Direction. Many times, school–family communication tends to be unidirectional, as the teacher sends information to the family through notices or reports without the expectation of a response (Todd et al., 2014), which can add to a sense of tension in the collaborative relationship. Communication can and should travel in two directions. Schools have a responsibility to communicate with parents, and it is essential that families take an active role in articulating to the school behaviors that manifest in home settings.

One-way communication is limited because it occurs in a straight line from sender to receiver and serves to inform, persuade, or command. Two-way communication, on the other hand, includes feedback from the receiver to the sender, and it also lets the sender know the message has been received accurately. In two-way communication, both the sender and receiver listen to each other, gather information, and are willing to make changes wherever necessary to work together harmoniously.

T.I.P. – Theory Into Practice 3.2

ASSESS YOUR COMMUNICATION STYLE

1. Look at the statements below and circle the ones that describe you the best. Circle all that apply.

Receiving Messages	Sending Messages
Reading:	**Writing**:
I understand well most things that I read.	I enjoy keeping a daily journal, calendar, or planner.
I look at a newspaper or book every day.	I recopy information that I want to remember or understand better.
I like to spend free time reading.	
I'd rather read the book than watch the movie.	I prefer to write down my ideas before I say them.
To learn how to do something, I like to read the instructions.	I take a lot of notes at meetings.
Reading is relaxing.	I keep in touch with people by writing notes and letters.

(Continued)

(Continued)

Receiving Messages	Sending Messages
Listening:	**Speaking:**
I keep the iPod/music or TV on for company.	I like to tell stories.
I like to close my eyes and really take in the sounds around me.	I like to take part in conversations.
I like to listen to stories about people and their lives.	I learn well by discussing my ideas with others.
I remember almost everything I hear.	I love to spend time on the telephone.
To learn to do something, I like to watch and listen to someone demonstrate it.	I like to ask questions to understand better.

2. The left two boxes represent your preference for *receiving* information. The top left quadrant may indicate that you prefer to receive information and learn best by reading it. The bottom left indicates you learn best by listening.

3. The right two boxes represent your preference for *sending* information. The top right quadrant represents a preference for sending messages in writing. The bottom right indicates a preference for sending messages through speaking.

4. Look at your responses above. In which quadrant have you circled the most statements?

5. The quadrant in which you have the most items circled may be your preferred communication style.

6. Give an example of how you have used your preferred communication style in your work.

7. What does this information suggest for future communication in school–family partnerships?

RESPONDING TO COMMUNICATION DIFFERENCES

Efforts to improve school–family communication should focus on developing effective communication skills. There are things you can do to strengthen your relationships with parents, such as maintaining a posture of active listening. Communication really involves the capacity to listen, pay attention, perceive, and respond in ways that demonstrate to the speaker that you have attended, listened, and accurately perceived (Gorman, 2004). To demonstrate that you have truly heard parents' message, Gorman suggests that you (1) ask open-ended questions; (2) be an active listener; (3) clarify thoughts; (4) respond to the primary message; and (5) summarize important points.

Nonverbal behaviors are also important in making parents feel understood and helped. This includes maintaining eye contact, occasional head nodding and smiling, and having an open posture. Notice when a parent may be stressed, and try to put him or her at ease. "You should be aware of the emotions behind the thoughts and respond accordingly" (Gorman, 2004, p. 22). Acknowledge feelings, provide support, and guide the parent to the appropriate solution whenever possible. Exhibiting these behaviors, even when parents may be intent on expressing their dissatisfaction with any aspect of the school or your teaching, will likely result in a parent who is more open to working with you in a positive way. These helpful reminders for communicating your interest and concern to parents will serve you well.

Cramer (2006) offered several suggestions for how to develop good lines of communication with family members that can strengthen the connection between school and home and create a shared commitment to learning. Establishing a daily classroom hotline is one example. Cramer suggested that teachers have a dedicated classroom phone line, with an answering machine. Each day, the teacher records a new message that includes information about what took place in school that day, homework assignments due the next day, and information about school events (long-term assignments, school field trips, school events, etc.). Parents can call the school at their own convenience to quickly find out what they need to know, and they can leave questions or comments on the phone message system (Cramer, 2006).

Another idea Cramer (2006) proposed was a home–school technology connection, which can be useful in facilitating contacts between teachers and parents. Many homes have access to computers, which allows for communications at any time without the need to find a mutually convenient meeting time that works around the family's work schedule or other obligations. When it is difficult for family members to coordinate travel to school, you can conduct Web conferences or connect through Skype or Facetime, which allows opportunities to involve family members that extend beyond the face-to-face format (Cramer, 2006).

Whether face-to-face or via computer/Skype, we should be considerate about creating a meeting in which people feel comfortable and free to share ideas (Cramer, 2006). To ensure that parents or caregivers feel equal to each professional who is present, invite parents to share stories and provide suggestions for their child, and provide ample opportunity for parents to discuss any suggestions that are made (Sheehey & Sheehey, 2007), rather than simply talking *at* parents or providing one-directional communication. Sheehey and Sheehey ask educators to

> be prepared to lend a sympathetic ear to parents, to listen to their stories and to respond to them with gentleness. Your primary responsibility is to discover how you will be able to assist not only the children with disabilities in your class, but their parents as well. Parents need to know that you are in their corner, that you will stand up for their child and seek what is best for the family. (p. 4)

Understand that parents might have difficulty receiving information, for any number of reasons, and be proactive to provide assistance where necessary.

INDIVIDUAL PARENT AND FAMILY FACTORS

Understanding Individual Parent and Family Factors

Building effective long-term partnerships requires that we understand the differing perspectives that parents bring to the relationship and that we work toward support for parents and improvement in our collaborative efforts for the benefit of our students with ASD.

Current life contexts. Sometimes parents may simply lack the available time, energy, or resources to participate because of work or family responsibilities. Parents might be struggling to fulfill their job and family obligations, and they might not have available time to devote to attend school meetings, volunteer at school, or participate in other activities (Hornby & Lafaele, 2011; Murray et al., 2014; Wegmann & Bowen, 2010). Work and scheduling issues were the most frequently reported barriers to parent involvement in Murray et al.'s research (2014). One parent in Gorman's (2004) experience indicated that "although he wished he could attend school functions as other parents did, he could not, because he worked both a day job and a night job in order to provide for his family of seven" (p. 81). Parents who work sometimes have difficulty attending critical IEP meetings, which are usually held during school/work hours (Burke, 2013). And although some jobs allow flexibility for taking time off for school-based involvement, sometimes parents may simply be too tired at the end of the day to attend meetings, help with homework, or participate in school activities (Hornby & Lafaele, 2011). Finally, limited resources, such as lack of transportation, could also limit a parent's ability to be involved (Murray et al., 2014).

Perceptions of inequality. Some parents might limit their involvement with schools because they feel intimidated by the school or because they feel inadequate or lacking the necessary expertise to be of any help (Burke, 2013; Hornby & Lafaele, 2011). They may feel they have not developed sufficient academic competence to help their children, or they may lack confidence that their involvement will bring about positive outcomes (Hornby & Lafaele, 2011). Parents may feel unwelcome, feel there is a power differential, or feel that their roles are minimized (Burke, 2013). When they sense inequality in the collaborative relationship, parents may feel intimidated and unwelcome at school and therefore avoid participation.

> ## Family Voices 3.3
>
> "Teachers don't think to include me as much as I would like. Teachers don't have as much education about ASD as I do. Many teachers hold the view that parents should 'just be parents' instead of empowering them."

Expectations. It may be natural for parents to have any number of expectations for the public school system, which, when unmet, can contribute to their dissatisfaction. Some might hold the school solely responsible for their child's education, believing the school staff members are the "experts" (Gorman, 2004). They expect the school system to do what is best for their child. Parents may feel disappointment with their child's lack of progress and therefore question different instructional methods or approaches that the school may or may not be able to provide (Gorman, 2004). No matter the source of dissatisfaction, the burden lies with school staff to respond in a professional manner when their practices are questioned.

RESPONDING TO INDIVIDUAL PARENT AND FAMILY FACTORS

Build upon strengths. A strengths-based approach to partnering with families can support and empower families to collaborate with school personnel (Bryan & Henry, 2008). By empowerment, we mean that families feel valued and included in the school, and they share a sense of purpose and confidence in their ability to see their children succeed in school. Seek to recognize families as assets and build upon the strengths that families bring to the partnership, rather than focusing on problem reduction and correction (Bryan & Henry, 2008).

Ideally, "principals, teachers, counselors, and all school personnel recognize and affirm strengths by developing a culture in which they intentionally find ways to celebrate all children and their families and let parents know that their efforts are appreciated even when their children are struggling in school" (Bryan & Henry, 2008, p. 150). When you see what appears to be limited parent involvement, instead of assuming the parents don't care to be involved, you can think of the resilience parents must have, given the challenges they face in raising a child with a disability. Be diligent in making parents feel welcome in the school and seeing themselves as assets in their children's education (Bryan & Henry, 2008).

Know your parents. Gorman (2004) offers several guiding principles for responding when parents seem nonparticipatory. (1) Get to know the parents. By getting to know parents, you can better facilitate their cooperation. You may be able to persuade their involvement by focusing on what is important to them. (2) Be creative with invitations. For example, if parents have not responded to handwritten notes, consider sending an e-mail. Or a class project to work on computer skills can become a way to send personalized invitations or requests to see work in progress. Or offer simple refreshments to parents who participate in school functions. (3) Help parents participate. Some may be unable to participate because of real concerns, such as being unable to leave their job or challenges finding a babysitter for their children. Work with them to overcome some of these barriers.

Build trust. Trust is critical in a collaborative relationship. The primary way to bring two different viewpoints together is for parents and teachers to become aware of each other's problems and work together (Todd et al., 2014). To build trust, we should strive to establish rapport with parents, listen with empathy, invite parents to engage in a partnership, and create a safe environment for open discussions. We should work toward allowing parents to feel less threatened and improving trust in the relationship. Effective communication is at the heart of managing conflict and engaging in constructive problem solving (Wellner, 2012).

T.I.P. – Theory Into Practice 3.4

NONPARTICIPATION: REFLECTING ON YOUR TEACHING

Although you may identify parents who you feel are not as involved as they could be, you can use the following questions to reflect on your teaching and to guide you in seeking participation from parents:

1. How much do you want parents to be involved?

2. How does your school help or hinder parent involvement?

3. Identify specific steps you can take to increase the participation of culturally and linguistically diverse parents.

4. Are there any groups of parents you find it difficult to communicate and be involved with? How can obstacles to involvement be addressed?

5. In what ways have you tried to get to know the parents of your students?

Source: Adapted from Gorman, J. C. (2004). *Dealing with challenging parents of students with special needs.* Thousand Oaks, CA: Corwin.

Focus on the problem, not the person. How should you respond when, for example, a parent expresses concern over some part of the IEP or the entire plan? What if parents ask that their child receive educational services in the general-education classroom and resist services that do not support that goal when the team agrees that special education is a more appropriate environment for the child? What if their dissatisfaction leads them to question your teaching practices or to seek an alternative placement for their child? What if a parent insists on a specific program or services that were beneficial to another child and demands that the school provide the same service for their child?

When dealing with parents who are discontent, Gorman (2004) offers three principles. Principle 1: Focus on the problem, not the person. Try not to respond to the negativity, even if they are blaming you for the problem. Try not to take the parents' complaints personally. Rather, think rationally about the problem, take the time to get as much information as you can, and seek to identify solutions. Principle 2: Ask for parents' solutions. Getting parents to think about a solution can help change the mindset from complaining to collaboration. If they do offer a solution, be respectful of it, rather than communicating that you think it's not feasible. Principle 3: Focus on the end goal. Rather than focusing on the complaint or becoming defensive, put the focus on the desired outcome (skills improvement, academic improvement, etc.). One parent in Gorman's (2004) report reflected that when she shared positive information about the child when confronted by the parents, "I don't think I did anything special. I think they finally felt like they were listened to" (p. 75). Listening goes a long way toward resolving a disagreement.

T.I.P. – Theory Into Practice 3.5

CONFLICT: REFLECTING ON YOUR TEACHING

Although conflict occurs in all relationships and should be expected, it can be difficult to deal with parents who are angry. Use the following questions to reflect on your teaching and guide you in dealing with parents who express their anger:

1. To what extent do you feel comfortable with conflict or confrontation?

2. How do you usually try to handle your own anger or that of someone else?

3. Are there any parents you continue to feel anger toward, although the original incident has passed, and how might this impact your current relationship?

4. Make a list of ways to respond to conflicts with parents that you can use if confronted with such a situation.

Source: Adapted from Gorman, J. C. (2004). *Dealing with challenging parents of students with special needs.* Thousand Oaks, CA: Corwin.

CONCLUSION

Forming collaborative partnerships with families of children with ASD means that the partners have shared decision-making (Bryan & Henry, 2012). Yet "in schools, students' and families' voices are typically silenced, and programs and interventions are designed for rather than with students and families" (Bryan & Henry, 2012, p. 409). This chapter is about building bridges rather than walls so that when we collaborate effectively our students with ASD benefit.

Parents should have an equal voice and have the ability to participate in decision-making, planning, and implementation of educational solutions. To accomplish this, schools have to intentionally involve families in the partnership process, purposefully diminishing their roles as "experts"; respect families' knowledge and insights; regard each other as valuable resources and assets; involve family members in mutual and equitable decisions; and refuse to blame each other (Bryan & Henry, 2012). Work diligently to provide a variety of opportunities for families to become involved in the school. Such opportunities should be based on the family's strengths and expertise that they can contribute to the partnership.

Educators are mandated to partner with families of students with special needs. This is a significantly demanding and challenging responsibility. If barriers are identified and understood, they can be addressed, and educators can maintain their commitment to the partnership and fulfill their legal obligations.

SUMMARY STATEMENTS

- Although parents and professionals desire to engage in collaborative partnerships, they sometimes have difficulty establishing a level of collaboration that benefits children with disabilities.

- There are a number of reasons why parents who are from cultures that differ from that of school personnel might be reluctant to be involved in collaboration, including language barriers, interpersonal values, and the attitudes and perceptions of school personnel.

- To effectively interact with families of diverse cultures, we must gain understanding of specific cultures, learn about their families, and learn to value people of different cultures.

- Differences in communication patterns and preferences can impede collaborative efforts.

- Sometimes, parents may simply lack the available time, energy, or resources to participate in school–family collaboration.

- Some parents might limit their involvement with schools because they feel intimidated by the school or because they feel inadequate or lacking the necessary expertise to be of any help.

WHAT WOULD YOU DO?

Look back at the case study about Henry, Nina, and Mr. Acosta presented at the beginning of the chapter. Based on what you have read in this chapter, in previous chapters, and in your own experiences, how would you respond to the following questions?

1. How do you imagine Mr. Acosta feels in this situation? What about Nina?

2. Which of the potential barriers to collaboration do you think play a role in this scenario?

3. How does your own communication style differ from Nina's, and how is it similar? What advice would you give Mr. Acosta about communicating with Nina?

4. Do you think Nina might feel a sense of inequality with the staff of Henry's school? Why, or why not?

5. What can the school do to encourage Nina to engage in meaningful collaboration? What ideas from this chapter would you suggest, and what ideas have you learned about from other sources that might be helpful?

6. What training do you recommend the school staff receives that could facilitate greater parent involvement in general?

CHAPTER REFLECTION QUESTIONS

1. Which of the potential barriers to collaboration have you seen in your observations?

2. Explain the two different vantage points from which professionals and parents can see collaboration.

3. How does cultural and linguistic diversity influence parents' desire to collaborate with schools?

4. What are some ways that educators can respond to cultural and linguistic diversity to promote collaboration?

5. How can life contexts, beliefs about involvement, and perceptions of inequality contribute negatively to collaborative efforts?

RECOMMENDED RESOURCES

Websites

- Autism Speaks: Parents & providers collaboration to build a better autism medical home. Available at https://www.autismspeaks.org/science/science-news/parents-providers-collaborate-build-better-autism-medical-home

- Special Education Guide: The Parent–Teacher Partnership. Available at http://www.specialeducationguide.com/pre-k-12/the-parent-teacher-partnership

Publications

Cheatham, G. (2006–2007). Providing culturally and linguistically appropriate services for students with ASD. *Impact, 19*(3), 10. Retrieved from https://ici.umn.edu/products/impact/193/193.pdf

Cox, J. (n. d.). Parent–teacher collaboration strategies that work. *Teach Hub*. Retrieved from http://www.teachhub.com/parent-teacher-collaboration-strategies-work

Gorman, J. C. (2004). *Dealing with challenging parents of students with special needs.* Thousand Oaks, CA: Corwin.

Hedeen, T., Moses, P., & Peter, M. (2011). *Encouraging meaningful parent/educator collaboration: A review of recent literature.* Eugene, OR: Center for Appropriate Dispute Resolution in Special Education (CADRE). Retrieved from http://files.eric.ed.gov/full text/ED536983.pdf

REFERENCES

Bacon, J. K., & Causton-Theoharis, J. (2013). It should be teamwork: A critical investigation of school practices and parent advocacy in special education. *International Journal of Inclusive Education, 17*, 682–699.

Bryan, J., & Henry, L. (2008). Strengths-based partnerships: A school–family–community partnership approach to empowering students. *Professional School Counseling, 12*(2), 149–156.

Bryan, J., & Henry, L. (2012). A model for building school–family–community partnerships: Principles and process. *Journal of Counseling & Development, 90*, 408–420.

Burke, M. M. (2013). Improving parental involvement: Training special education advocates. *Journal of Disability Policy Studies, 23*(4), 225–234.

Cramer, S. F. (2006). *The special educator's guide to collaboration: Improving relationships with co-teachers, teams, and families* (2nd ed.). Thousand Oaks, CA: Corwin.

Dabkowski, D. (2004). Encouraging active parent participation in IEP team meetings. *TEACHING Exceptional Children, 26*, 34–39.

Friend, M., & Borsuck, W. (2009). *Including students with special needs: A practical guide for classroom teachers* (5th ed.). Upper Saddle River, NJ: Pearson Education.

Friend, M., & Cook, L. (2010). *Interactions: Collaboration skills for school professionals.* Upper Saddle River, NJ: Pearson Education.

Gorman, J. C. (2004). *Dealing with challenging parents of students with special needs.* Thousand Oaks, CA: Corwin.

Hornby, G., & Lafaele, R. (2011). Barriers to parental involvement in education: An explanatory model. *Educational Review, 63*(1), 37-52.

Individuals With Disabilities Education Act (IDEA), 20 U.S.C. §§ 1400 et seq. (2004 & Supp. V. 2011).

Jung, A. W. (2011). Individualized education programs (IEPs) and barriers for parents from culturally and linguistically diverse backgrounds. *Multicultural Education, 18*(3), 21–26.

Koro-Ljungberg, M., Bussing, R., Wilder, J. A., & Gary, F. (2011). Role of communication in the context of educating children with attention-deficit/hyperactivity disorder: Parents' and teachers' perspectives. *Journal of School Public Relations, 32*, 41–75.

Lasky, B., & Karge, B. D. (2011). Involvement of language minority parents of children with disabilities in their child's school achievement. *Multicultural Education, 18*(3), 29–36.

Murray, K. W., Finigan-Carr, N., Jones, V., Copeland-Linder, N., Haynie, D. L., & Cheng, T. L. (2014). Barriers and facilitators to school-based parents involvement for parents of urban middle school students. *Sage Open, 4*(4), 2–12.

Sheehey, P. H., & Sheehey, P. E. (2007). Elements for successful parent–professional collaboration: The fundamental things apply as time goes by. *TEACHING Exceptional Children Plus*, *42*(2), 1–12.

Todd, T. A., Beamer, J., & Goodreau, J. (2014). Bridging the gap: Teacher–parent partnerships for students with autism spectrum disorders. *LEARNing Landscapes*, *8*(1), 287–304.

Trainor, A. A. (2010). Diverse approaches to parent advocacy during special education home–school interactions. *Remedial and Special Education*, *31*(1), 34–47.

Wegmann, K. M., & Bowen, G. (2010). Strengthening connections between schools and diverse families: A cultural capital perspective. *Prevention Researchers*, *17*(3), 7–10.

Wellner, L. (2012). Building parent trust in the special education setting. *Leadership*, *41*(4), 16–19.

4

Linking Assessment to Instructional Planning

LEARNER OBJECTIVES

After reading this chapter the learner should be able to do the following:

- Describe the components of complete assessment/evaluation for students with ASD.

- Discuss what goes into developing an IEP for students with ASD.

- Explain how to create goals and objectives in an IEP and develop SMART goals.

- Define and describe evidence-based practices for meeting IEP goals for students with ASD.

- Identify at least one thing general-education teachers can do to make classroom instruction more accessible for students with ASD.

- Outline ways to encourage parent participation in an IEP meeting.

CASE STUDY

Jacob is an 8-year-old boy with ASD who spends part of his school day in the general-education classroom with the help of a personal aide so that he can have interactions with his peers. Jacob rarely initiates conversations or makes eye contact with other individuals. When he does engage in conversation with his peers, they feel he talks "at" them rather than "with" them. Most often, Jacob talks about his favorite subject, baseball, and seems to have little awareness of what his conversation partner may be expecting or thinking. Peers say that Jacob talks in ways that seem like a lecture rather than a conversation, giving endless details others find repetitive or uninteresting.

Periodically, Jacob becomes very upset and loses his temper during classroom instruction and when transitioning to recess or lunch, and staff have been unable to determine what might prompt such behavior. The IEP team developed a goal for Jacob to increase social skills and to manage his behavior during transitions. To accomplish this goal, Jacob's teacher has been incorporating Social Stories into her instruction. While the IEP team is impressed with this strategy overall, they feel it has done little to help him with the acquisition of academic content, so they want to try new strategies. Jacob's teacher uses a lot of collaborative learning in her instruction, but she wonders whether that type of environment works well for Jacob. She wonders if she needs to change the way she delivers instruction to accommodate his needs.

The IEP team plans to meet again in the near future to discuss Jacob's progress and to establish new goals for him. His general-education teacher supports inclusion for Jacob, but she doesn't know what strategies to implement that would help Jacob further develop his social and academic skills. She knows she should establish a structured environment in her classroom and that students with ASD can benefit from a focus on the visual aspects of each lesson, but she lacks the knowledge of how to incorporate more visual aids into her instruction.

....

INTRODUCTION

The best instructional planning relies on accurate and useful assessment information. By utilizing a systematic process of gathering accurate and useful assessment data, we can then make diagnostic and educationally relevant decisions for students that can help them reach their full potential. Useful assessment data will be the basis for the goals and objectives established in the individualized education program (IEP) and, ultimately, the instructional practices we will implement to help students achieve the goals that were specified in the IEP.

This chapter will provide a summary of how assessment data is gathered, with a focus on collecting data from multiple sources, across multiple settings or contexts. The process of developing an IEP based on the assessment data will be described. The focus will be on writing goals that are SMART—specific, measurable, utilizing action words, realistic and relevant, and time-limited. Research-based interventions designed to help students with ASD meet their IEP goals and objectives will be discussed briefly. The chapter will also provide tips for creating successful inclusive classrooms in which students with ASD are often educated. Finally, the chapter will close with ways to partner with families and encourage their active participation in the IEP process and making sound educational decisions.

GATHERING ASSESSMENT DATA

Identification and Evaluation

Assessment is more than administering a battery of tests. It is a much broader concept, conceptualized as a process of gathering information for use in making diagnostic and educational decisions. Most importantly, assessment of students for whom ASD is suspected should be comprehensive and rely on multiple sources of data.

At the core of the assessment process should be a formal psychological assessment conducted by a psychologist experienced in evaluating students with ASD. There is no single, definitive assessment that will identify ASD, so clinicians must observe behavior and development to make an appropriate diagnosis. Data should be collected from multiple sources, across multiple settings or contexts, and through multiple strategies.

Finally, strategies for assessment should include observations, administration of formal and informal measures, and the completion of rating scales and inventories by individuals familiar with the child and his or her day-to-day functioning, such as parents and teachers.

A complete diagnostic evaluation should include a minimum of the following, according to the California Department of Developmental Services (CDDS) (2002) and other governing bodies throughout the United States. A review of relevant background information is necessary, as well as parent or caregiver interviews, a medical evaluation, behavior observations, and cognitive assessment. Adaptive functioning tests (measures of personal and social self-sufficiency and problem solving in real-life situations) are also necessary for completing a comprehensive evaluation.

DIAGNOSTIC ASSESSMENT

Diagnostic assessments are used to evaluate whether the individual child meets the criteria for an ASD diagnosis. The complete diagnostic process includes an assessment of social and communication skills, restricted and repetitive interests, and patterns of behavior. There should also be a comprehensive interview with parents or caregivers, formal observation, interviews with previous teachers and staff, and informal observations in natural settings to complement the one-on-one assessments with the child who has been referred. Clinical psychologists or psychologists who have experience and training in the diagnosis of ASD are typically the individuals who administer the assessments.

Standardized cognitive and developmental testing, including the assessment of language, is used to distinguish ASD from other developmental difficulties. When carefully selected and administered by experienced clinicians, the assessments should provide information about the child's overall level of ability and functioning in verbal and nonverbal areas, which provides a necessary starting point for a clinician to make a careful diagnosis and begin the planning of the most appropriate interventions. It is important to assess both verbal and nonverbal functioning because many children with ASD show stronger nonverbal skills than we would expect from their language skills or play, confounding the assessment data to the untrained professional.

Family Voices 4.1

"I think a lot of parents are terrified of receiving a diagnosis. For us, it was the best thing that happened to us. It helped us understand our son better, and it opened the door to specialized therapies he couldn't have access to before the diagnosis. We didn't panic. We got support, and we knew we were not alone in this."

When we also include parent and teacher reports and observations across settings, along with the cognitive and behavior assessments with clinical judgments, we have a much more comprehensive picture of the child. Such a thorough data-gathering process allows educators and families to make more informed decisions about individualized instructional programs for the child.

Parent interviews and questionnaires. Trained clinicians can administer comprehensive parent interviews using a variety of checklists and forms, and parents can be involved in self-ratings as well. For instance, the Social Communication Questionnaire (formerly known as the Autism Screening Questionnaire; Berument, Rutter, Lord, Pickles, & Bailey, 1999) is a parent report questionnaire with two versions available: (1) the lifetime version, helpful for screening and diagnostic purposes, and (2) the current version, appropriate for evaluating change over time in an individual (Ozonoff, Goodlin-Jones, & Solomon, 2005). Parents can also complete the Gilliam Autism Rating Scale (Gilliam, 1995), which consists of four scales to measure social interaction, communication, stereotyped behaviors, and developmental differences (Ozonoff et al., 2005).

Diagnostic assessment. There are a number of available diagnostic instruments used by clinicians. The Autism Diagnostic Observational Schedule, Second Edition (ADOS-2) (Lord, Rutter, DiLavore, & Risi, 2012) is a tool commonly used in the diagnostic process, considered the "standard protocol" among clinicians. The ADOS is a semistructured assessment of communication, social interaction, and play for individuals aged 12 months through adulthood who are suspected of having ASD. The ADOS consists of activities that allow the examiner to observe the occurrence or nonoccurrence of behaviors that have been identified as criteria for an ASD diagnosis. The focus of ADOS is on observation of social behavior and communication and is not designed to assess specific cognitive abilities (Lord et al., 2012). The Childhood Autism Rating Scale (Schopler, Reichler, & Renner, 1988) is another instrument often used to rate behavior observed during development evaluation, and it has also been adapted for use as a parent rating scale (Ozonoff et al., 2005).

The Screening Tool for Autism in Toddlers and Young Children (STAT, n.d.) is another popular tool used to provide information about ASD. The STAT assessment is an interactive measure developed to screen for autism in children between 24 and 36 months of age, and it is designed for use by community professionals who work with young children. Activities assess key social and communicative behaviors, including imitation, play, requesting, and directing attention. This tool allows users to identify children at an earlier age who are at risk for an ASD diagnosis and to refer them for further assessment and intervention.

Cognitive and language assessments. Cognitive functioning is another important area to be assessed. The goals of cognitive assessments include generating a profile of the child's cognitive strengths and weaknesses, facilitating education planning, and determining eligibility for certain services (Ozonoff et al., 2005). Professionals should estimate a child's cognitive potential to determine the current level of functioning, the potential response to treatments, and the expected range of progress (CDDS, 2002). The Wechsler Intelligence Scale (Wechsler, 2003) is commonly used to assess cognitive abilities in children who have spoken language. Also, the Peabody Picture Vocabulary Test (Dunn & Dunn, 1997) is often used to measure expressive and receptive language abilities.

The use of both standard and informal measures of functioning is recommended to ascertain where the child is functioning relative to his or her same-age peers. Formal cognitive testing measures include an assessment of verbal and nonverbal functions. Informal measures can also be used to determine levels of functioning through parent reports and direct observations. Informal observation can be used to strengthen confidence in estimating the child's cognitive level (CDDS, 2002).

Adaptive behavior assessment. Another essential component of the assessment battery for students with ASD involves examining adaptive behavior. Adaptive behaviors are those age-appropriate behaviors necessary for independent living and functioning in daily life. They include skills such as grooming, dressing, school rules, money management, making friends, and various personal responsibilities. Determining whether an individual requires constant supervision or can achieve some level of independence is largely a function of adaptive behavior measures. The most widely used measure of adaptive behavior is the Vineland Adaptive Behavior Scales (Sparrow, Balla, & Cicchetti, 1984), and it assesses communication, daily living skills, and socialization.

In summary, the primary purpose of a comprehensive evaluation and possible diagnosis of ASD is to provide guidance for developing interventions most appropriate for each individual child. A high-quality evaluation of ASD should include the use of instruments designed to assess multiple domains of functioning and behavior, the inclusion of parent and caregiver interviews and interactions, observations across multiple contexts, a consideration of developmental factors, and a thorough review of available records. Data from these assessments inform professionals about specific deficits and skills across the core impairment categories (social, communication and play skills, and restricted, repetitive, and stereotyped behaviors). Results from this battery of assessments should then be used to plan appropriate interventions.

T.I.P. – Theory Into Practice 4.1

STOP AND THINK

Why do you think a diagnosis of ASD would involve so many different forms of assessment?

LINKING ASSESSMENT TO INTERVENTION

After performing a complete battery of assessments, professionals are then in a position to make informed instructional decisions based on the resulting data. An individualized education program (IEP) is developed so that educational interventions are specifically tailored to the unique needs of each child. The IEP is developed using input from the child's caregivers and thorough assessments completed by different professionals, including teachers, psychologists, occupational therapists, speech and language therapists, and more. The IEP is written to establish measurable goals for the child and to plan the overall special education experience of the child with a disability, the services the school will provide, and how progress will be measured.

DEVELOPING THE IEP

The assessment process provides data that can then be used to develop an IEP for the student. The IEP is the written document that spells out the special education and related services that are to be provided to best meet the specific needs of a child with a disability. It should include these important parts:

1. *Present level of performance.* This section describes how the child is currently doing in school. It explains how the disability affects his or her performance in class and its purpose is to identify priority educational needs.

2. *Annual goals and objectives.* Once the child's needs have been identified, the IEP team will work to develop appropriate goals that will address each of those needs. Annual goals describe what the child is expected to learn or do within a 12-month period.

3. *Measuring and reporting progress.* Each IEP must contain a description of how the child's progress toward meeting the annual goals will be measured and when it will be reported to caregivers.

4. *Special education services.* The IEP must also contain a description of the special education services that will be provided to the child, the related services, and the supplementary aids or services to be provided to the student. The IEP also describes services that will be provided to supplement the educational services. Some children may also need extra help in one area or another, such as speaking or moving, and so they may participate in occupational, physical, and/or speech and language therapies. These are called related services.

5. *Educational placement.* The IEP must also contain an explanation of the extent to which the child will participate with nondisabled students in the regular class and in other school settings. This is to ensure that children are educated in the least restrictive environment to the greatest extent appropriate.

If the classroom setting is not a general education classroom, the IEP should specify the amount of time the child will participate, if any, in the general-education classroom and what amount will be spent participating in special education services.

6. ***Program and testing modifications***. IDEA requires that students with disabilities take part in state or district-wide assessments. The IEP team will decide if the student needs accommodations for the test or whether the student should take another type of assessment entirely, and they will state why these accommodations are necessary. Such modifications can include having an aide in the classroom, obtaining special equipment or teaching materials, or other accommodation.

7. ***Length and duration of services***. The IEP should specify the starting and ending dates of goals, objectives, and related services. It should also include the frequency of the services, where they will be delivered, and how long they will be provided.

8. ***Statement of transition***. Beginning no later than age 16, the IEP must include measurable goals for the student's anticipated postsecondary program and the services needed for the child to reach those goals. Transition goals and services focus on the instruction and support needed to help the student move from the school environment into a job or college or other programs designed to promote independent living.

CREATING ANNUAL GOALS AND OBJECTIVES

Annual goals and objectives should be based on comprehensive assessment data collection as mentioned in the previous section. Goals in the IEP should address the following areas: social functioning; nonverbal communication skills; receptive, expressive, and pragmatic language; fine or gross motor skills; academic skills; and behavioral skills. Annual goals and objectives should clearly state what the student is expected to accomplish; they should be worded as a positive statement, and they should be clearly observable and measurable. The chart that follows provides several sample IEP goals for developing a student's social skills.

Sample IEP Goals for Social Skills

1. _____ **will develop social understanding skills as measured by the benchmarks listed below.**

   a. _____ will raise his/her hand and wait to be called on before talking aloud in group settings in four or five opportunities to do so.

   b. _____ will work cooperatively with peers in small-group settings (i.e., share materials and allow peers to share different thoughts) in four or five opportunities to do so.

Sample IEP Goals for Social Skills

  c. _____ will develop an understanding of the relationship between his/her verbalizations and actions/effect on others in four or five opportunities to do so.

  d. _____ will engage in appropriate cooperative social-play interactions initiated by others in four or five opportunities to do so.

  e. _____ will engage in appropriate turn-taking skills by attending to peer's turn and waiting for own turn in four or five opportunities to do so.

  f. _____ will appropriately acknowledge an interaction initiated by others by giving an appropriate response, either verbal or nonverbal.

  g. _____ will develop an understanding of the rationale for various social skills by stating the reason when asked (i.e., Why do we say excuse me?).

2. **_____ will increase social-emotional skills as measured by the benchmarks listed below.**

  a. _____ will identify various emotional states in others in four or five opportunities to do so.

  b. _____ will state why a person might be feeling a particular emotion in four or five opportunities to do so.

  c. _____ will identify various simple emotional states in self in four or five opportunities to do so.

  d. _____ will state why he/she might be feeling a particular emotion in four or five opportunities to do so.

  e. _____ will state what would be an appropriate response to a particular emotional state in four or five opportunities to do so.

3. **_____ will increase social communication skills as measured by the benchmarks listed below.**

  a. _____ will initiate communicative interactions with others in four or five opportunities to do so.

  b. _____ will initiate varied appropriate topics with others in four or five opportunities to do so.

  c. _____ will initiate communicative interactions with others by asking questions in four or five opportunities to do so.

  d. _____ will engage in conversational turn-taking with others across three to four conversational turns in four or five opportunities to do so (topics initiated by self or others).

  e. _____ will ask questions of others regarding topics initiated by self or others to sustain conversation for conversational turn-taking in four or five opportunities to do so.

  f. _____ will identify and understand various nonverbal social communication behaviors (i.e., tone of voice, personal space, vocal volume, body orientation, and facial expressions) by stating their implied meaning in four or five opportunities to do so.

(Continued)

(Continued)

Sample IEP Goals for Social Skills

4. **_____ will increase narrative discourse skills to objective criteria as measured by the benchmarks listed below.**

   a. _____ will state the main idea of the story, video, or situation in four or five opportunities to do so.

   b. _____ will relate information (i.e., past events, stories, situations, etc.) sequentially in four or five opportunities to do so.

   c. _____ will identify what happened first, in the middle, and last regarding a previously read story, past event, or situation.

   d. When relating information, _____ will provide an initial background statement, include important pieces of relational information, and leave out irrelevant details.

Source: Adapted from National Association of Special Education Teachers. Original file available at http://www.naset.org/fileadmin/user_upload/Autism_Series/Examples_IEP_Goals_Objectives_for_ASD.pdf

Well-written goals and objectives should be objective, observable, and measurable, and they should include answers to the following questions:

1. Who will demonstrate the behavior or skills?

2. How will the skill be demonstrated?

3. Where or under what conditions will the skill be demonstrated?

4. How frequently will the skill be demonstrated?

5. By when will the skill be demonstrated?

IEPs should contain goals that are SMART: **s**pecific, **m**easurable, use **a**ction words, **r**ealistic and relevant, and **t**ime-limited. The following table breaks down a sample goal into its SMART parts:

Sample IEP Goal for Social Skills: Shawna

By the end of Semester 2, Shawna will increase her social communication skills as measured by the benchmarks listed below: (f) Shawna will ask questions of others regarding topics initiated by self or others to sustain conversation for conversational turn-taking in four or five opportunities to do so.	
Specific	Ask questions of others regarding topics initiated by self or others

Sample IEP Goal for Social Skills: Shawna	
Measurable	Increase in four or five opportunities to do so
Action words	Ask, sustain
Time-limited	By the end of the second semester

IEPs should contain goals and objectives that are specific and measurable. Specific goals are designed to target certain areas of academic achievement or functional performance, and they should include clear descriptions of the knowledge and skills to be taught and how progress toward those goals will be measured. "Tyler will increase study skills," is not specific, whereas "Tyler will demonstrate the following study skills: highlighting appropriate passages in social studies materials" is more specific. Measurable goals are those that can be counted or observed, and they will, therefore, allow parents and educators to know how much progress the child has made since the last measurement. A sample measurable and observable goal is, "Given second-grade material, Owen will read a passage of text orally at 110–130 words per minute with no more than three errors."

SMART goals are realistic, relevant, and time-limited, as they address the child's unique needs that result from his or her disability. A specific, measurable, and realistic goal is something like this: "Kimberly will improve her writing skills so that she can write a paragraph of at least three sentences, including compound and complex sentences that are clearly related." SMART goals are also time-limited, stating what the child should know or be able to do after a certain period. Time-limited goals permit practitioners the ability to monitor progress at regular intervals.

For the sake of argument, let us look at a few examples of poorly written goals in the following chart. In the right column, we can see the improved version. Notice how the improved goal includes the components discussed in this section of the chapter (specific, measurable, contains action words, realistic, and time-limited).

SMART Goals and Objectives	
Poorly Written Goal	**Improved Goal**
Matthew will learn to type.	At the end of the second semester, Matthew will be able to type a passage of text at a speed of 40 words per minute, with no more than five errors, on a 5-minute timed test.
Megan will learn to read.	After 1 year of specialized instruction, Megan will be able to decode words with no more than two errors, as measured by the decoding score of the Gray Oral Reading Test (GORT).

(Continued)

(Continued)

SMART Goals and Objectives	
Poorly Written Goal	**Improved Goal**
Mia will learn to read at the first-grade level.	After 1 year of individual tutoring for 1 hour per day, Mia will read at the first-grade level, as measured by the global composite score of the Gray Oral Reading Test.
Benjamin will successfully complete a math worksheet.	When presented with a worksheet containing 20 problems, Benjamin will correctly identify the place value of each number independently (tens, hundreds, thousands) in at least 4 out of 5 trials over three consecutive weeks, as measured by work samples.
Amanda will write two sentences correctly.	Given a picture of interest, Amanda will be able to write two sentences using correct punctuation and capitalization in at least 3 out of 4 trials in a 2-week period, as measured by work samples.

To test yourself, try finding the SMART components of each improved goal. The first one is done here for you: At the end of the second semester, Matthew will be able to type a passage of text at a speed of 40 words per minute, with no more than five errors, on a 5-minute timed test.

Specific: *type a passage of text*

Measurable: *at a speed of 40 words per minute; no more than five errors; on a 5-minute timed test*

Action words: *type*

Time-limited: *at the end of the second semester*

T.I.P. – Theory Into Practice 4.2

REWRITE THE FOLLOWING GOALS

Poorly Written Goal	Improved Goal
1. Jimmy will improve his communication skills with peers at recess.	
2. Irene will increase her letter recognition.	
3. Hayden will follow directions given by the teacher.	
4. Amelia will write one correct paragraph.	

1. Consider a personal behavior you would like to change (i.e., lose weight, eat healthier, get more exercise, read more, write in your journal, visit with friends, ride your bike, etc.).

2. Create a SMART plan to increase, decrease, or maintain the present behavior, developing goals and objectives that are specific and measurable, use action words, and are realistic and time-limited.

Example 1: I will lose 10% of my body weight in 12 weeks by reducing calorie consumption by 600 calories per day and burning 300 calories a day through exercise.

Example 2: I will write two pages per day in my journal following 10 minutes of prayer or meditation in the morning before going to school.

3. Consider implementing the plan and measuring your results.

EDUCATIONAL INTERVENTIONS TO MEET IEP GOALS

We will address specific educational interventions in more detail in subsequent chapters. What is important to discuss here is that interventions based on scientific research should be the priority. With the growing increase in the rate of ASD diagnoses, the field of educational interventions is also growing. Not all interventions have been validated through research, however, and therefore, educators must be knowledgeable about the range of educational practices available, choosing evidence-based interventions, methodologies, and accommodations to implement. Evidence-based practices, according to the IDEA (2004), are based on research that employs systematic and empirical methods that draw on observation or experiment and involve rigorous data analysis to test the hypotheses and justify the general conclusions drawn. A peer-reviewed journal should have accepted reports of evidence-based practices or practices approved by a panel of independent experts.

The program of instruction for each student with ASD should be individualized and appropriate for his or her specific needs. ASD is complex, and each student with ASD possesses a varied array of strengths and areas of need. There are numerous possible educational interventions to help students make progress toward meeting the IEP goals and objectives set for them. For now, we will summarize potential areas of focus for those educational interventions. They include social skills development and peer interaction, communication, activities of daily living, play and leisure, attention, executive functioning, academic performance, motor skills, sensory processing, and behavior.

This chapter outlines a few of these areas of instructional focus. Areas of focus for intervention in social development include joint attention, peer interaction, turn-taking, sharing, group interaction, and social rules, among others. Instructional-focus areas of communication include motivation to communicate, the function of communication, means of communication, and ability to understand and use nonverbal communication. Daily living instructional areas include personal hygiene, dressing, eating, organization, task completion, schedules, and routines, among others. Executive-functioning instructional strategies include goal setting, planning, sequencing, organization, pacing, and self-monitoring, among others. Academic areas can include reading, math, or any content area. Motor skills include motor control, muscle tone, handwriting, cutting, and so on. Strategies to address these and other areas will be discussed in more detail in subsequent chapters.

EVIDENCE-BASED PRACTICES

Identifying and using effective instructional practices with students with ASD is the responsibility of educators. Unfortunately, some of the educational methods developed for students with ASD are "promoted to result in rapid, all encompassing, and dramatic improvements, or to actually restore an individual with an autism-related disability to normalcy" (Simpson, 2005, p. 141). We must be careful in our evaluation of potential educational interventions.

It is understandable that parents and practitioners who work with children with ASD are willing to consider approaches that *promise* improved outcomes or restore individuals to normal functioning (Simpson, 2005). Choosing to believe in interventions that are not evidence-based can have serious implications. In fact, Simpson (2005) stated, "Dependence on and uncritical use of miracle cures and unproven methods have encouraged unhealthy, unrealistic, and improbable expectations and have, in all too many cases, retarded the progress of students with ASD" (p. 141). The solution, then, is to identify and use methods that are based on scientific evidence. To qualify as an appropriate intervention, the method should have reliable evidence of the program's effectiveness.

In this textbook, we will discuss in depth only those interventions that are scientifically based. In some cases, approaches that have little scientific backing will also be discussed, for the sake of illustration. For now, we will discuss how educators can work to facilitate successful inclusion for students with ASD, followed by a discussion about forming effective school–family partnerships in developing IEPs for students with ASD. Subsequent chapters will discuss, in more detail, the most commonly used research-based interventions.

EDUCATING STUDENTS WITH ASD IN INCLUSIVE CLASSROOMS

Many times, progress toward meeting IEP goals and objectives can be made in inclusive classrooms. As mentioned in previous chapters, IDEA requires that students with disabilities be placed in the least restrictive environment (LRE). LRE means that, to the greatest extent appropriate, students with disabilities should be educated in the general-education classroom. The requirement is that students with special needs are educated alongside their peers, and they are given appropriate support services, rather than placing them in separate special education classrooms.

Advocates for this model believe that the benefits are increased expectations by teachers, behavioral modeling of typically developing peers, increased learning, and potential increases in self-esteem. There are a few issues that will be covered only briefly here. Given the mandate to provide services to students with disabilities in the least restrictive environment, this chapter provides a brief discussion of inclusive classrooms as a means to make progress in meeting IEP goals and objectives.

Student needs. Deficits in social communication, social interaction, and in navigating peer relationships and social situations make success in school settings a challenge for students with ASD (Able, Sreckovic, Schultz, Garwood, & Sherman, 2015). Students are often expected to participate in group work and cooperative-learning activities in which they may not function well without proper support from the teacher. They are frequently asked to respond aloud to discussion questions or make class presentations, which could be overwhelming to a student with ASD. In secondary school, they are asked to change classrooms and make a multitude of other transitions throughout the day, and they are expected to participate in various social networks in and out of school. We must make efforts to provide appropriate supports to students who need our assistance in these areas.

Family Voices 4.3

"The authorities tell us Madeline's needs can be met in a mainstream classroom. But the reports say she needs specialists to work with her. It feels like they're saying, 'Just bring her into classroom and it will all be fine.' But I don't think it will be 'fine.' Must I include Maddie if she won't get the help she needs there?"

The salient characteristics of ASD, including deficits in social skills and communication, as well as restricted interests and/or repetitive behaviors, can be viewed as "misaligned with social success in school settings" (Able et al., 2015, p. 45). In Able et al.'s (2015) research, teachers felt that social isolation, insistence on rule following, limited self-advocacy skills, and difficulties with transitions between settings interfered with the full inclusion in the classroom for students with ASD.

Teacher needs. Inclusive classrooms present challenges for teachers as well. General-education teachers may feel ill-prepared to meet the multifaceted needs of children with ASD in inclusive classrooms (Able et al., 2015), perhaps because their teacher-training program included too little instruction in how to meet the needs of students with ASD. Research suggests teachers' lack of confidence and self-efficacy in working with students with special needs necessitates greater support in instructional strategies and understanding characteristics of children with ASD.

The chart below outlines important considerations for you as you work toward developing a successful inclusive experience for students with ASD. Hopefully, the strategies you learn throughout this textbook will enable you to enter a special education or a general-education or inclusive classroom with confidence and that you have the tools to collaborate in meaningful ways with other professionals and with families of students with ASD. You will have the tools necessary for implementing meaningful educational practice in special education or general-education or inclusive classrooms while partnering with families for the benefit of students with ASD. The focus of this text is to prepare you to be a successful teacher of students with ASD in general or special education classrooms so that you do not feel, one day, that you were "ill-prepared" in your teacher-training program.

Inclusion Tips
CREATING A SUCCESSFUL INCLUSIVE CLASSROOM

1. Condense information from the IEP to highlight each student's characteristics, needs, and corresponding classroom accommodations.

2. Collaborate with professionals to share goals and strategies.

3. Create a "retreat" space. To help remove students from overwhelming situations and to give them a space and time to "cool down," create a space where a student can go to escape and regain control.

4. Develop routines and procedures, especially for transition times. Transitions can be challenging for students with ASD, and they are oftentimes when the most disruptive behavior occurs. Plan carefully

how to transition students from one activity to another.

5. Use nonverbal cues and visual aids as much as possible. Many students with ASD have difficulty processing verbal language. Since so much discussion and so many lesson presentations in a classroom are verbal, students can become frustrated in inclusion classrooms. Nonverbal cues help students understand the sequence of activities, clarify expectations, and understand what is happening next. Use signs, gestures, picture cues, and other visuals to communicate directions, and incorporate visual aids, such as pictures and graphic organizers, into lessons.

6. Reinforce abstract concepts with concrete examples. For example, look at a map while learning compass directions, or have a student store where they can practice the concepts they've learned about money or about

interacting with people in professional environments.

7. Promote active, hands-on learning experiences. Instead of receiving the same worksheet where students label the parts of a plant, give students stick-on labels with terms (i.e., stem, roots, leaves, etc.), and instruct students to label the parts of a real plant.

8. Implement Universal Design for Learning (UDL). UDL is an approach to curriculum planning that makes learning engaging and accessible to a range of learners with different strengths and needs. UDL builds on Howard Gardner's theory of multiple intelligences, which calls for utilizing multiple modalities in teaching and in student responses. It recognizes that we all learn and express our learning in different ways—we can use our strengths to learn and express ourselves.

PARTNERING WITH FAMILIES

Encouraging Parent Participation in the IEP Meeting

Teachers are required to consider parents as equal partners in the education of students with disabilities. However, there are sometimes barriers to the collaborative process, such as limited communication between schools and families, insufficient knowledge of parents about special education practices, and limited participation of parents in IEP meetings (Hebel & Persitz, 2014; Tucker & Schwartz, 2013), which has been discussed in other chapters in this text. When schools and parents do not collaborate in decision-making, the IEP might be less responsive to the unique needs of students. IEP teams might, therefore, want to consider what they can do to improve parent participation.

Create Opportunities for Families to Provide Input

1. Ask for parent input into the IEP draft. If you wait to show parents the finished draft without including their input, they will not feel they are a valuable part of the process.

2. Understand parents' priorities. Understanding what parents want can assist teams in the educational planning process. Some parents desire a focus on teaching social skills, others want schools to create inclusive opportunities for their child, others might want schools to focus on teaching communication skills, and still others want access to highly trained staff or trained behavior specialists. Take these desires and others into consideration when planning the IEP.

3. Include parent suggestions in the IEP. Plan and write goals and objectives with parents. Include their suggestions in the final product.

4. Provide regular communication. Maintain regular communication with parents about their child's progress. Also determine ahead of time what that regular communication will look like.

5. Make collaboration a school priority. School professionals are in a position of leadership and are expected to set the tone for collaboration in IEP teams. Collaboration should not be considered an afterthought when things go wrong or conflict ensues. Be quick to respond to phone calls and e-mails from parents, and look actively for ways to facilitate family involvement. Recognize that partnering with families takes work—it does not happen by accident.

6. Take action to resolve conflict. Talk on the phone, allow parents to bring an advocate to meetings, meet in person, or do whatever it takes to make parents feel supported. Consider parents' preferences when planning for conflict resolution.

T.I.P. – Theory Into Practice 4.4

PARENT COLLABORATION QUESTIONNAIRE

Consider offering this brief questionnaire to parents to help you to better understand how they want to be involved in the collaborative IEP process.

What school practices and behaviors would allow you to feel like you were a welcome member of the IEP team?

☐ Asking for my input into the IEP draft

☐ Providing regular communication about my child's progress

☐ Including me in the planning and writing of goals and objectives

☐ Responding promptly to my telephone calls or e-mails

☐ Inviting my attendance at IEP meetings

☐ Taking my suggestions into account regarding my child's IEP or educational interventions

☐ Helping me gain access to resources and training

□ Helping my child gain access to trained behavior specialists or other service providers

    □ Listening to me or letting me talk through things when I need it

    □ Remaining open and honest with me

    □ Keeping up to date and knowledgeable about my child's disability

□ Working actively and compassionately to resolve any conflicts

□ Helping me understand special education law and my rights as a parent

□ Facilitating meetings or gathering with other parents

□ Other: _____
_____

PREPARING FAMILIES TO BE PARTNERS IN MAKING EDUCATIONAL DECISIONS

Many times parents have not acquired the knowledge base necessary for making the best educational decisions for their child. To provide parents with the knowledge necessary for carrying out their responsibilities of participating with educators in the decision-making process, Turnbull and colleagues (2010) suggest that educators prepare knowledge-to-action guides for parents. This practice is based on knowledge of relevant evidence-based practices that support each parent's role as a decision maker that can be inaccessible to parents.

Moving knowledge through a funneling process so that it is usable to practitioners and families involves some effort on the teacher's part. First, needs must be identified (e.g., preventing aggressive behavior). Next, gather resources from multiple sources, including the Internet (i.e., Google search) and a library's peer-reviewed academic articles. Then, evaluate the resources to ensure their quality, and select which resources could be used in decision-making. Through this process, explained in more detail in their article (Turnbull et al., 2010), families can be empowered to combine knowledge with action.

T.I.P. – Theory Into Practice 4.5

KNOWLEDGE-TO-ACTION GUIDES

1. Locate one or all of these helpful resources to help in the preparation of a knowledge-to-action guide for practitioners and parents:

    a. Beach Center on Disability: http://www.beachcenter.org/wisdom_based_action/default.aspx

(Continued)

(Continued)

b. Graham, I. D., Logan, J., Harrison, M. B., Straus, S. E., Tetroe, J., Caswell, W., & Robinson, N. (2006). Lost in knowledge translation: Time for a map? *Journal of Continuing Education in the Health Professions, 26*, 13–24. Retrieved from http://pram.mcgill.ca/seminars/i/Graham_2006_Lost_in_Knowledge_Translation.pdf

c. The Knowledge to Action Cycle. Available at http://ktclearinghouse.ca/knowledgebase/knowledgetoaction

d. Turnbull, A., Zuna, N., Hong, J. H., Hu, X., Kyzar, K., Obriemski, S., . . . Stowe, M. (2010). Knowledge-to-action guides: Preparing families to be partners in making educational decisions. *TEACHING Exceptional Children, 42*(3), 42–53.

2. Using the framework or another appropriate adaptation of the framework, select an identified need to research and adapt to the *funneling process*.

3. Identify the need, gather resources, evaluate the knowledge, select the knowledge, make it useful, and make it available for an end user (practitioner or parent).

SUMMARY STATEMENTS

- Multiple assessment tools should be utilized to ensure accurate findings. Data should be collected from multiple sources, across multiple settings or contexts, and through multiple strategies.

- Components of an IEP include present level of performance, annual goals and objectives, how progress will be measured and reported, a description of special education services and placement, necessary program and testing modifications, length of services to be provided, and a transition plan.

- Well-written goals and objectives are observable and measurable and should discuss who will demonstrate the behavior, how the skill will be demonstrated, under what conditions the skills will be demonstrated, and by when. SMART goals are specific and measurable, contain action words, and are time-limited.

- Educators should use interventions that are evidence-based when instructing students who have ASD.

- Many times progress toward meeting IEP goals and objectives can be made in inclusive classrooms.

- Working toward increasing active parent participation in the IEP planning process and preparing them to make sound educational decisions will ultimately benefit our students with ASD.

WHAT WOULD YOU DO?

Look back at the case study about Jacob presented at the beginning of the chapter. Based on what you have read in this chapter, what you have read in previous chapters, and your own experiences, how would you respond to the following questions?

1. Do you think it is appropriate for Jacob to learn to "manage his behavior"? Why, or why not?

2. How do you think the goal in Jacob's IEP to manage behavior during transitions is linked to his strengths and/or weaknesses?

3. What should the IEP team establish as Jacob's next goal? Help the IEP team establish the new goal for Jacob by writing the goal in SMART format.

4. What items should you include in a knowledge-to-action guide for Jacob's family?

5. In what ways can you suggest that the general-education teacher work toward developing a successful inclusive classroom experience for Jacob?

CHAPTER REFLECTION QUESTIONS

1. What are the components of a complete assessment battery for ASD, and why is it important to use multiple sources of data?

2. What should be included in an IEP?

3. What are SMART goals, and why is it important to write goals in SMART form?

4. Why is it important to use evidence-based practices for students with ASD?

5. How would you advise a general-education or inclusion teacher to meet the needs of students with ASD in his or her classroom?

6. In what ways can educators prepare families to be partners in making educational decisions?

RECOMMENDED RESOURCES

Websites

- CAST. Resources for understanding Universal Design for Learning. http://www.cast.org

- Beach Center on Disability. Several sample knowledge-to-action guides are available here:

http://www.beachcenter.org/default.aspx?JScript=1

- KT Clearing House. A discussion of the knowledge-to-action cycle can be found here, where users can click each part of the graphic for more information. http://ktclearinghouse.ca/knowledgebase/knowledgetoaction

Articles/Publications

- Autism Speaks Inc. (2011). Individualized education program (IEP): Summary, process and practical tips. Retrieved from http://www.autismspeaks.org/sites/default/files/iep_guide.pdf

- Los Angeles Unified School District. (n.d.). *Conducting an effective IEP meeting.*

Available at http://achieve.lausd.net/Page/3344

- Turnbull, A., Zuna, N., Hong, J. H., Hu, X., Kyzar, K., Obriemski, S., . . . Stowe, M. (2010). Knowledge-to-action guides: Preparing families to be partners in making educational decisions. *TEACHING Exceptional Children*, *42*(3), 42–53.

REFERENCES

Able, H., Sreckovic, M. A., Schultz, T. R., Garwood, J. D., & Sherman, J. (2015). View from the trenches: Teacher and student supports needed for full inclusion of students with ASD. *Teacher Education and Special Education*, *38*(1), 44–57.

Berument, S. K., Rutter, M., Lord, C., Pickles, A., & Bailey, A. (1999). Autism screening questionnaire: Diagnostic validity. *British Journal of Psychiatry*, *175*, 444–451.

California Department of Developmental Services. (2002). *Autism spectrum disorders: Best practice guidelines for screening, diagnosis, and assessment.* Retrieved from http://www.dds.ca.gov/Autism/docs/ASD_Best_Practice2002.pdf

Dunn, L. M., & Dunn, L. M. (1997). *Peabody Picture Vocabulary Test* (3rd ed.). Circle Pines, MN: American Guidance Service.

Gilliam, J. E. (1995). *Gilliam Autism Rating Scale.* Austin, TX: PRO-ED.

Hebel, O., & Persitz, S. (2014). Parental involvement in the individual educational program for Israeli students with disabilities. *Internal Journal of Special Education*, *29*(3), 58–68.

Individuals with Disabilities Education Act (IDEA), Amendments of 2004, 20 U.S.C. § 1400.

Lord, C., Rutter, M., DiLavore, P. C., & Risi, S. (2012). *Autism Diagnostic Observation Schedule, Second Edition (ADOS-2).* Los Angeles, CA: Western Psychological Services.

Ozonoff, S., Goodlin-Jones, B. L., & Solomon, M. (2005). Evidence-based assessment of autism spectrum disorders in children and adolescents. *Journal of Clinical Child and Adolescent Psychology*, *34*, 523–540.

Schopler, E., Reichler, R., & Renner, B. (1988). *The Childhood Autism Rating Scale (CARS).* Los Angeles, CA: Western Psychological Services.

Screening Tool for Autism in Toddlers and Young Children (STAT). (n.d.) Retrieved from http://stat.vueinnovations.com/about

Simpson, R. L. (2005). Evidenced-based practices and students with autism spectrum disorders. *Focus on Autism and Other Developmental Disabilities*, *20*(3), 140–149.

Sparrow, S., Balla, D., & Cicchetti, D. (1984). *Vineland Adaptive Behavior Scales.* Circle Pines, MN: American Guidance Service.

Tucker, V., & Schwartz, I. (2013). Parents' perspectives of collaboration with school professionals: Barriers and facilitators to successful partnerships in planning for students with ASD. *School Mental Health*, *5*, 3–14.

Turnbull, A., Zuna, N., Hong, J. H., Hu, X., Kyzar, K., Obriemski, S., . . . Stowe, M. (2010). Knowledge-to-action-guides: Preparing families to be partners in making educational decisions. *TEACHING Exceptional Children*, *42*(3), 42–53.

Wechsler, D. (2003). *Wechsler Intelligence Scale for Children* (4th ed.). San Antonio, TX: Psychological Corporation.

Introduction to Applied Behavior Analysis

5

CASE STUDY

Curtis attends school at Esperanza Middle School in Mr. Hooper's general education language arts and history class block. Curtis is not able to make appropriate social greetings or to respond when others initiate greetings, and the team is concerned about increasing social isolation and peer rejection. Curtis does not greet or acknowledge teaching staff or other adults at school or in the community, nor does he interact with his same-age peers. He has a good vocabulary and seems capable of engaging in basic conversations with adults and peers but seems to avoid doing so on most occasions.

Curtis also seems easily frustrated in class when he's not given access to computer time. As a reward for good behavior, Mr. Hooper often allows students a few minutes of extra free time on the computer to play any approved games or explore approved websites. Sometimes in the middle of silent reading, Curtis blurts out, "I want computer time." Mr. Hooper responds, "Not yet, Curtis. Maybe after you've read the assignment." Curtis responds, "I want it now!!!" To avoid a "meltdown," sometimes Mr. Hooper says, "Okay, but just for a few minutes. Please be quiet. You are disturbing the other students who are reading."

Mr. Hooper and Curtis's parents would like to teach Curtis to greet others (i.e., saying "hello" when he meets his peers or adults or responding to greetings initiated by others, rather than imitating what they've said). They

LEARNER OBJECTIVES

After reading this chapter, the learner should be able to do the following:

- Describe the seven dimensions of applied behavior analysis.

- Explain the difference between respondent and operant behavior.

- Describe positive and negative reinforcement and positive and negative punishment.

- Describe prompting, modeling, shaping, and fading.

- Explain discrete-trial teaching and incidental teaching.

have been working with Curtis by prompting him to exchange the greeting when he meets a familiar person, such as his teacher, parent, grandparents, or ABA therapist. Later, they would like Curtis to spontaneously greet anyone he is not familiar with, such as store clerks, restaurant workers, or schoolmates he does not yet know.

The team has been using video modeling to teach Curtis how to greet and interact with others. The video shows one boy meeting another as they arrive at school. The first boy initiates the interaction by saying, "Hello, how are you?" Next in the video, there is a prompt that says, "Can you say, 'I'm fine. How are you?'" So far, Curtis has responded to greetings initiated by others by repeating what they said. For example, when a teacher says, "Good morning, Curtis. It's so nice to see you at school today," he responds by saying, "Good morning, Curtis. It's so nice to see you at school today."

The team defined appropriate social greetings to include (1) making eye contact with an unknown person; (2) acknowledging the other person (looking in the direction of the other person); (3) offering a verbal response to the other person's greeting (i.e., saying "hello"); (4) responding reciprocally with a wave or smile; and (5) maintaining appropriate distance between himself and the other person.

....

INTRODUCTION

Applied behavior analysis (ABA) refers to a group of techniques used to bring about meaningful, positive changes in behavior. It is a science devoted to understanding and improving human behavior (Cooper, Heron, & Heward, 2007). What distinguishes ABA from other forms of behavior intervention is the scientific method of inquiry. Procedures are to be implemented in a systematic, technological manner designed to make meaningful improvement in behavior (Cooper et al., 2007). ABA is the systematic, controlled, empirical investigation of socially important behavior using empirically validated, research-based, and acceptable practices (Baer, Wolf, & Risley, 1968; Cooper et al., 2007).

ABA is widely recognized as a safe and effective treatment for autism that is used to foster skills such as listening and imitating, reading, conversing, and understanding another person's perspective (Alberto & Troutman, 2013; Cooper et al., 2007). ABA has a strong research base demonstrating its effectiveness. Several studies have demonstrated improvements in communication, social relationships, play, self-care, academics, and employment in groups of participants ranging from preschoolers to adults as a result of ABA (Cooper et al., 2007; Donaldson, 2014; Joseph, Alber-Morgan, & Neef, 2015; Meadan, Ostrosky, Zaghlawan, & Yu, 2009; Minjarez, Williams, Mercier, & Harden, 2011; I. Smith, Flanagan, Garon, & Bryson, 2015). It is important to note that

ABA is not an intervention; it is the science of learning how to increase or decrease socially significant behaviors.

ABA, as a science, is quite complex, as we will discuss in this chapter. Completion of lengthy, formal training programs and testing are required for the certification of an ABA therapist. ABA therapy is conducted in clinics or in school settings by school psychologists or certified ABA therapists. For those reasons, we will not consider this chapter to be a complete and comprehensive text on ABA training. Rather, the chapter will provide an overview of ABA; then, we will move to a discussion of how special educators and general educators can incorporate principles of ABA into their teaching so that the behavior of your students can reflect positive changes.

APPLIED BEHAVIOR ANALYSIS

In ABA, trained therapists identify clearly defined target behaviors; develop goals for improving behavior; collaborate with parents, families, caregivers, and educators; develop a treatment plan for each individual's specific needs; and then carefully carry out the plan. Practitioners provide services such as conducting behavioral assessments, analyzing data, writing and revising treatment plans, overseeing others who implement treatment plans, and training others to implement treatment plans ((Behavior Analyst Certification Board [BACB], 2016).

An ABA therapy session is usually 2 to 3 hours long, using structured time and frequent breaks to conduct incidental teaching and opportunities to practice skills in new environments. Every aspect of ABA is customized for each student's skills, needs, interests, and situation. The intensity of ABA is usually about 25 to 40 hours per week, depending on the needs of the child.

Family Voices 5.1

"I'm not going to lie . . . at first ABA was very hard for me to watch. Therapists came in with their regimented procedures. My kid would cry during those initial sessions . . . I mean really cry hysterically. I would have to go to another room, shut the door, and put my headphones in to drown out the cries—I couldn't bear to hear him cry. But after a while, he started responding. It has made a huge difference in his behavior, and now I'm a fan."

APPLIED BEHAVIOR ANALYSIS—SEVEN DIMENSIONS

Applying principles of behavior, in hopes of improving a specific behavior, and then evaluating whether or not any changes noted in the behavior can be attributed to the process of the application is what ABA is all about. In 1968, Baer, Wolf, and Risley, in their seminal article, established the principles on which the scientific study of behavior is based. The seven dimensions of applied behavior analysis introduced by Baer and colleagues describe the fundamental characteristics of a behavioral intervention, which includes that it is applied, behavioral, analytic, technological, conceptually systematic, and effective, and it should display some generality. Treatments that do not feature all seven dimensions are considered incomplete and potentially compromised in their effectiveness. Interventions based on the science of ABA should follow these guidelines.

An intervention that is *applied* refers to the behavior under study and its importance or significance to society (Baer et al., 1968). The concept most important here is how socially important the behavior change is for a given individual. The behaviors we target should have a real-life application for the person we are working with to allow an individual to successfully function within his or her environment (i.e., communication, social skills, eating, sleeping, physical skills, disruptive behaviors, etc.). If a skill being addressed by an intervention has social significance to the individual, then the intervention fits the component of applied under the seven criteria.

To fit into the applied criterion, goals and interventions should be selected because they are related to the needs of the client and/or stakeholders, such as parents or teachers. What is important to the client should directly relate to the goals of the intervention or program to be implemented. This is also why sometimes the intervention takes place at home, in the most natural environment, and sometimes in the classroom.

For an intervention to be considered *behavioral*, we must define the behaviors to be addressed in observable and measurable terms. That means the behavior can be seen and recorded, and the changes can be measured over time. Behaviorism is the foundation of ABA and behaviors are the focus. ABA focuses on what the child should or should not do, rather than what they should or should not think or feel. Moreover, ABA should focus on getting a child to exhibit a new behavior, not just stop a problematic one (e.g., you would teach a child to raise his hand, instead of teaching the child to stop interrupting the teacher).

ABA is *analytic*. This means that data are collected, daily or weekly, to determine whether the intervention is effective in improving the target behavior. This will reveal whether the intervention is responsible for the behavior change. If data do not show a change as expected (target behavior does not increase or decrease in the way in which it was expected), then the intervention may need to be changed in some way. An intervention that is having no impact on behavior may therefore be considered a waste of time and money and should be discontinued.

An intervention should be *technological*. This means that the techniques being used should be clearly and completely identified and described. The behavior to be changed should be defined precisely, and all of the procedures and methods used should be described clearly. Techniques and procedures that are used should be so plainly described that anyone could read them and understand what to do. For instance, instead of saying, "Reinforce David when he uses nice words to speak to peers," a more technological description would be, "When David uses please or excuse me, provide him with high fives."

"The best rule of thumb for evaluating a procedure description as technological is probably to ask whether a typically trained reader could replicate that procedures well enough to produce the same results, given only a reading of the description" (Baer et al., 1968, p. 95). Techniques that are clearly defined and described increase the likelihood that Person A will implement the intervention the same as Person B. Techniques, procedures, and strategies implemented should be so clearly explained that anyone could read them and understand how to implement the intervention.

An intervention should be *conceptually systematic*. It should contain a description of procedures that are precisely technological and explained in terms of basic principles of behavior. Everything implemented in an ABA program should relate to research-supported concepts, such as shaping, positive reinforcement, and errorless teaching. Other behavioral terms that make an intervention conceptually systematic include positive and negative reinforcement, extinction, fading, differential reinforcement, prompting, and chaining.

An intervention should be *effective*. If the application of behavioral techniques does not produce significant effects, then the application is considered a failure. In other words, if a technique shows positive results in raising a classroom grade from a D– to a D, it is not an obvious example of applied behavior analysis (Baer et al., 1968). The power in altering behavior enough to be socially important is the essential nature of this criterion (Baer et al., 1968). Baer and colleagues (1968) pointed out that in evaluating whether a certain intervention has produced enough behavioral change to deserve the label effective, we should ask, "How much did that behavior need to change?" An important point to note about an intervention's effectiveness is from whose vantage point you are looking. Consider a parent's perspective—one that wanted screaming to be reduced by 100%. If your intervention reduced screaming behavior by 25%, but the parent wanted 100%, then your behavior plan was not effective.

Finally, to be considered ABA, the skills learned in the intervention should be *generalized*. We want to know if the child can display the skills he learned across settings, people, or stimuli. We should look at whether the behavior changes persist over time and generalize to other environments. For instance, can the child correctly label a red apple flashcard and a red apple at the grocery store? If the child learned to say "please" 3 months ago, can he say "please" today? If a student is able to use the skill he learned in a variety of environments, the behavior is considered generalized. Moreover, the best way to determine whether the skills are generalized is to track data across environments.

Seven Dimensions of Applied Behavior Analysis	
1. Applied	The work conducted must have social significance.
2. Behavioral	Precise and reliable measurement of behavior should be attainable.
3. Analytic	It must be shown that the treatment led to behavior change and not something else, such as chance.
4. Technological	Procedures used should be clearly described and identified.
5. Conceptually Systematic	Procedures should be described in terms of their principles.
6. Effective	Procedures should improve the behaviors being addressed to a practical degree.
7. Generalized	Positive changes should extend over time, environments, and behaviors.

ABA is critical in the education of students with ASD. It is committed to teaching behaviors or skills that are practical and effective and can be generalized to other settings, people, or stimuli (Baer et al., 1968). Every educational program in ABA is selected according to whether it is appropriate, meaningful, and functional for the individual. Questions the researcher should ask include the following: (1) Are the skills likely to be maintained in the everyday, natural environment? (2) Will the responses help improve the quality of a person's life? And (3) can the skills be used outside the teaching situation or learning environment? (Ryan, 2011).

The words of Baer et al. (1968), the researchers who established the key concepts of ABA discussed here, provide a concise summary of ABA:

An *applied* behavior analysis will make obvious the importance of the behavior changed, its quantitative characteristics, the experimental manipulations which analyze with clarity what was responsible for the change, the technologically exact description of all procedures contributing to that change, the effectiveness of those procedures in making sufficient change for value, and the generality of that change. (p. 97)

Now that we have learned the critical components of applied behavior analysis, let us move on to discuss some basic behavioral terms, followed by the teaching methods used in ABA.

BEHAVIORAL CONCEPTS USED IN ABA

Two Kinds of Behavior: Respondent and Operant

A respondent behavior happens in *response* to some stimuli and is characterized by involuntary action. Respondent behaviors are reflexive responses that are elicited by stimuli over which individuals have little or no control, such as sneezing, blinking, hiccups, and the like. Pulling your hand away from a hot surface and being startled by loud noises are other examples of respondent behavior. Emotions fall into respondent behavior as well. Respondent behavior can be elicited in response to a new stimulus; new associations can be learned between a stimulus and the response.

Operant behavior, on the other hand, *operates*, or acts on the environment and is controlled by the consequences that follow the behavior. Consequences control our behavior because they have an influence on the frequency of the behaviors they follow. The consequence of being given access to a preferred activity immediately after a response occurs will most likely increase the likelihood of the same response in the future. For example, a child who is praised for helping with a chore is more likely to help again in the future; a child who is allowed to push another child down and take his toy is more likely to be aggressive to others in the future. The child's helping is considered the operant behavior, controlled by the consequence of praise or reward in these examples.

REINFORCEMENT AND PUNISHMENT

Reinforcement. Reinforcement refers to the motivating events or rewards given to a person who engages in a behavior. Every behavior we perform results in some consequence. When our behavior results in a desirable consequence, this motivates us to continue behaving that way (Alberto & Troutman, 2013). For example, I wake up each morning and make myself something for breakfast. When the behavior of making breakfast results in the desirable consequence of satisfying my hunger, I am motivated to continue behaving that way in the future. More than likely, I will repeat the same behavior tomorrow morning. Yesterday, I took an aspirin for my headache. My behavior (taking the aspirin) resulted in the favorable consequence of eliminating my headache, and I will therefore repeat that behavior next time I have a headache.

Reinforcement can be positive or negative. *Positive reinforcement* is a procedure in which a stimulus or positive reinforcer is delivered immediately following a response that serves to increase likelihood of a future occurrence of that response. Positive reinforcement is *adding* something that will motivate the child to increase the likelihood he will engage in that behavior again. For example, a teacher gives her student praise for completing his homework. The praise is the positive reinforcement (something we added) for doing the desired behavior (homework). Being able to watch a favorite TV show after doing all of your homework is another example of positive reinforcement. Other reinforcers for students could be playing with games or favorite toys, hearing praise, obtaining tokens or tickets, eating a preferred snack, getting candy or stickers, obtaining high fives, or anything preferred by the student.

Negative reinforcement happens when a stimulus is *removed*, taken away, or withdrawn immediately following a behavior that serves to increase the future occurrence of that behavior. Negative reinforcement should not be thought of as punishment. With negative reinforcement, you are increasing a behavior by removing or taking away something that motivates the child. Taking an aspirin to soothe your headache is another example of negative reinforcement. (It reinforces your pill-taking behavior by removing the pain.)

Negative reinforcement is a concept that many consider difficult to conceptualize. Negative reinforcement involves the removal of something already present, immediately following that behavior. That behavior will increase in the future, as a result, because it created an outcome that the student considered to be favorable. For example, Benjamin doesn't want to eat carrots, but his parents keep trying to get him to eat them. When he is served his dinner, if there are any carrots on his plate, he will scream until they are taken off his plate. His parents give in to the screaming tantrums and take away the carrots because they don't like hearing him scream. Why is this negative reinforcement? The carrots were present before Benjamin had a tantrum. His tantrum caused his parents to remove the carrots. Benjamin's tantrums are getting more severe; this behavior is increasing. Therefore, the tantrums are being negatively reinforced by the removal of the carrots. Both kinds of reinforcement, positive and negative, will increase a behavior. Punishment, as we will see later, is used to decrease a behavior.

It is important to remember that anything that serves as a reinforcer for one student can be entirely different for another. The effectiveness of the reinforcer is an individual preference for each child. We can ask students what they would like to receive as a result of their achievement, depending on the child's level of functioning, or we can provide a "menu" of appropriate choices for students to rank in order of preference (Alberto & Troutman, 2013). For the reinforcer to be effective, we should make sure to provide the reinforcer only after the student performs the target behavior.

Choice of reinforcers. There is evidence that shows that children with ASD engage in more on-task behavior and less disruptive behaviors when they are provided with opportunities to make choices about the task or activities, as opposed to when another person (the teacher or a parent) selects the activity (Elliott & Dillenburger, 2016). Because of those findings in the literature, Elliott and Dillenburger (2016) assessed whether allowing for reinforcer choice in discrete trial teaching resulted in lower rates of maladaptive behavior for students with ASD. Preferred reinforcer items were identified with the participants. In the nonchoice conditions, the therapist provided one of the three preferred items when an accurate response was given; in the choice condition, the child could choose one of the three preferred items after the response. Choice of a reinforcer did not have an effect on motivation for two children in the investigation, but it did increase accurate responding for one of the children (Elliott & Dillenburger, 2016). These results show that choice influences behavior in some children with ASD but not all. For some, choice makes a big difference in motivating appropriate behavior. The fact that reinforcer choice increased the positive effects for even one child has implications for those working with children with ASD (Elliott & Dillenburger, 2016) and is worthy of consideration.

Family Voices 5.2

"I'd like to commend the therapists for working hard to find out what was a reinforcer for my Nico. Once they established what he wanted, he worked hard to get it. They found his motivation."

1. Make a list of common behaviors that you exhibit (e.g., arriving on time for job, taking a class, taking an aspirin, turning on the water faucet, eating your lunch, etc.).

2. Also, list the positive or negative reinforcers that provide motivation for engaging in that particular behavior.

Punishment. Punishment procedures are used to *decrease* a behavior. It is a process whereby a consequence immediately follows a behavior, which will decrease the frequency of that behavior. Like reinforcement, there are two kinds of punishment, positive and negative. *Positive punishment* works by *presenting* a negative consequence after an undesired behavior is exhibited. For example, a child who grabs a toy from another child is sent to time-out. The boy grabbing (behavior) is met with time-out (punishment). It can be difficult to consider time at as a positive. Getting a speeding ticket is considered positive punishment. (Speeding is the behavior; the ticket is the negative consequence or punishment, meant to reduce the likelihood that you will speed again in the future.) Think of it this way: remember that *positive punishment* involves *presenting* a negative consequence following an undesired behavior, making the behavior less likely to be repeated in the future.

Negative punishment happens when something is *removed* after an undesired behavior is exhibited, making the behavior less likely to be repeated in the future. For example, if a child acts inappropriately, he loses a token that he could later cash in for a prize from the class treasure box. The token was removed (negative punishment) so that he is less likely to act inappropriately in the future. When a child has her toy taken away for fighting with her brother, that is an example of negative punishment. If taking away the toy decreases the probability of her screaming in the future, then it serves as a negative punisher.

T.I.P. – Theory Into Practice 5.2

STOP AND THINK

The concept of *punishment* often conjures up bad thoughts. In ABA, punishment decreases the chances that a particular behavior will occur again, as opposed to reinforcement, which increase the likelihood of behavior. How would you describe punishment to a parent who has asked that you never "punish" her child?

With punishment, remember that the end result is to decrease the undesired behavior. Positive punishment involves *adding* a negative consequence after an undesired behavior, whereas negative punishment involves *removing* a desired item or activity after the undesired behavior occurs. ABA therapists often employ principles reinforcement (positive and negative) and punishment (also positive and negative) in their behavioral interventions.

Reinforcement and Punishment			
		Stimulus	
		Presented	*Removed*
Probability of behavior	*Increase*	Positive Reinforcement	Negative Reinforcement
	Decrease	Positive Punishment	Negative Punishment

The table shows the relationship between positive and negative reinforcement and punishment. In positive reinforcement, a stimulus is presented immediately following the target response, which helps increase the future likelihood of the target response occurring. In negative reinforcement, an aversive stimulus is removed immediately following the target response to increase the future likelihood of the target response occurring. *If you want to increase a behavior, provide positive or negative reinforcement.* In the table, we also see punishment conceptualized. Positive punishment involves adding something that serves to decrease future occurrences of a behavior, and negative punishment involves taking something away to decrease future occurrences of a behavior. *If you want to decrease a behavior, provide positive or negative punishment.*

With an understanding of the behavioral concepts used in ABA, let us now move to an introduction to the implementation of ABA.

Family Voices 5.3

"Is ABA the best thing for my child? Well, honestly, it's the only therapy the insurance would cover, and that's what got us interested in the first place. But with the insistence on planning, order, and charting progress, it all made me feel like there was some order to our child's day and it helped him make progress."

TEACHING WITH APPLIED BEHAVIOR ANALYSIS

Functional Analysis

All ABA work should begin with an analysis of the function of a behavior prior to treatment (Kruger et al., 2015). We should determine whether the behavior is one of excess (e.g., aggression, disruption, or too much screaming) or deficit (e.g., the child does not give a correct response when presented with an instructional task or poor match skills). ABA is useful for decreasing or increasing any behavior (Alberto & Troutman, 2013). Before a behavior change program can be initiated, the behavior analyst must describe the target behavior clearly. This initial analysis helps us determine the behavior that the intervention will address.

Functional analysis of behavior is described in more detail in the next chapter of this text. As a reminder, let us consider possible functions of a behavior. Students may exhibit a behavior to gain something (e.g., attention from an adult or peer; a tangible object, activity, or event; or sensory stimulation) or to escape from something (e.g., attention from a peer or adult; social interaction; a demanding or boring task; or painful or discomforting sensory stimulation). To understand the function of a behavior, we could ask these questions: (1) Is there a pattern of events or behaviors that usually occurs prior to the behavior? (2) Is there a pattern of events or behaviors that consistently follows the occurrence of the behavior? And (3) can the student be taught an alternative, appropriate behavior to accomplish the same function as the inappropriate behavior? (Alberto & Troutman, 2013). Based on the function of the behavior, we can then move to developing the behavior support plan.

DISCRETE-TRIAL TEACHING

Discrete-trial teaching involves dividing a target behavior into smaller components or target responses and teaching each component separately. Those smaller target responses are taught in a clear, distinct manner in a carefully planned shaping procedure that teaches new behaviors in discrete trials or "learn-units" (Elliott & Dillenburger, 2016). In a meticulously planned procedure, we follow a three-step pattern: (1) a *stimulus* is presented, (2) followed by a given target *behavior*, which is (3) immediately followed by a *consequence* or positive or negative reinforcer.

In other words, a cue is given, the child responds, and a reward is given for a correct response. In everyday school life, we might see the following playground situation: One child holding a soccer ball approaches another child and says, "Hi!" The second child says, "Hi!" in response. The first child smiles and says, "Let's go," and the two begin kicking the soccer ball to each other. Children with autism might not have the skills to respond socially with other people. Discrete-trial teaching can address underlying skill deficits by breaking down the skill into discrete parts so that weak areas can be strengthened. Prompts can be given, whether verbal, physical, or modeled, until a successful interaction occurs that can be reinforced.

Interestingly, typical literacy instruction in general-education classrooms follows a similar three-step pattern. Teaching students to spell correctly might involve the following learning trials: (1) the teacher orally presents a word printed on a flashcard and prompts the student to look at the word and spell it along with him or her (stimulus), (2) the student spells the word (behavior/response), and (3) the teacher provides performance feedback (consequence). On the next learning trial, the teacher removes the flashcard and asks the student to spell the word on his or her own, the student spells the word, and the teacher provides praise for correct responses and corrective feedback for incorrect responses (Joseph et al., 2015).

We can think of discrete-trial teaching as a series of teaching attempts, with each attempt called a *discrete trial*. For example, say we want to teach Tricia to learn to identify red and blue cards when they are placed on the table. In Discrete Trial 1, the teacher would place one red and one blue card on the table. The teacher might say, "Point to red," and Tricia would respond by pointing to the red card. The teacher would then say, "Yes, that's right!" That is considered one discrete trial. In another session, the teacher would place one red and one blue card on the table and ask Tricia to "point to blue." Tricia responds by pointing to the blue card, and the teacher says, "Yes, you are correct. Good job!" This represents Discrete Trial 2.

In this example, the teacher saying, "Point to red" was the antecedent stimulus. Prior to this trial, Tricia would not have been able to point to red without the stimulus. The teacher's request to point to a color card is considered the antecedent (A). Tricia's response, pointing to the colored card, is considered the behavior (B). This is the response that should be reinforced with a consequence (C). The consequence for the correct response, or reinforcement, could be in the form of verbal praise, as in the prior example, or it could have been delivery of a tangible reinforcer, like candy or stickers. For incorrect responses, no reinforcement would be given. Instead, the teacher would provide correction, perhaps by saying, "No, that is not correct," and then begin a new trial.

Each trial should be carefully scripted and should involve the exact same procedures each time. By running each teaching trial the same way, it allows the behavior analyst to identify why a trial might not be working and modify it. If every trial was run differently, it would be impossible to know whether it is working or whether other variables were introduced that made the change.

Discrete-trial teaching helps increase motivation and learning for children with ASD for a number of reasons. First, each trial is usually short, and many trials can be completed, which allows for numerous learning opportunities. Second, the one-to-one teaching in discrete-trial teaching allows for individualized instruction that meets the needs of each child specifically. Third, the strict adherence to procedures in discrete-trial teaching helps provide the structure to which students with ASD respond well (T. Smith, 2001). It is important to note that ABA uses discrete-trial training as one method, and there are many others, such as incidental teaching, which we will discuss next.

INCIDENTAL TEACHING

Incidental teaching is used to facilitate the student's use of language. It occurs within the context of an interaction between two people in a natural environment. In incidental teaching, the student specifies an individual reinforcer, the teacher prompts a language response from the student, and then the teacher reinforces the language response. For example, if a child wants to have a piece of fruit, and we want her to make a verbal request for the fruit instead of her pointing and grunting to get it, we can tell her to say "orange," and when she says it, bring her the orange. This interaction increases the likelihood that she will maintain a language response after several incidences.

An example of incidental teaching is in the following scenario. The instructor is near the student. The student initiates a request for the orange by pointing and grunting. The instructor would remove the desired item for a brief time. The instructor would then ask for a correct verbal response. The instructor would then wait for a few seconds for the learner to respond, or the instructor would provide a prompt. When the child responds by saying, "orange," the instructor will use an enthusiastic tone of voice and provide access to the desired object (the orange, in this case).

SHAPING

In shaping, we reinforce successive approximations toward a desired behavior. For example, a child can learn to stay in his seat when the teacher initially reinforces sitting behavior when it occurs for short periods of time and gradually increases the sitting time required to earn the reinforcer. Many behaviors are taught through shaping, such as when parents praise a child the first time she dresses herself, even if her dress is on backward. Later, the child will earn the compliment only if she puts the outfit on correctly.

Shaping involves gradually modifying the existing behavior in small steps toward the desired behavior. For example, if you have a young boy who only engages with a pet dog by hitting it, you could hold his hand and turn the hit into a stroking motion and perhaps add the prompt, "Gentle ... pet gently." Pair this with positive reinforcement by saying, for example, "It's so nice when you are gentle with Bella!"

TASK ANALYSIS

Task analysis is the process in which a task is analyzed into its parts so that those parts can be taught through the use of chaining. We do a task analysis so that skills are taught in an orderly and systematic manner in which one skill builds on another, rather than being taught haphazardly (Joseph et al., 2015). For example, literacy instruction often proceeds from a task analysis. Literacy tasks are broken up into steps, and each step is taught until the student masters each task (i.e., students learn to make letter–sound correspondences, moving on to whole words and, from there, to reading sentences) (Joseph et al., 2015).

T.I.P. – Theory Into Practice 5.4

TRY A TASK ANALYSIS

1. Take a simple task, such as putting on a jacket or making a peanut butter and jelly sandwich, and list its component parts in the correct sequence. List all of the steps you can think of (i.e., take out bread, take out knife, spread peanut butter on one slice of bread, spread jelly on the other slice of bread, etc.).

2. Read your step to a friend while he or she does exactly as you have written.

3. Think about how you might need to add steps or rearrange the order to make the task more easily performed. (e.g., we left out "open the bread wrapper and take out two pieces of bread" in the list).

USING ABA IN THE INCLUSIVE CLASSROOM

Gongola and Sweeney (2012) advocate for the use of discrete-trial teaching as an intervention that can be implemented in classroom settings. Ideally, discrete-trial teaching occurs in highly structured environments, but delivery can occur in inclusive classrooms, in an area with minimal distractions, or away from a group where transitions occur. Perhaps scheduling the discrete-trial session in the class during lunch break or in the cafeteria the first thing in the morning when it remains uninhabited is best. "As a student's attention to task and readiness skills increase, the teaching environment should begin to shift to become more like the general teaching environment"

(Gongola & Sweeney, 2012, p. 185). Some skills should be taught in a separate, quiet environment, and some skills can be embedded into planned activities in the inclusive classroom. The learned skill can be practiced in small-group situations with careful monitoring and attention to detail (Gongola & Sweeney, 2012).

Inclusion Tips

DISCRETE-TRIAL TEACHING

1. Evaluate whether discrete-trial teaching is the most appropriate approach.

2. Gather a cohesive instructional team.

3. Organize a system of data collection.

4. Determine student preferences for reinforcers.

5. Gain student attention.

6. Begin discrete-trial teaching, with prompts, student responses, and consequences.

7. Gradually increase teaching opportunities in inclusive classrooms.

PARTNERING WITH FAMILIES TO IMPLEMENT ABA

It can be very beneficial—or even necessary—for parents to implement ABA strategies at home. We have established in other chapters of this text that when parents are active participants in their child's treatment, positive outcomes are achieved. When we can help parents extend the learning and intervention practices from school to home, we increase the likelihood of generalizing their child's newly learned skills.

Determine family needs. The first step of parent-implemented ABA is to determine the strengths, needs, and priorities of the family. Gain a full understanding of the child's behaviors that impact family functioning, the nature of parent–child interactions, and family activities, for example. Gather information, being responsive and sensitive to the unique context of each family.

Select goals. Next, professionals and families work together to select goals. From the data you gathered in the first step, help parents identify the specific goals the child will work toward achieving. These goals should address areas of concern for the family, should have a positive impact on family functioning while not causing any additional stress to the family, and should be appropriate for parent implementation. Make sure parents have input into goal selection.

Develop the intervention plan. Once we have developed goals, we can create the intervention plan, which provides specific steps for parents to implement easily. Make sure to spell out a plan that includes (a) instructional strategies broken down into step-by-step directions, (b) the frequency and duration of instruction, (c) the prompts and reinforcers that should be utilized, (d) when and where parents should provide instruction, and (e) how progress will be monitored.

Train parents. Once you have developed a plan in collaboration with parents, you will want to provide structured training. You might consider having a parent group-training session, individual training sessions, or a combination of both. Training can be conducted in the child's home, in the community, in a clinic setting, or at school. In the training, provide sufficient feedback and coaching as they practice implementation. Model specific procedures as you demonstrate how to implement a plan. Consider role-playing as a way for parents to practice the intervention. Coach parents in data collection and documentation as well. Or consider asking parents to watch and review videos of sample strategies being implemented. Several studies have demonstrated positive outcomes when training parents to implement ABA interventions (Meadan et al., 2009; Minjarez et al., 2011; Reagon & Higbee, 2009; Smith et al., 2015).

Implement the intervention. Once you move to implementation, also take care to monitor progress and make adjustments to the plan as needed. You want to ensure that the practice is implemented correctly and consistently, so we suggest ongoing discussions throughout the plan's implementation. Review the data and documentation, and solicit parent feedback about the plan. We want to know whether the intervention is impacting target skills, or if the intervention should be adjusted where needed.

Parent-Implemented Intervention

1. Determine the needs of the family.
2. Select goals.
3. Develop the intervention plan.
4. Train parents.
5. Implement the intervention, monitor progress, and adjust as needed.

SUMMARY STATEMENTS

- Applied behavior analysis is a systematic approach utilized to improve socially important behavior through the identification of related environmental variables and the production of behavior change techniques that make use of those findings.

- The seven dimensions of applied behavior analysis introduced by Baer and colleagues describe the fundamental characteristics of a behavioral intervention, which includes that it is applied, behavioral, analytic, technological, conceptually systematic, and effective, and it should display some generality.

- A respondent behavior happens in response to some stimuli and is characterized by involuntary action. Respondent behaviors are reflexive responses that are elicited by stimuli over which individuals have little or no control.

- Operant behavior, on the other hand, *operates*, or acts on the environment and is controlled by the consequences that follow the behavior.

- Reinforcement refers to the motivating events or rewards given to a person who engaged in a behavior. Every behavior we perform results in some consequence. When our behavior results in a desirable consequence, this motivates us to continue behaving that way.

- Punishment procedures are used to *decrease* a behavior. It is a process whereby a consequence immediately follows a behavior, which will decrease the frequency of that behavior.

- Discrete-trial teaching involves dividing a target behavior into smaller components or target responses. Those smaller target responses are taught in a clear, distinct manner in a carefully planned shaping procedure that teaches new behaviors in discrete units.

- Ideally, discrete-trial teaching occurs in highly structured environments, but delivery can occur in inclusive classrooms, in an area with minimal distractions, or away from a group where transitions occur.

- It can be very beneficial—or even necessary—for parents to implement ABA strategies at home.

WHAT WOULD YOU DO?

Look back at the case study about Curtis presented at the beginning of the chapter. Based on what you have read in this chapter, what you have read in previous chapters, and your own experiences, how would you respond to the following questions?

1. Based on what we know from this case study, how does the video modeling technique the team currently uses fit into the seven dimensions of an ABA intervention?

2. How could we use discrete-trial teaching to help Curtis increase social interactions or reduce screaming for computer time?

3. Would you suggest reinforcement or punishment to increase Curtis's social interactions, and why? Would reinforcement or punishment be better to address Curtis's screaming? What reinforcers or punishers would you suggest for Curtis?

4. Do you think incidental teaching could be helpful to teach Curtis how to initiate social interactions or decrease screaming? Why, or why not?

5. In what ways could we use functional analysis, modeling, prompting, shaping, and differential reinforcement to help with Curtis's social interactions and screaming behaviors?

CHAPTER REFLECTION QUESTIONS

1. Mr. Cooper has started using stickers that can be traded for free time to help Mia, one of his kindergarten students who becomes easily frustrated and cries a lot when she is asked to work independently. Mr. Cooper gives her a sticker whenever she works independently for a few minutes. He reports that Mia is crying less, so the sticker program appears to be working. Is Mr. Cooper practicing applied behavior analysis? Why, or why not?

2. What is an example of a skill that could be taught using discrete-trial training?

3. In what ways could ABA be used in general-education or inclusive classrooms?

4. How can we work with parents to implement components of ABA at home?

RECOMMENDED RESOURCES

Websites

- Association for Behavior Analysis International. Available at https://www.abainternational.org/welcome.aspx

- Autism Speaks: Applied behavior Analysis. Available at https://www.autismspeaks.org/what-autism/treatment/applied-behavior-analysis-aba

- Center for Autism: Applied Behavior Analysis. Available at http://www.centerforautism.com/aba-therapy.aspx

Articles/Publications

Cooper, J. O., Heron, T. E., & Heward, W. L. (2007). *Applied behavior analysis* (2nd ed.). Upper Saddle River, NJ: Pearson Education.

Gongola, L., & Sweeney, J. (2012). Discrete trial teaching: Getting started. *Intervention in School and Clinic, 47*(3), 183–190.

Joseph, L. M., Alber-Morgan, S., & Neef, N. (2015). Applying behavior analytic procedures to effectively teach literacy skills in the classroom. *Psychology in the Schools, 53*(1), 73–88.

REFERENCES

Alberto, P., & Troutman, A. C. (2013). *Applied behavior analysis for teachers* (9th ed.). Upper Saddle River, NJ: Pearson Education.

Baer, D. M., Wolf, M. M., & Risley, T. R. (1968). Some current dimensions of applied behavior analysis. *Journal of Applied Behavior Analysis, 1*, 91–97.

Behavior Analyst Certification Board (BACB). (2016). *About behavior analysis.* Retrieved from http://bacb.com/about-behavior-analysis

Cooper, J. O., Heron, T. E., & Heward, W. L. (2007). *Applied behavior analysis* (2nd ed.). Upper Saddle River, NJ: Pearson Education.

Donaldson, A. L. (2014). Team collaboration: The use of behavior principles for serving students with ASD. *Language, Speech, and Hearing Services in Schools, 45*, 261–276.

Elliott, C., & Dillenburger, K. (2016). The effect of choice on motivation for young children on the autism spectrum during discrete trial teaching.

Journal of Research in Special Educational Needs, 16(3), 187–198.

Gongola, L., & Sweeney, J. (2012). Discrete trial teaching: Getting started. *Intervention in School and Clinic, 47*(3), 183–190.

Joseph, L. M., Alber-Morgan, S., & Neef, N. (2015). Applying behavior analytic procedures to effectively teach literacy skills in the classroom. *Psychology in the Schools, 53*(1), 73–88.

Kruger, A. M., Strong, W., Daly, E. J., III, O'Connor, M., Sommerhalder, M. S., Holtz, J., …Heifner, A. (2015). Setting the stage for academic success through antecedent intervention. *Psychology in the Schools, 53*(1), 24–38.

Meadan, H., Ostrosky, M., Zaghlawan, H. Y., & Yu, S. Y. (2009). Promoting the social and communicative behavior of young children with autism spectrum disorders: A review of parent-implemented intervention studies. *Topics in Early Childhood Special Education, 29*(2), 90–104.

Minjarez, M. B., Williams, S. E., Mercier, E. M., & Harden, T. (2011). Pivotal response group treatment program for parents of children with autism. *Journal of Autism and Developmental Disorders, 41*(1), 92–101.

Reagon, K. A., & Higbee, T. S. (2009). Parent-implemented script fading to promote play-based verbal initiations in children with autism. *Journal of Applied Behavior Analysis, 42*, 659–664.

Ryan, C. (2011). Applied behavior analysis: Teaching procedures and staff training for children with autism. In T. Williams (Ed.), *Autism spectrum disorders—From genes to environment* (pp. 191–212). Rijeka, Croatia: InTech. Retrieved from http://cdn.intechopen.com/pdfs-wm/19204.pdf

Smith, I. M., Flanagan, H. E., Garon, N., & Bryson, S. E. (2015). Effectiveness of community-based early intervention based on pivotal response treatment. *Journal of Autism and Developmental Disorders, 45*, 1858–1872.

Smith, T. (2001). Discrete trial training in the treatment of autism. *Focus on Autism and Other Developmental Disabilities, 16*, 8–92.

6   Promoting Behavioral Changes in Children With ASD: Functional Behavioral Assessment and Behavioral Intervention Plans

LEARNER OBJECTIVES

After reading this chapter, the learner should be able to do the following:

- Describe the purpose of a functional behavioral assessment (FBA).

- Describe how to identify the function of problem behaviors.

- Describe the antecedent, behavior, and consequence of a given behavior and be able to complete an ABC analysis for the behavior.

- Develop a hypothesis statement.

- Design a behavior intervention plan based on the functions of problem behaviors.

- Develop a rationale for why it is important to collaborate with families to implement a behavior plan.

- Become familiar with ways to ensure that inclusive classrooms can conduct FBAs and BIPs.

"We can teach appropriate behavior skills to children!"

—DIXIE JORDAN

CASE STUDY

Ethan is a student with ASD enrolled in Mr. Carter's sixth-grade classroom. Ethan is educated in an inclusive classroom along with his peers. Ethan enjoys art and reading, and he does not seem to like group activities or large crowds. He is above grade level in reading and enjoys extensive time reading alone whenever he is allowed. Many of Ethan's classmates would describe him to be good-natured, outgoing, and humorous. Although he prefers to spend time alone, it is obvious that Ethan likes to make his classmates laugh.

Ethan lives at home with his mother, father, grandmother, and a younger brother who is 2 years old. Ethan is new to his current school. His family had to move in the middle of this school year due to his father's job transfer to this city.

Occasionally, during small-group activities, Ethan appears to have a "meltdown." He engages in verbal outbursts, throwing classroom materials onto the floor after being given an academic task, using profanity, and telling other students to "be quiet" during group work. Ethan sometimes makes attempts to run from the classroom when he becomes frustrated.

Mr. Carter thinks that Ethan engages in such behaviors to gain caregiver or teacher attention or to escape something he finds unpleasant. Mr. Carter feels that on average, he is spending at least an hour per day dealing with Ethan's difficult behaviors, which interferes with Ethan's and his peers' learning. Many times, Mr. Carter sends Ethan to the principal after an outburst, but Ethan returns to class and repeats the same behaviors.

Mr. Carter has tried to prevent Ethan's outbursts by offering rewards if he does not engage in the disruptive behavior. Ethan's behavior has not improved through this tactic, and it has been difficult for Mr. Carter to find an appropriate reward that might help.

Mr. Carter has not had any training in behavior analysis. He feels that his classroom management strategies that seem to work with other students have been unsuccessful in managing Ethan's behaviors, and he'd like to learn behavior approaches that might be more helpful to Ethan. Another teacher, Mrs. Williams, suggested to Mr. Carter that perhaps Ethan is not misbehaving intentionally or in order to get his way, but rather, such behaviors are Ethan's attempt to communicate something. Perhaps the function of Ethan's behavior is to avoid a situation he feels is difficult. "We need to find the function of Ethan's behaviors," said Mrs. Williams. Mr. Carter would like to learn more about why Ethan's behavior occurs and learn to develop more appropriate behaviors. "Maybe Mrs. Williams is onto something with this behavior analysis stuff," Mr. Carter thought to himself.

....

INTRODUCTION

Some students with ASD will display challenging behaviors that can make it difficult for them to learn, cause harm to the child or others, or isolate them from their peers. They may engage in self-harming behaviors or aggression toward their peers, they may be sad or anxious, or they may not have learned positive ways to express their needs or have them met. Any of these behaviors can interfere with a student's ability to learn the skills he or she needs to be successful. We must, therefore, find ways to teach new behaviors to our students with ASD. As Dixie Jordan said in the opening quote, "We can teach appropriate behavior skills to children!" (Jordan, n.d., p. 1). We do that by assessing the behavior and developing appropriate interventions to match the data we gather.

Functional behavioral assessment (FBA) is a problem-solving process that looks beyond the behavior itself to identify factors associated with the behavior and select interventions that directly address the problem behavior. This process offers a better understanding of the function or purpose behind student behavior. Behavior intervention plans that are based on an understanding of "why" a student misbehaves are extremely useful in addressing a wide range of problem behaviors (Center for Effective Collaboration and Practice [CECP], 2001). FBA allows us to understand a student's purpose for engaging in a particular behavior, so we can then implement interventions that teach replacement behaviors. Once we understand the purpose of a student's behavior through FBA, that information is then used to plan an effective behavior intervention.

PROBLEM BEHAVIORS

A brief review of what we mean by *problem behaviors* is in order, before proceeding to the steps in conducting a functional behavioral assessment and implementing a behavior intervention plan. Problem behaviors include any response that we target for a reduction in the frequency, intensity, or duration of its occurrence. Problem behaviors are usually those that threaten the safety or disrupt the learning of the student or others and do not include those that are purely academic in nature (such as reading words incorrectly). Behaviors that could be problematic for students with ASD fall into the following categories:

- Verbal and physical aggression toward self or others

- Repetitive and inflexible behaviors

- Socially inappropriate behaviors

- Inattentive, disorganized behavior

- Withdrawal or refusal to participate

Such behaviors are likely to interfere with teachers' or parents' attempts to promote learning and therefore should be addressed with evidence-based strategies. For behaviors that do not interfere with learning or that do not cause harm to anyone, we would not conduct an FBA.

Examples of behaviors that can interfere with learning are those that involve self-injury (e.g., biting or hitting self), aggression toward others (e.g., hitting, kicking, scratching, or biting others), escaping (e.g., running from the classroom unattended), and tantrum behaviors (e.g., crying, screaming, or yelling). Other problematic behaviors include bizarre vocalizations (e.g., talking to someone who was not physically present), defiance, property destruction (e.g., throwing objects, banging objects, or knocking over furniture), elopement (leaving an area or room without permission), inappropriate vocalizations (e.g., making comments that are rude or off topic), and off-task behavior (e.g., engaging in some behavior other than assigned tasks).

An important thing to remember about the behavior of children with ASD is this: Most problem behaviors in a child with ASD, even the aggressive behaviors, are not intended to hurt others. Instead, the behaviors might be related to the student's limited ability to control her emotions, including silliness, anger, and anxiety. These behaviors should not be interpreted as malicious. When stressed, some children with ASD might have difficulty regulating their emotions. This means "that the child must be taught how to cope with stress and how to calm herself. Helping a child learn this is one of the greatest gifts you can give her" (Fein & Dunn, 2007, p. 245).

BEHAVIORS SERVE A FUNCTION

To better understand the FBA process, let us first consider that all behavior serves a function, or purpose, for a child. Our responsibility is to collect data to help understand why a child exhibits problem behaviors and then seek ways to address them. We know that all behaviors serve a purpose: They allow students to (1) get something desirable (i.e., social attention, teacher attention, or access to tangible objects or preferred activities) or (2) to escape or avoid something undesirable (i.e., escape an unpleasant situation or avoid a task that is too challenging).

Sometimes, the reason for a behavior is to gain social attention or a reaction from others. For example, a child might engage in a behavior to get others to look at him, laugh at him, or play with him. Other behaviors occur so that the person can obtain a tangible item or gain access to a desired activity. For example, a child might scream and shout until her parents buy her a new toy (a tangible item) or allow her access to a computer game (an activity). Other behaviors might occur because the person wants to get away from or avoid something. For example, a child engages in aggressive behavior so his teacher stops giving him difficult assignments. Finally, some children engage in a behavior not to rely on anything external to the person but to do something internally pleasing. These *self-stimulating behaviors* are often demonstrated when the person gets some kind of internal sensation that is pleasing to the student or to remove an internal sensation that is displeasing (e.g., pain). For example, the student might rock back and forth because it is enjoyable or because the environment seems overwhelming. That child did not engage in the behavior to obtain attention or tangible items or to escape any demands placed on him.

Behaviors occur for a reason. It bears considering that people engage in all kinds of behaviors, but they will repeat behaviors that serve some kind of function for them. By *function*, we mean "why" a behavior occurs. And while it might be difficult to understand why a person does something, we know there will always be an underlying function. For example, if Derek has a fight at school (behavior), he will likely get suspended (consequence). If we know that Derek dislikes school, we may also come to the realization that he has learned that fighting is a good way to get sent home. The next time Derek does not want to be in school, what behavior do you think he will use? In this case, the behavior (fighting) earned Derek the desired consequence (suspension). "Any time a child uses a behavior that is successful in meeting a need, the behavior is likely to be repeated. The behavior serves a function for the child" (Jordan, n.d., p. 3).

IDENTIFYING THE FUNCTION: FUNCTIONAL BEHAVIORAL ASSESSMENTS (FBAS)

The elements of an FBA include describing the problem behavior, identifying the antecedents or consequences that control the behavior, developing a hypothesis about the behavior, and testing the hypothesis. In other words, FBA is a process for determining the reason or reasons why a student engages in inappropriate behaviors. As the function of the behavior becomes more apparent, we can teach new behaviors that will accomplish the same outcome for the student. Identifying the function of a behavior ultimately helps us understand how to decrease problem behavior and strengthen more desirable behavior.

Functional behavioral assessment is based on several assumptions: (1) Problematic behaviors do not occur in a vacuum—there is a reason for their occurrence; (2) behaviors occur in response to an identifiable event or stimuli; (3) behaviors are governed by the consequences that follow them; (4) behavior is a form of communication—the action might be saying, in a nonverbal fashion, "I am tired," "I am bored," or, "I'm upset at what happened"; and (5) all behaviors demonstrated by a person serve a function and have a purpose. If the student didn't see a benefit after showing a certain behavior, then she would eventually stop doing that behavior.

Family Voices 6.1

"You can ask me anything. Please, ask me anything. Ask about spectrum disorder and stimming and medication and early intervention. I will tell you everything I know. See, in our house, autism is not a secret. It is not a buzzword or a vague, underground rumor. It is true and vibrant and powerful. It is living within my son."

Source: Author Carrie Cariello, in, "As a parent of a child with autism, this is what I want you to know about my family," in the Independent news, available at: http://www.independent.co.uk/voices/comment/as-a-parent-of-a-child-with-autism-this-is-what-i-want-you-to-know-about-my-family-10081619.html

The following table outlines the steps involved in conducting an FBA. We will discuss each of these steps in this section of the chapter.

Steps in Conducting a Functional Behavioral Assessment

1. Define the behavior.
2. Gather behavioral information.
3. Develop hypothesis statements.

4. Create a behavior support plan.
5. Implement the intervention.
6. Evaluate the success of the intervention.

Define the Behavior

The team will collaborate to provide a description of the behavior. We want a description that is specific enough so that a person hearing about it for the first time would be able to act it out in a way that is much similar to what the student does (Scott, Alter, & McQuillan, 2010). Saying a student is "lazy" or he or she is "being difficult" is not specific enough to define the behavior. One teacher, described in Scott et al. (2010), first said that a student was "driving me and everyone else in the class crazy" (p. 89). When prompted to act it out, she soon realized that her description of the behavior was unclear. She was then able to provide a more precise definition of the behavior as "a series of high-pitched noises in short bursts." If you can't "act it out," you know that your description is ambiguous.

The team should define the problem behavior that needs to change in observable and measurable terms. It is important to define the behavior using concrete statements. Instead of saying, "Max had a tantrum," it is more concrete to say, "Max threw his notebook to the floor and attempted to hit his teacher three times." Rather than saying a student was aggressive, we can say the student pushed a classmate off the swing on the playground. Finally, rather than saying a student exhibited "destructive behavior," we can instead say, "The student tears instructional materials when presented with an assignment."

T.I.P. – Theory Into Practice 6.3

IDENTIFY THE BEHAVIOR

Look back at the case study presented at the beginning of the chapter.

1. Define one of Ethan's behaviors that should be addressed.

Gather Behavioral Information: ABCs

Once the problem behavior is defined in clear terms, the team should collect data about the variables that impact the student's behavior. We want to know when the behavior is most likely to occur and not occur. We can refer to this as *describing the context* of a particular behavior. Scott et al. (2010) provided a helpful question to answer in this phase of the FBA: "If I were going to come and visit tomorrow and wanted to see the behavior, when should I be there and what would be happening?" (p. 90). In gathering this information, we should look at three pivotal parts of the behavior: the *antecedent*, the *behavior*, and the *consequence*. The team will gather information that will help understand and identify the antecedent or consequent events that control the behavior (an ABC analysis). An observer notes what happens right before the behavior occurs (the **antecedent**), what the student does (the **behavior**), and what happens directly after the behavior (the **consequence**).

Family Voices 6.2

"My daughter is especially sensitive to criticism. When you point out what she did wrong in front of the whole class, you're going to see a different behavior—one that you might not like. Please don't punish her for that behavior. Don't give her a consequence for the behavior that resulted from her feeling criticized. Please, let's work together to provide feedback in a way that meets her needs rather than causes a problem behavior. I know my daughter, and I'd be glad to work on solutions to the behavior you don't want to see."

Antecedents. Scott et al. (2010) call antecedents the *when and where* of a behavior. Antecedents are any event, action, or object that signals a behavior to occur. Antecedents refer to the environment in which the behavior occurs, the circumstances that surround the occurrence, and when the behavior occurs. Antecedents can be grouped into two main types: setting related and event related. Setting-related antecedents include things such as schedule changes, staff changes, medication changes, irregular sleep patterns, temperature changes, and difficulties on the school bus. Setting events tend to slowly chip away a student's tolerance and ability to perform and often result in what we perceive as problematic behaviors. Event-related antecedents are those that immediately precede a challenging behavior. They include asking a student to do a nonfavored task, an irritating noise, the behavior of others, being interrupted during preferred activities, and transitions.

When attempting to determine the antecedent, we should ask, "Is there something in the environment that may be leading to the behavior (e.g., escaping loud noises, a person who always presents a demand, a change in routine that might seem frightening to the child, etc.)?" We want to identify anything that seems to have a causal relationship or that contributes to the behavior's occurrence. Common antecedents include too much noise, being asked to do something he or she does not want to do, difficult tasks, being told "no," limited attention, changes or transitions, and difficulty communicating wants or needs.

Consequences. A consequence is everything that happens after the behavior, including how people respond to the behavior. Consequences are responses that follow a behavior that serve to maintain it, also called the *function* of a behavior. Scott et al. (2010) call this the *purpose*. Students exhibit a particular behavior to get a desired consequence (escaping or avoiding something or gaining access to something).

Students continue to engage in behaviors because it allows them to get something they want or to escape something undesirable. Consequences are anything that sustains the behavior. For example, Ivan destroys a worksheet because it is too difficult for him, and he therefore escapes doing the difficult task. Avoiding the work is the consequence to the behavior. Typical consequences include escaping a stimulation, getting out of doing something requested of him or her, having the ability to continue doing something preferred, avoiding a difficult task, and gaining attention.

The following chart, taken from the Virginia Department of Education (VDE) (2011), shows a sample ABC chart. The earlier vignette about Ivan has been added to the chart provided by VDE:

From the ABC analysis, the team can begin to consider the function of the behavior, or what purposes the behavior serves for the child. The team will ask questions such as, "Is the student trying to obtain something, such as attention, activities, or

Sample ABC Chart		
Antecedent *(When and Where)*	**Behavior** *(What's Happening)*	**Consequence** *(Purpose)*
Joe was told to line up for mathematics class.	Joe hit a peer in line.	Joe was moved to the end of the line.
Joe was told to line up for lunch.	Joe pulled a peer's hair.	Joe was moved to the end of the line.
Ivan was given a math worksheet to complete.	Ivan tore up his worksheet and threw it in the trash.	Ivan did not do his math worksheet.

objects? If so, what exactly is he or she trying to obtain?" Or "Is the student trying to escape or avoid something, such as tasks or activities? If so, what exactly is he or she trying to escape or avoid?" Answers to these questions will help the team form a hypothesis about the student's behavior. This hypothesis will be used to formulate a behavior intervention plan.

Family Voices 6.3

"Be aware that some girls on the spectrum may effectively hide or camouflage their symptoms, but doing so consumes a great deal of their mental energy. Check in with them occasionally even if they appear to be blending in with the class."

Develop a Hypothesis Statement

Next, the team will develop a hypothesis about why the behaviors occur. The hypothesis will be used to drive the behavior intervention that the team will later implement. The discussion here centers on describing why students behave as they do. Rather than using the word *function*, Scott et al. (2010) recommend that we consider *how the behavior is working for the student*. "The idea is that rather than asking if there is a function, get people talking about what's in it for the student—focusing on what the function is" (Scott et al., 2010, p. 90).

The hypothesis should describe (1) the setting, the immediate antecedents, and the immediate consequences that surround the problematic behavior; (2) the behavior that is occurring; (3) the function of the behavior; and (4) any other relevant information. An example of a hypothesis, provided by the Virginia Department of Education (2011) is as follows: "Tricia swears out loud when asked to answer a question during history class. She is most likely to do this if the question is difficult. When Tricia swears, she is taken to the principal's office. Tricia's swearing behavior is likely to attempt to escape the demand of answering a question in front of the classroom" (p. 54).

When you can develop a hypothesis about the behavior and you can list potential underlying causes, you have successfully completed a functional behavioral assessment. "In truth, a functional behavioral assessment is done when you have gathered sufficient information so that a trend in the behavior begins to emerge and a behavioral support plan logically evolves" (Pratt, 2008, p. 172). After a hypothesis statement is developed, the team will create and implement a behavior support plan based on the data-gathering phase.

T.I.P. – Theory Into Practice 6.4

DEVELOP A HYPOTHESIS STATEMENT

For the following behaviors, formulate a hypothesis about what function the behavior serves for the student. The first one has been done as an example.

Behavior: When presented with a set of math worksheets, Carla bunches them up and throws them in the trash. Carla is then sent to the principal's office.

Hypothesis: When Carla bunches up math worksheets and throws them away, she is likely doing so to escape the demand of completing work that is too difficult.

Behavior: During silent reading time, Jackson leaves his seat and wanders in the classroom yelling out random comments that cause his peers to laugh.

Hypothesis:

Behavior: Anna makes smart-aleck remarks when her teacher calls on her in class.

Hypothesis:

Behavior: Nathan regularly fails to bring his homework to class and therefore has to stay in at recess most mornings.

Hypothesis:

BEHAVIOR INTERVENTION PLANS

Once a functional behavioral assessment is complete (i.e., you've collected and analyzed enough information to identify the function of a student's behavior and formulate a hypothesis statement), the IEP team will use that data to develop a behavior intervention plan. When we think of creating a behavioral intervention, our focus shifts from assessment to intervention. Through the FBA assessment process, we defined the behavior, identified the contexts and conditions under which it occurs, and considered why the student would want to continue engaging in the behavior (essential components of FBA). We would then use that information to develop an intervention plan to address the problem behavior.

The behavior intervention plan (BIP) provides a description of the intervention procedures that will decrease inappropriate behaviors and increase appropriate alternative behaviors. The plan should describe the setting events and antecedents, desired replacement behaviors, the consequences to be used that will decrease the problem behavior and increase (reinforce) appropriate replacement behaviors. The BIP should include strategies to teach the student more acceptable ways to get what he or she wants, decrease future occurrences of the misbehavior, and address any repeated episodes of the misbehavior. We use the FBA to develop the BIP.

Elements of a Behavior Intervention Plan

1. List the antecedents, problem behavior, consequences, and function of the problem behavior.

2. Identify the alternative behavior that results in the same consequence that the problem behavior serves.

3. Ensure the alternative behavior is easier to perform than the problem behavior.

4. Identify antecedents and consequences that would decrease the effectiveness of the problem behavior.

Developing a BIP, derived from information gathered during a functional behavioral assessment, allows us to implement interventions designed to reduce problem behaviors and teach alternative methods for addressing the function of the behavior. The behavior intervention plan (BIP) may include teaching more acceptable behaviors, changing setting events, manipulating antecedents or consequences, or changing the curriculum or instructional strategies. Outcomes of the BIP include teaching more acceptable methods to get needs met, reducing further occurrences of problematic behavior, and providing necessary supports for success. See a sample of a simple behavior plan for Kaylani and Jeffrey, which demonstrates how we would use an FBA to plan an intervention.

Sample BIPs	
Kaylani	
Target (Problem) Behavior	Kaylani stays at the computer playing after her time is up and requires adult prompting to end and move to the next activity.
Perceived Function	Kaylani wants to continue engaging in her preferred activity.

Sample BIPs	
Kaylani	
Possible Replacement Behavior	Kaylani independently leaves the computer at the end of her allotted time and turns off the power switch.
Intervention Strategies	• If Kaylani leaves immediately, praise her for following her schedule and place a "check mark" on her data sheet. • If Kaylani does not leave immediately, prompt her to read her schedule, and place an *x* on her data sheet.
Jeffrey	
Target (Problem) Behavior	Jeffrey constantly interrupts the teacher. When other students are working independently, and the teacher is working with individual students, Jeffrey makes animal noises to get the teacher's attention. Jeffrey does not get work done independently and distracts other students.
Perceived Function	Jeffrey wants the teacher's attention.
Possible Replacement Behavior	Jeffrey will display a "help" card when help is needed.
Intervention Strategies	Provide attention when Jeffrey displays his "help" card (even if to say, "I'll be there in a minute"). Ignore all noises.

Scott et al. (2010) suggest a helpful structure for finding a functional replacement behavior by using a table of two columns, one for the student and one for the teacher. In column one, we ask, "What behaviors would work for the student?" and in column two, we ask, "What behaviors would work for the teacher?" Under the first column, we would list all of the behaviors that the student could engage in that would give him or her the thing he or she wants. We list the behaviors that the student uses to access or avoid a particular situation or event. For example, Scott et al. (2010) suggest items for column one, behaviors that work for the student, to be throwing a book at the teacher, tipping over the desk, yelling loudly, and banging on the desk. Conceivably, these behaviors work for a student to get what he or she wants.

In the second column, we would list all of the things the teacher is willing to accept in this situation as an alternative to the problem behavior. Scott et al. (2010) suggest that items in column two could include: sitting quietly, turning a yellow card over on his desk, raising hand, waiting for the teacher to ask a question, or writing the question down for later. Then, we would look at which items are common to both columns to help define appropriate replacements. Once a replacement behavior is identified, we move to teaching the replacement behavior to the student. Teaching the replacement behavior involves telling the student what is desired, when it should occur, and why it should occur (Scott et al., 2010). Effective instruction includes more than simply telling the student what to do. "Effective instruction sets students up to be successful" (Scott et al., 2010, p. 92).

The process of creating a behavior support plan involves determining how to teach and reinforce a replacement behavior that serves the same function as the problem behavior you identified in the initial steps of the FBA. The focus is on ensuring that the student gets what he wants when using the replacement behavior and that he is not getting what he wants when using the inappropriate behavior.

T.I.P. – Theory Into Practice 6.5

ETHAN'S BEHAVIOR SUPPORT PLAN

1. Based on what you know about creating a behavior support plan, how would you approach creating a plan for Ethan in the case study presented at the beginning of the chapter?

2. How could you involve Ethan's family in creating the plan?

To determine which type of intervention will be best suited for the student, first ask yourself two questions: (1) Can the student perform the replacement behavior? Determine whether the student *can't* do the behavior or *won't* do the behavior. And (2) is there anything you can change in your classroom to increase the likelihood that the new behavior will occur? Such changes might include modifying the room arrangement, teacher instructions, instructional materials, or anything else that might act as a trigger to promote the replacement behavior. You may need to adjust the antecedents to increase the likelihood of the replacement behavior occurring, or you may need to modify the consequence to reinforce the replacement behavior.

The *process* of teaching the replacement behaviors will be covered more in depth in subsequent chapters. For this chapter, the focus has been on assessment, to define the inappropriate behavior in terms of its function, and on identifying appropriate replacement behaviors. We will discuss strategies for implementing behavior interventions in subsequent chapters.

SCHOOL-FAMILY COLLABORATION IN FBA

The most successful approaches to reducing problematic behaviors are based on efforts to understand the function of behavior before attempting intervention (LaRocque, Brown, & Johnson, 2001). Knowing the function of a behavior, as we have discussed throughout this chapter, allows practitioners and families to teach more socially acceptable replacement behaviors. It is important to involve families in such assessments and interventions. This is because families and caregivers have firsthand information about the functions that specific behaviors may have in the home (LaRocque et al., 2001). "While professionals can intervene with positive outcomes for children with problem behaviors without parental involvement, a more durable outcome can be achieved with a meaningful home–early intervention partnership" (LaRocque et al., 2001, p. 61).

Families and caregivers have the knowledge and personal experiences with their children that can be valuable in our efforts to provide effective interventions. Incorporating parental input into the FBA and the BIP increases the possibility that interventions can be carried out at home. Engaging parents as partners in collaboration can positively affect children's behavior (LaRocque et al., 2001). The active involvement of caregivers in functional assessment and analysis, in the development of hypotheses from the assessment results, and in the intervention can be very successful, especially when the interventions are utilized with caregivers in natural settings (e.g., the home).

In many cases, family involvement in the process of FBA has been restricted to the identification and hypothesis development stages (Peck-Peterson, Derby, Berg, & Horner, 2002). Families have played a limited role in the hypothesis-testing phase. There are fewer examples of applications of FBA in home settings, where parents deliver consequences for problem behavior or reinforce appropriate behaviors. "It may be wise for parents to play an integral role in evaluating the environmental variables maintaining a child's problem behavior and in designing and implementing interventions to improve children's behavior" (Peck-Peterson et al., 2002, p. 8).

Family Voices 6.4

"My daughter's teachers did a functional behavior assessment. I disagreed with the report, however, because they did not interview me and get my opinion. The behavior analysis never asked me anything. I guess I just have to trust that the program plan they develop from this assessment is appropriate. I would have liked to be involved in planning the program . . . don't I have that right?"

Let us consider how we can engage caregivers in the collaborative FBA process. In the hypothesis development phase, caregivers could serve the role of providing the details regarding the antecedents, consequences, and a history of reinforcement for the problem behavior. During the hypothesis-testing phase, caregivers may collect data from direct observations and help to inform intervention design with coaching and guidance from behavior analysts. Caregivers can help during the intervention design phase to ensure that the intervention is consistent with their values, skills, schedule, resources, and support systems (Peck-Peterson et al., 2002). When the intervention has been implemented, caregivers can play a role in ongoing evaluation. They can indicate what works and doesn't work and participate in data interpretation and intervention redesign.

How Caregivers Can Participate in FBA	
Phase	**Role**
Hypothesis Development	Provide details about antecedents, consequences, and reinforcement of problem behavior.
Hypothesis Testing	Collect data from direct observations that inform intervention design.
Intervention Design	Ensure the intervention is consistent with family values, skills, schedule, resources, and support systems.
Intervention Implementation	Provide ongoing evaluation. Indicate what works and doesn't work. Interpret data. Redesign the intervention if necessary.

It is vital that we work toward increasing the contribution of caregivers in the FBA and BIP process. With shared information, caregivers and educators are better able to examine the functions of their children's behavior and examine the best instructional methods for replacing problematic behaviors and increasing strengths (LaRocque et al., 2001). Caregivers are valuable sources of information. They can inform the IEP team what their children are capable of in different environments, and they can provide insights into behavior problems so that the entire team can develop strategies for the schools, the communities, and the homes in which students live (LaRocque et al., 2001). If we conduct FBAs without the full inclusion of caregivers, we ignore a critical and knowledgeable source of information regarding the child. "Staff members who do not include parents' contributions in the assessment and development of interventions jeopardize successful outcomes" (LaRocque et al., 2001, p. 67).

INCLUSION TIPS

Many general-education teachers report that dealing with challenging behaviors is one of the most difficult and stressful aspects of their jobs (Stoiber & Gettinger, 2011). Functional assessment is one way to deal effectively with problematic behaviors. By challenging behaviors, we mean those that interfere with children's learning and adjustment, such as being disruptive, noncompliant, or aggressive. Understanding which classroom variables serve as potential triggers for problematic behaviors can contribute to the development of behavioral support strategies that may prohibit those behaviors that can often interfere with learning.

Stoiber and Gettinger (2011) implemented professional development for teachers to help them conduct FBA and develop positive behavioral supports in their study with 70 teachers, and their results provide promising evidence that in-service educators can develop instrumental knowledge in FBA and PBS to improve student social competence and behavioral outcomes. FBA and PBS can improve classroom environments, decrease challenging behaviors, and strengthen positive behaviors (Stoiber & Gettinger, 2011).

There is a growing body of evidence that suggests that general-education teachers can be trained to use FBA and develop behavior intervention plans. The direct observation of students in authentic settings can provide valuable information that teachers can then use to replace problem behaviors with more appropriate behaviors (Fallon, Zhang, & Kim, 2011). One important training gap for classroom teachers has been in the area of assessment and treatment of students' aggressive, disruptive, emotional, and other severe behaviors (Fallon et al., 2011). It is therefore important that we work to train inclusive teachers to conduct a functional assessment and develop a related intervention plan. Understanding and identifying students' challenging behaviors is a necessary skill for teachers who work with students with ASD.

Inclusion Tips

STEPS FOR FBA AND POSITIVE BEHAVIOR SUPPORTS

Step 1: Conduct a Functional Behavioral Assessment

1. Identify the behavioral concern.
2. Describe the context for the behavior of concern.
3. Indicate conditions related to the behavior (triggers).
4. Identify functions of the behavior (the payoff).
5. Describe previous strategies and their effectiveness.
6. Identify alternative positive behaviors to strengthen.
7. Write a summary and hypothesis statement.

Step 2: Establish Goals

1. Establish a target date for goal attainment.
2. Describe what the child is expected to do.
3. Describe the context for performance of goal behavior.

Step 3: Design the Behavior Intervention Plan

1. Develop strategies linked to the FBA information.
2. Determine appropriate alternative response strategies.

Step 4: Implement the Intervention Plan and Monitor Progress

1. Implement the behavior support plan as intended.
2. Collect data to monitor progress.
3. Revise the plan as needed. Document revisions.

Step 5: Summarize and Evaluate Outcomes

1. Summarize progress, and determine what components of PBS contributed to progress and what was not effective.
2. Make decisions about revised goals as necessary; record decisions.
3. Summarize and incorporate revisions.

When students exhibit challenging behaviors in the classroom, teachers in both inclusive and special education classrooms are responsible for providing effective interventions to decrease these behaviors. We have seen in this chapter how conducting a functional behavioral assessment and then matching an intervention to the data gathered in the assessment can be effective in reducing challenging behaviors. Functional behavioral assessment has been established as an evidence-based practice to address challenging behaviors (Cooper, Heron, & Heward, 2007; Dutt, Chen, & Nair, 2016). FBAs are conducted with the aim of developing a behavioral intervention plan to manage challenging behaviors that interfere with the student's or others' learning. An analysis of the function of behavior is necessary for the selection of the most effective intervention for a student. When we understand the function of a behavior, we can better select and teach an appropriate behavior to replace the inappropriate behavior that shares the same function. This highlights the critical link between assessment and intervention (Dutt et al., 2016).

SUMMARY STATEMENTS

- A functional behavioral assessment (FBA) is a problem-solving process that looks beyond the behavior itself to identify factors associated with the behavior and select interventions to directly address the problem behavior.

- Problem behaviors include any response that we target for a reduction in the frequency, intensity, or duration of occurrence. Problem behaviors are usually those that threaten the safety or disrupt the learning of the student or others.

- Behavior serves a purpose and can be replaced by a more appropriate behavior that serves the same function.

- An ABC analysis allows the observer to note what happens right before the behavior occurs (the *antecedent*), what the student actually does (the *behavior*), and what happens directly after the behavior (the *consequence*).

- Families or caregivers have knowledge and personal experiences with their children that can be valuable in our efforts to provide effective interventions.

WHAT WOULD YOU DO?

Look back at the case study about Ethan presented at the beginning of the chapter. Based on what you have read in this chapter, what you have read in previous chapters, and your own experiences, how would you respond to the following questions?

1. Describe what Ethan is doing that is interfering with his learning or the

learning of his peers. Be specific in describing the problem behavior.

2. What are the benefits of conducting an FBA to address Ethan's problem behaviors?

3. Complete an ABC analysis for Ethan to understand potential antecedents, behaviors, and consequences related to

the problematic behaviors. What do you think is the function of Ethan's behavior?

4. Give an example of a more desired behavior(s) that would serve the same function.

5. What can you do to modify Ethan's behavior (i.e., what would you include in his BIP)?

6. What things would you look for to know whether the intervention has been successful?

7. Why would it be important that Ethan's caregivers implement a plan at home? What would you suggest that Ethan's family try at home to address his problematic behavior?

CHAPTER REFLECTION QUESTIONS

1. For what kinds of behaviors would we conduct an FBA, and for what behaviors would we not conduct an FBA?

2. Explain the concept that all behaviors have a function.

3. How would we conduct a functional behavioral assessment?

4. What is an ABC analysis? What are antecedents and consequences, and why should we be concerned with them?

5. How does an FBA help us develop an intervention to teach replacement behavior?

6. Why should we partner with caregivers in the FBA process?

RECOMMENDED RESOURCES

Websites

• Center for Parent Information and Resources, Behavior Assessment, Plans and Positive Supports. Available at http://www.parentcenterhub.org/repository/behavassess

• PBIS World. Available at http://www.pbisworld.com/tier-2/functional-behavior-assessment-fba

Articles/Publications

• Crone, D. A., Hawken, L. S., & Horner, R. H. (2015). *Building positive behavior support*

systems in schools: Functional behavioral assessment (2nd ed.). New York, NY: Guilford Press.

• Gresham, F. M., Watson, T. S., & Skinner, C. H. (2001). Functional behavioral assessment: Principles, procedures, and future directions. *School Psychology Review, 30*(2), 156–172.

• Loman, S., & Borgmeier, C. (n.d.). *Functional behavioral assessment training manual for school-based personnel: Participant's guidebook.* Retrieved from http://www.pbis.org/common/cms/files/pbisresources/practicalfba_trainingmanual.pdf

REFERENCES

Center for Effective Collaboration and Practice (CECP). (2001). Functional behavioral assessment. Retrieved from http://cecp.air.org/fba/default.asp

Cooper, J. O., Heron, T. E., & Heward, W. L. (2007). *Applied behavior analysis* (2nd ed.). Upper Saddle River, NJ: Pearson Prentice Hall.

Dutt, A. S., Chen, I., & Nair, R. (2016). Reliability and validity of skills and needs inventories in functional behavior assessments and interventions for school personnel. *Journal of Special Education*, *49*(4), 233–242.

Fallon, M. A., Zhang, J., & Kim, E. J. (2011). Using course assessments to train teachers in functional behavior assessment and behavioral intervention techniques. *Journal of International Association of Special Education*, *12*(1), 50–58.

Fein, D., & Dunn, M. A. (2007). *Autism in your classroom: A general educator's guide to students with autism spectrum disorders.* Bethesda, MD: Woodbine House.

Jordan, D. (n.d.). *Functional behavioral assessment and positive interventions: What parents need to know.* Retrieved April 14, 2016, from http://www.wrightslaw.com/info/discipl.fba.jordan.pdf

LaRocque, M., Brown, S. E., & Johnson, K. L. (2001). Functional behavioral assessments and interventional plans in early intervention settings. *Infants and Young Children*, *13*(3), 59–68.

Peck-Peterson, S. M., Derby, K. M., Berg, W. K., & Horner, R. H. (2002). Collaboration with families in the functional behavior assessment of an intervention for severe behavior problems. *Education and Treatment of Children*, *25*(1), 5–25.

Pratt, C. (2008). Teaching a different way of behaving: Positive behavior supports. In K. D. Buron & P. Wolfberg (Eds.), *Learners on the autism spectrum: Preparing highly qualified educators* (pp. 161–181). Shawnee Mission, KS: Autism Asperger Publishing Co.

Scott, T. M., Alter, P. J., & McQuillan, K. (2010). Functional behavior assessment in classroom settings: Scaling down to scale up. *Intervention in School and Clinic*, *46*(2), 87–94. doi:10.1177/1053451210374986

Stoiber, K. C., & Gettinger, M. (2011). Functional assessment and positive support strategies for promoting resilience: Effects on teachers and high-risk children. *Psychology in the Schools*, *49*(7), 686–706.

Virginia Department of Education, Office of Special Education and Student Services. (2011). *Models of best practice in the education of students with autism spectrum disorders.* Retrieved April 14, 2016, from http://www.doe.virginia.gov/special_ed/disabilities/autism/technical_asst_documents/autism_models_of_best_practice.pdf

Positive Behavior Supports

7

"Most students with ASD want to behave appropriately and follow the rules but have a great deal of trouble applying their rote memory to real situations", especially when they are anxious, impulsive, or confused."

—(PIERANGELO & GIULIANI, 2008, P. 165)

CASE STUDY

Xavier is a third-grade student with ASD who comes to Mr. McMichael's general-education classroom for morning meeting, language arts, and math. Mr. McMichael has worked very carefully with special education teachers to set up the classroom environment and provide instruction in ways that meet Xavier's needs. Xavier learns best in school environments that are structured, predictable, and quiet and that permit him to work in small groups.

Xavier is often by himself at school and doesn't seem to have many friends. Because he has not yet acquired the skills necessary to gain teacher attention appropriately or communicate his needs, he engages in what could be perceived as "problem behaviors" to get his needs met. These problem behaviors do not occur when Xavier is working in isolated areas, where there is little or no movement by others, or when working on preferred tasks or routines that are kept brief and predictable.

Xavier has difficulties with transitions, and the team has therefore created a picture schedule that hangs on the board at the front of the room. The schedule contains pictures of the different instructional activities that will occur during Xavier's time in Mr. McMichael's classroom. These include individual seatwork, small-group work, and

LEARNER OBJECTIVES

After reading this chapter, the learner should be able to do the following:

- Explain what is meant by positive behavior supports.

- Describe what is involved in teaching replacement behaviors.

- Explain the concept of reinforcing appropriate behaviors.

- Explain the importance of evaluating the success of a behavioral intervention and what the evaluation team should look for.

- Describe the benefits of working with families to implement PBS.

- Describe how a general-education teacher can implement PBS.

solitary reading. After each activity is completed, Xavier moves the picture and puts it in a pocket next to the schedule. The team believes this activity helps prepare Xavier for transitions. Also, the team has created color-coded materials so that Xavier can easily access them for a particular activity with limited assistance. Additionally, Xavier participates in peer-mediated instruction in Mr. McMichael's classroom.

Recently, despite these preventative practices put in place in Mr. McMichael's classroom, Xavier has been yelling during whole-group instruction and getting out of his seat without permission, many times attempting to leave the classroom altogether. Mr. McMichael doesn't know what to do to decrease the interfering behavior, and he is growing increasingly frustrated with his inability to instruct the rest of the class when Xavier is yelling.

The team conducted a functional behavioral assessment to determine what might be causing Xavier to engage in this behavior. Results indicate that Xavier does not yell at home and that Mr. McMichael responds to Xavier each time he yells by saying, "Xavier, no yelling." They determined that Xavier might be yelling to get Mr. McMichael's attention.

The team decided to use an index card system to try to reduce Xavier's yelling behavior. He will have an index card on his desk that reminds him to raise his hand instead of yelling. Each time he raises his hand, he will get a check mark in the box on his index card. After three checks, Xavier can earn a special reward. After three weeks of consistently trying to implement the index card intervention, Xavier's behaviors have escalated. Now, after yelling, Xavier tries to leave the room. The team thinks that another FBA is appropriate for determining more specifically why Xavier might be engaging in these behaviors.

After conducting the second FBA, the team will need to develop an individualized behavior plan that will outline what practices will be used to decrease the problematic behavior, when the practices will be implemented, and how the intervention will be monitored.

....

INTRODUCTION

The opening quote for this chapter, provided by Pierangelo and Giuliani (2008), serves as the rationale for including a chapter in this text about behavioral supports for students with ASD. Because children with ASD want to behave appropriately, we, in turn, should want to provide the supports necessary to help them develop the behaviors that are considered appropriate in classroom and home settings. A positive behavior support, or PBS, offers the structure with which we can modify the environment to prevent problem behavior and maximize positive behavior outcomes.

Positive behavioral interventions are used to modify the classroom or home environment so as to prevent the occurrence of problematic behaviors that interfere with learning and to teach the child to engage in more appropriate, alternative behaviors (Neitzel, 2010). Research has shown that PBS is effective in reducing challenging behaviors for children with ASD (Buschbacher, Fox, & Clarke, 2004; National Research Council, 2001; Neitzel, 2010; Turnbull et al., 2002).

How does a discussion of positive behavior supports fit with the previous chapters on applied behavior analysis (ABA) and functional behavioral assessment (FBA)? Admittedly, all of these acronyms can create a lot of confusion about how these pieces fit into the puzzle of addressing problematic behaviors. First, reviewing the definition of ABA is in order. Applied behavior analysis, which was examined separately in Chapter 5, is a highly technical and intensive approach designed to teach new skills and eliminate problem behavior. A trained ABA therapist first does a functional behavior analysis, designs a program, and delivers services over many hours in order to make positive changes in a student's behavior (Fein & Dunn, 2007). ABA is "a science devoted to the understanding and improvement of human behavior" (Cooper, Heron & Heward, 2007, p. 2). It is "guided by the attitudes and methods of scientific inquiry," and is "implemented in a systematic, technological manner" (Cooper et al., 2007, p. 20). ABA is different from PBS in that it should be administered only by formally trained behavior therapists over a long period of time.

We can think of PBS as an approach that has "evolved" from ABA or is an "extension" of ABA. ABA is considered a very technical approach to behavior intervention that is usually implemented by certified professionals who have had a considerable amount of formal training. On the other hand, PBS is a relatively nontechnical intervention model that service providers who have not had such formal training in ABA can implement (Johnston, Foxx, Jacobson, Green, & Mulick, 2006). Researchers consider PBS to be an approach that emerged from ABA principles, which offers interventions that are much like ABA but do not require the level of formal training and certification as ABA. Turnbull et al. (2002) think of PBS as an extension of ABA, by saying,

> As an extension of applied behavior analysis, PBS does not have a sole and discrete focus of remediating a student's inappropriate behavior in a clinical setting through the expertise of a clinician using a functional analysis. Rather, PBS emphasizes a lifestyle focus in natural settings implemented by teachers, families, and perhaps others, using an array of assessment and support procedures. (p. 377)

In this chapter, we will look at PBS, the "less technical" version of ABA that does not require that practitioners receive significant amounts of graduate-level training to implement a scientific approach to behavior modification.

USING POSITIVE BEHAVIOR SUPPORTS
TO ADDRESS PROBLEM BEHAVIOR

Positive behavior supports start with a functional behavioral assessment, which we discussed in the previous chapter, followed by the design, implementation, and evaluation of a behavior intervention plan, which will be the focus of this chapter. The plan that the IEP team develops should include a number of interventions designed to address the behaviors that were identified in the FBA. The plan will teach the student more acceptable ways to get what he or she wants, to decrease future occurrences of the misbehavior, and to address any repeated episodes of the misbehavior (CECP, 2000).

The focus of PBS is on modifying the classroom or home environment to prevent the occurrence of problematic behaviors and to teach the child to engage in more appropriate behaviors (Neitzel, 2010). "The primary goal of PBS is to improve the quality of life for children by increasing their appropriate behaviors and adjusting the learning environment to prevent interfering behaviors from first occurring or reoccurring" (Neitzel, 2010, p. 248).

Typically, PBS involves three levels of support: universal support (provided to all students), group support (provided to smaller numbers of students), and individual support. Universal support is the least intense component, and the next two categories include increasingly intensive support (Turnbull et al., 2002). Each of the three areas

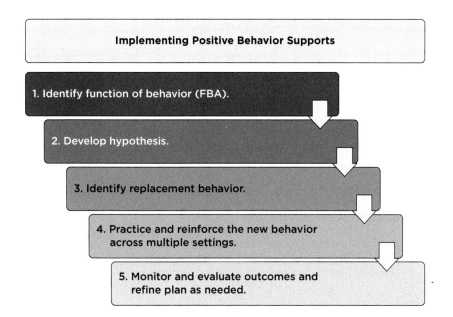

Implementing Positive Behavior Supports

1. Identify function of behavior (FBA).

2. Develop hypothesis.

3. Identify replacement behavior.

4. Practice and reinforce the new behavior across multiple settings.

5. Monitor and evaluate outcomes and refine plan as needed.

should be implemented, and all students who require support within each area should receive the appropriate degree of intensity (Turnbull et al., 2002).

Universal support is taught to all students, regardless of identification or referral for specific problem behaviors. The goal of universal support is to eliminate as many problem behaviors and increase as many appropriate behaviors for as many students in the school as possible. Group support recognizes that some students' behaviors are not sufficiently addressed through universal support. This setting is more appropriate for students who need more intense intervention than universal support, but do not need individual support. The most intensive level of support, or individual support, is meant for children whose behaviors impede his or her learning or the learning of others. An IEP team must develop positive behavior supports to address those behaviors on an individual basis (Turnbull et al., 2002). We will focus on the more intensive individual support category in this chapter.

TEACHING REPLACEMENT BEHAVIORS

In the functional behavior assessment, we identified the function of a behavior. Now staff can plan an intervention that will teach appropriate replacement behaviors to the student. The new behaviors should serve the same function for the student, showing more appropriate ways to achieve the same outcome. For example, instead of yelling out in class during group instruction, as in the opening case study about Xavier, he can be taught to raise his hand as a way of gaining access to the same function (whatever the team has identified to be the function of the inappropriate behavior). Raising his hand to gain attention from the teacher, for example, is the replacement behavior.

Pierangelo and Giuliani (2008) provided a simple list of how to develop a plan and teach positive behavior:

1. Identify a replacement behavior.

2. Teach the behavior using methods that match the student's learning style and needs.

3. Teach cues to signal the appropriate behavior (e.g., when the teacher raises his hand with the palm out, it means to stop talking).

4. Practice the behavior through repeated trials.

5. Reinforce the desired behavior (e.g., verbal praise, reward points).

6. Practice and reinforce the behavior across multiple settings.

We should be intentional about teaching replacement behaviors because "most students will continue to demonstrate inappropriate behaviors unless taught an appropriate behavior to replace the inappropriate one" (Pierangelo & Giuliani, 2008, p. 174).

T.I.P. – Theory Into Practice 7.2

STOP AND THINK

Why do you think teaching a replacement behavior works better than giving punishment or consequences to eliminate a problem behavior?

Identify a replacement behavior. Once the purpose of a behavior is determined (e.g., to escape or to obtain), an alternative means for achieving the same purpose should be identified and taught. We first determine what the replacement behavior should be, and then teach the new behavior. The new skills should produce a positive effect the same or as close to the same function as the challenging behavior, thus making the child's problematic behaviors less effective or useful. For example, if a student has tantrums in order to gain attention from the teacher, that student must have a way to gain the same results from the person he or she desires. Think of this new behavior as a way to answer the question, "What do we want them to do instead?"

A replacement behavior is the new behavior that you want the child to exhibit instead of the problem behavior. An effective replacement behavior will have a similar consequence that provides the same function. If the problem behavior is one that seeks attention, for example, you should find an appropriate way for him or her to get that attention. If the target (problem) behavior is the student leaving his seat during instruction, the replacement behavior might be keeping his feet on the floor under his desk.

Replacement Behaviors	
Challenging Behavior	**Replacement Behavior**
When presented with challenging tasks, Eric buries his head in his arms on the desk and refuses to engage in the assignment.	Eric will raise his hand and ask his teacher a question about a difficult math problem.
Lorraine struggles to verbalize her requests, and so, she has severe tantrums to get tangibles and activities.	Lorraine will be taught to use a communication book showing pictures of preferred toys and activities.
Geoffrey displays severe aggressive behavior (hitting, biting, kicking, and property damage) to escape difficult math tasks.	Geoffrey will respond to questions from the teacher (i.e., "Would you like a short break?") by indicating "yes" or "no."
Jeremy talks to a neighbor during teacher instruction and independent work when presented with new material.	Jeremy will raise his hand and ask for assistance on the assignment from the teacher.
When Christian has difficulty doing an assignment, he swears and shouts during independent work time.	Christian will ask for help from a peer partner when he feels he can't do a problem.

We learned previously that challenging behavior serves a purpose for a child. Identifying that purpose is the goal of the functional behavioral assessment (FBA) we discussed in the previous chapter, and we use that information to identify a replacement behavior. Perhaps a child has a tantrum, and you've identified that the behavior usually occurs when he or she is unable to express feelings or needs. You can teach him or her to point to a picture instead, one that communicates, "I'm feeling very mad," for example, rather than rolling on the floor and screaming. Or if the child has a tantrum in response to something (e.g., not getting something he or she wants, being asked to perform a certain activity, or to avoid something he or she doesn't want to do), ask yourself, What more appropriate behavior will serve the same function? If the function of screaming for Mark is to get attention, you can teach him that raising his hand or lightly tapping someone on the shoulder results in more attention than the screaming behavior.

T.I.P. – Theory Into Practice 7.3

REPLACEMENT BEHAVIOR

1. Think of a challenging behavior you have observed in your fieldwork or classroom.

2. Hypothesize what the function of that behavior might be for the child you observed.

3. Identify a replacement behavior that would serve the same function.

Teach the new behavior. When the support team has identified a new skill or behavior to teach, the team must also identify a method of instruction and follow the steps required to implement that procedure in a systematic fashion. The key in teaching the new behavior is consistency and repetition. New behaviors should be taught throughout the day, whenever the child is not engaging in challenging behavior, using the exact same instructional procedures each time. The skill should be taught throughout the day at school and at home. When teaching new behaviors is done systematically and consistently, the potential for successful behavior change becomes increased.

Teaching a replacement behavior must be very systematic. Appropriate behaviors should be modeled, prompted, cued, and reinforced (i.e., shaping the behavior). There are four basic steps to follow when teaching new behaviors: (1) modeling, (2) role-playing, (3) performance feedback, and (4) generalization and maintenance. In modeling, we should keep it simple, demonstrating one skill at a time, using repetition. Role-playing teaches students what to do and how to do it. Feedback comes in the form of positive reinforcement for enacting the role-playing behavior.

When teaching the new behavior, consider using prompts or cues to help the child learn new skills. Sometimes, children will need a variety of visual, verbal, or physical cues. Verbal prompts can include clear instructions of what to do next. You can use gestures as a prompt as well. Demonstrate a behavior, and consider saying, "Now, you do it."

Replacement Skills for Behaviors Intended to *Obtain*: Attention, Objects, or Activities	
• Modify task length or assignment expectations.	• Schedule access to desired object, event, or activity.
• Modify materials.	• Provide choice of activity, material, or partner.

Replacement Skills for Behaviors Intended to *Obtain*: Attention, Objects, or Activities

- Modify mode of response.
- Provide an activity schedule.
- Provide a contingency of activity completion.
- Schedule time with an adult or peer.
- Use video modeling.
- Offer more assistance when presenting new or difficult tasks.
- Teach students to wait longer periods of time without getting adult attention.
- Instead of a student grabbing materials, teach him or her to hand a picture of the desired material or activity to staff.

- Provide peer support.
- Provide frequent offers of assistance.
- Include the use of manipulatives.
- Incorporate the student's interests.
- Implement social skills groups.
- Use Social Stories to address inappropriate behaviors.
- Use gestures or proximity prompts with minimal verbal directions.

Replacement Skills for Behaviors Intended to *Escape*: Activities, Demands, and Social Interactions

- Modify task length.
- Modify expectations.
- Modify materials.
- Modify mode of response.
- Break task down into smaller parts.
- Provide choice.
- Provide an activity schedule.
- Teach how to appropriately terminate a preferred task without talking out or disrupting (e.g., raise hand; wait to be acknowledged; then say, "stop please").
- To address behaviors like running out of the room, teach the student to use a break card to go to a designated "time away" area.

- Select a reinforcer prior to the activity.
- Incorporate the student's interests.
- Use a time.
- Develop self-management systems.
- Provide peer supports.
- Add manipulatives.
- Provide visual supports.
- Followed the "least preferred" with the "most preferred."
- Modify seating arrangements.
- Reduce distractions.

CONSEQUENCE STRATEGIES

Every behavior plan must include guidelines for how the adults will respond to problem behaviors in ways that will not maintain the behavior. In addition, this part of the plan will include positive reinforcement strategies for promoting the use of new skills or more appropriate behaviors. We want to be careful to avoid reinforcing the challenging behavior while also intentionally reinforcing the new behavior.

How will I reward the child for doing the new skill that replaces the problem behavior (what reinforcers will I use)? In Mark's case, there is a greater likelihood of learning a new behavior (e.g., hand raising or shoulder tapping) when we ignore or turn away whenever he screams (problem behavior), prompt him to tap an adult on the shoulder (cueing), then turn back toward him and positively reinforce the desired behavior. If the reinforcement is effective, then the frequency of screaming should decrease and the hand raising should increase. It is less likely that Mark will use screaming behavior in the future as he learns that screaming is no longer an effective way to get attention. Reinforcement is a critical component of behavior change that will be discussed in more detail in the next section.

In a comprehensive behavior modification plan, the goals are to teach socially appropriate behaviors, organize consequences to prevent reinforcement of the problem behavior, and then organize consequences to maximize reinforcement of the appropriate behavior. Guidelines about how the adults will respond to problem behaviors in ways that will not maintain the behavior should be discussed, as should positive reinforcement strategies for promoting the use of new skills or appropriate behavior.

What is a *reinforcer*? A reinforcer is "anything that follows a behavior and increases the likelihood that the behavior will occur" (Aspy & Grossman, 2008, p. 174). Aspy and Grossman (2008) look at reinforcement as the most critical piece of a behavior intervention:

> The ultimate goal of any intervention plan is a change in behavior. If a decrease of an inappropriate behavior is sought, an alternative or replacement *behavior must be increased* to take the place of the problem behavior. If, on the other hand, the goal is to acquire a new skill to improve functioning, then the skill or *behavior must be taught and increased*. Only one element in an intervention ensures the increase of a behavior: *reinforcement*. (p. 174)

We should select procedures that will make the challenging behavior ineffective and less useful; rewards provided to the child for appropriate behavior should be either equal or better rewards than those for engaging in the challenging behavior.

Let us look at an example of reinforcing appropriate behavior. Lucas is a student who rarely turns in his assigned homework by the due date. The team conducted the FBA and hypothesized that Lucas's behavior was one of avoiding undesired activities (homework). Suppose the IEP team has identified the following target behavior for Lucas: Lucas will submit completed homework on time, or he will meet with the teacher before the due date to arrange an alternative due date and time. A goal related to the target behavior is that Lucas will use an assignment book to write down assignment details and due dates. The teacher will initial the notes in Lucas's assignment book and ensure that he understands them and has written them correctly. The team decided that a motivating reinforcer for Lucas is that he receives 15 minutes of extra time to work on the computer each day if his assignments are completed and turned in on time. Reinforcement (computer time) would be withheld if Lucas does not turn in his homework.

Types of reinforcement can include access to preferred activities or attention or opportunities to escape uncomfortable circumstances. For example, if a child makes inappropriate noises when adult attention is withdrawn or focused on other children, we can assume the behavior's function is to access teacher attention. We do not want to reinforce the inappropriate behavior by responding to the noises. It is better to ignore the noises, and provide attention only when the child asks for it appropriately (after you've taught her how to ask in an appropriate manner). If the child was taught to raise her hand and say, "Mrs. Robertson, I need help please," we would reinforce the appropriate attention-seeking behavior, even if to say, "one moment." In this case, the reinforcer was teacher attention, when sought in a more appropriate manner.

T.I.P. – Theory Into Practice 7.4

REINFORCING NEW BEHAVIORS

1. In the first TIP, you considered a challenging behavior, and you identified a replacement behavior that could serve the same function.

2. Using information from the child you observed for that activity, now identify a potential reinforcer for the new behavior.

It is most important to determine which reinforcer is important for a particular child. Reinforcers can vary considerably from person to person. What is most important is that you observe the child, noticing what he or she finds rewarding, so that you can give him what he wants after he has responded in the way you desire (Autism Speaks, 2012). You could find out what serves as a reinforcer for a child by asking caregivers or previous teachers or by noticing what the child does when left to his or her own devices. It is a good idea to identify several potential reinforcers because any given reward could lose its power over time (Fein & Dunn, 2007). Concrete rewards and activities can be potent reinforcers for children with ASD (toys, snacks, time for a preferred activity, etc.).

Family Voices 7.2

"When I was growing up, if someone was accused of being 'sensitive' it meant they were weak and should toughen up. Now that I have two children with autism who have several sensory and emotional sensitivities, I realize those are actually strengths. In our house, we refer to them as superpowers that we must learn to control and manage in order to do great things all around the world someday. If more people felt this way, we could tap into the natural gifts that people with autism have to offer the community at large."

A common assumption about reinforcement is that it simply involves giving a child whatever they want whenever they want it, for an unending period of time. In reality, that is not the case. Yes, the process initially involves rewarding positive replacement behaviors immediately and consistently, so we would work toward periods of reinforcement delay and less consistent schedules of reinforcement so that we shift gradually to "fading" of the reinforcement.

EVALUATING THE SUCCESS OF THE INTERVENTION

Once the behavior support plan is developed, and the team implements the plan itself, it is important to evaluate success. If the plan is not working, and we have been unsuccessful in decreasing problematic behavior and increasing replacement behaviors, we must determine what is at fault and then revise the plan accordingly. Data should be collected and reviewed periodically to make any needed adjustments. This ongoing data collection helps to ensure the child is making progress toward previously defined outcomes and that we, as teachers, have implemented the plan with integrity and consistency. We want to know if the plan resulted in any change in behavior or produced improvement in student outcomes. If it did not, then changes to the plan must be made.

Before the plan is implemented, strategies for monitoring the consistency and accuracy with which the intervention plan is implemented should be in place. We want to establish how the effectiveness of the plan will be determined, when it will be determined, and by whom. We should also know how the plan should be revised to address misbehavior, if necessary. Evaluation of the intervention should measure changes in the target behavior, from baseline (prior to starting the intervention) throughout the intervention. This is usually done through direct observation. The team may begin to see positive changes, negative changes, or no changes at all in behavior, and adjustments may be needed.

The team will observe the child during activities to note the occurrence of challenging behavior, as well as the replacement skills that are being taught. The observer will usually make written notes or place a mark on a data collection sheet and then transfer the mark to a corresponding chart or graph for further review. Reviewing the behavior support plan allows the team to notice any patterns or trends, such as whether the behavior is occurring more or less on particular days or at certain times of the day. The team should be able to evaluate whether the desired change in behavior has occurred, and if it has not, what could be the reason for the lack of change?

In the evaluation phase, you should be looking for what, if anything, might be in need of adjustment. Was the plan implemented with integrity? Was the plan implemented with consistency? Even under situations where the plan is implemented with utmost integrity and consistency, behavior support plans can require revision. There could be a new trigger influencing the student's behavior (e.g., a new staff person at school or a change in the daily routine). The support team may elect to add components to address new triggers, or they may need to conduct a new functional assessment and develop a revised behavior support plan.

PARTNERING WITH FAMILIES TO IMPLEMENT POSITIVE BEHAVIOR SUPPORTS

Positive behavior supports (PBS) can be used in a collaborative team to increase positive behavior while decreasing problem behavior at school and at home. A number of researchers have demonstrated positive effects of the positive behavior support process when used in home–school collaborative efforts (Blair, Lee, Cho, & Dunlap, 2011; Buschbacher et al., 2004; Garbacz et al., 2015; Preece, 2014), which we will discuss here.

It is important that educators support the families of children with autism in reducing problem behaviors. In a family-centered delivery model, "services are provided based on family needs and desires, and professionals build family competency and capacity via provision of resources and supports (Russa, Matthews, & Owen-DeSchryver, 2015, p. 96). When educators are a part of effectively managing behaviors in partnership with families, we see more favorable outcomes for the child, the family, and the schools.

The most important part of behavior collaborations involves training for parents. Many times, professionals who work with children on the autism spectrum who have challenging behavior routinely receive training in PBS, but such training is rarely provided for the parents of these children (Preece, 2014). Preece provided training to parents in positive behavior interventions, with favorable outcomes. Preece's (2014) parent training research suggests that parents who attended PBS training had increased confidence in understanding and managing their child's behavior.

Can partnering with caregivers help to address severe problem behaviors? Blair et al. (2011) would say, "yes." They worked with three young children on the more severe end of the autism spectrum, who had a long history of challenging behavior, to implement PBS in collaboration with their families. Aggressive behaviors, such as spitting, hitting, screaming, tantrums, head banging, and self-injury, were targeted in their research. Researchers trained parents to assist in implementing a behavior plan at home, which mirrored much of what we've learned about PBS in this chapter, and they were able to increase appropriate behaviors and decrease problematic ones.

Once the partnership has been initiated, research team members and families can identify the children's strengths, preferences, dislikes, and events that trigger problem behaviors (Blair et al., 2011). The team in Blair et al.'s (2011) research conducted a functional behavioral assessment, which we learned about in the previous chapter, and they identified target behaviors to address for each child. Using this information, the team developed a behavior support plan to teach replacement behaviors. The behavior plans (a) provided modified activities and materials based on the child's preference; (b) used visual schedules and choice boards; (c) provided peer proximity and modeling; (d) reinforced replacement behaviors by proving a preferred item, activity, or attention; and (e) withheld reinforcement when a problem behavior occurred. They found that less problem behavior occurred with children who had access to preferred activities and adult attention (Blair et al., 2011).

1. In the TIPs for this chapter, you considered a challenging behavior, you identified a replacement behavior that could serve the same function, and you identified a potential reinforcer for the new behavior.

2. Determine how you could involve family members in the process of finding the function, identifying a new behavior, and identifying an appropriate replacement for that particular child.

3. If you get a chance, ask the family if they would enjoy being a part of such collaboration, (if they are not already engaged in collaboration). (You don't need to actually conduct the collaborative identification process described here . . . just getting a feel for their desire to be involved is all that is necessary in this TIP.)

4. Alternatively, you could ask your fieldwork teacher if he or she involves parents in collaboration for behavior change. If so, find out to what extent and how he or she goes about partnering with families to assess behavior, identify replacement behaviors, and determine motivating reinforcers.

Garbacz and colleagues (2015) provided a promising model for engaging families to support student behavior. As opposed to one-directional communication, where school personnel provide the information about a child's behavioral functioning (e.g., newsletters, handbooks, or discipline reports) or when schools use parents as passive classroom volunteers, Garbacz et al. (2015) suggested a more collaborative form of family engagement in specific planning and problem-solving practices. They recommended that educators involve families in conducting assessments to identify strengths and needs and identifying practices that enhance home–school communication, as well as training and supporting parents' use of PBS strategies. Engaging families in the PBS leadership team to impact practices at home and at school provides enhanced outcomes for students, families, and educators (Garbacz et al., 2015).

INCLUSION TIPS

PBS is a comprehensive behavioral support aimed at producing a change in students who exhibit challenging behavior. PBS is appropriate for use in special education classrooms, and key components of PBS can be implemented in general-education classrooms as well. We understand that teachers have insufficient planning time, and they often have limited administrative support, so it is likely they wonder how they will find the time to provide positive behavioral support to the growing number of students who need it. Nevertheless, we outline here how all teachers can implement certain key components of PBS that may result in favorable outcomes. PBS can help educators determine the "what, where, when, and how" challenging behaviors occur, thus allowing for an appropriate intervention to reduce the challenging behaviors. The goal in PBS is not to "eliminate" behavior. Rather, it is to understand the behavior's purpose so that the student can replace it with new, appropriate behaviors that achieve the same purpose.

1. Understand the function of behavior.
   - What is the purpose of the student's behavior? Is the student trying to gain attention, avoid a certain task, or communicate a need? By understanding the reason for a behavior, we can implement appropriate interventions.
   - Define the challenging behavior in concrete terms. For example, rather than saying, "James is aggressive," say, "James often damages class materials and hits his peers."
   - Identify the circumstances under which the behavior is likely and unlikely to occur. Is James more likely to exhibit the challenging behavior right after being told to perform a difficult task? Is he less likely to do so during calm, peaceful afternoons?
   - Develop a hypothesis about the function of the behavior, describing the relationship between the behavior and the student's environment.

2. Teach alternative responses.
   - Teach one step at a time.
   - Use visual supports. Students may need visual reminders or cues to understand teacher expectations. Pictures or symbols help.
   - Model replacement behaviors.
   - Practice often.
   - Be consistent.

3. Notice and appreciate appropriate behavior.
   - Teach students to act in a certain way and reward them for correct behavior. (Also, make sure to determine the right reinforcer; decide what the student views as a reward.)
   - Reduce reinforcers over time.

4. Minimize the physiological, environmental, and curricular factors that might trigger challenging behavior.
   - Alter the classroom environment to remove or modify conditions that trigger challenging behaviors.
   - Increase predictability and scheduling. Uncertainty increases anxiety levels in many students.
   - Increase choice making. Some students with ASD are rarely provided with opportunities to make choices in their daily lives—they are told often what tasks to perform, with whom they can interact, and what rewards they may have. Providing choices can help lessen problem behaviors.
   - Make curricular adaptations. Sometimes, adjustments in difficulty level, length, or pace of an activity can increase motivation and reduce levels of off-task and disruptive behaviors. You can also vary tasks to allow for different modalities (auditory, visual, or tactile) of expression, take advantage of student interests, or adjust the mode of presentation to meet diverse needs.

5. Include others in the implementation. Parents and other faculty involved in the student's life should receive training on how to participate in PBS implementation and management. Techniques implemented by the general-education teacher can be implemented throughout the school, at home, and in the community.

SUMMARY STATEMENTS

- PBS offers the structure with which we can modify the environment to prevent the occurrence of problematic behaviors that interfere with learning, and to teach the child to engage in more appropriate, alternative behaviors.

- To teach replacement behavior, we identify the appropriate behavior, teach the new behavior systematically with repeated practice across multiple settings, and reinforce the desired behavior.

- A reinforcer ensures the increase of a replacement behavior. It is important to choose a reinforcer that is important for a particular child—what motivates one child will not necessarily motivate another.

- The team should evaluate the success of a behavioral intervention. If the plan is not working, and we are unable to decrease problematic behavior and increase replacement behaviors, we must determine what is at fault, and then revise the plan.

- When educators are a part of effectively managing behaviors in partnership with families, we see more favorable outcomes for the child, the family, and the schools.

- General educators can implement PBS. PBS can help educators determine the "what, where, when, and how" challenging behaviors occur, thus allowing for an appropriate intervention to reduce the challenging behaviors.

WHAT WOULD YOU DO?

Look back at the case study about Xavier presented at the beginning of the chapter. Based on what you have read in this chapter, what you have read in previous chapters, and your own experiences, how would you respond to the following questions?

1. What do you suppose the team might have learned when they conducted the second FBA?

2. Develop a hypothesis statement related to the function of Xavier's behaviors (yelling out during class instruction, leaving his seat, and attempting to leave the room).

3. Identify several potential replacement behaviors for Xavier.

4. What reinforcers do you think Xavier would find motivating?

5. How would you select reinforcers for Xavier?

6. How would you know if the intervention was successful?

7. How could you collaborate with parents to increase positive behaviors for Xavier?

8. What advice would you give Mr. McMichael about how to increase Xavier's positive behavior?

CHAPTER REFLECTION QUESTIONS

1. What is the goal of PBS?

2. Describe the steps in teaching replacement behaviors.

3. What is a reinforcer, and how is it used to develop appropriate behavior?

4. Why should the team evaluate the success of a behavioral intervention, and what should the evaluation team look for?

5. Why should educators partner with families to design and implement PBS?

6. How can general educators minimize the physiological, environmental, and curricular factors that might trigger challenging behaviors?

7. How can general educators support positive behavior?

RECOMMENDED RESOURCES

Websites

- Association for Positive Behavior Support: http://www.apbs.org/new_apbs/autismdesc.aspx

- Autism Classroom Resources: http://www.autismclassroomresources.com/positive-behavioral-support-what-does

- Autism Help: http://www.autism-help.org/intervention-positive-behavior-support.htm

- Autism Speaks: http://www.autismspeaks.org/sites/default/files/section_5.pdf

- Best Practices Autism. Positive behavior intervention and support. http://bestpracticeautism.blogspot.com/2010/02/positive-behavioral-support.html

Articles/Publications

- Neitzel, J. (2010). Positive behavior supports for children and youth with autism spectrum disorders. *Preventing School Failure, 54*(4) 247–255. Retrieved from http://glenwood.org/wp-content/uploads/2013/06/article-positive-behavior-supports-for-children-and-youth-with-autism.pdf

- Positive Environments Network of Trainers (PENT). (2013). *The BIP desk reference: A teacher and behavior intervention team's guide to developing and evaluating behavior intervention plans for behaviors that interfere with the learning of student and/or peers.* Retrieved from http://www.pent.ca.gov/dsk/BIPdeskreference2013.pdf

REFERENCES

Aspy, R., & Grossman, B. G. (2008). *The Ziggurat model: A framework for designing comprehensive interventions for individuals with high-functioning autism and Asperger Syndrome.* Shawnee Mission, KS: Autism Asperger Publishing Company.

Autism Speaks. (2012). What are the positive strategies for supporting behavior improvement? Retrieved May 10, 2016, from http://www.autismspeaks.org/sites/default/files/section_5.pdf

Blair, K. C., Lee, I., Cho, S., & Dunlap, G. (2011). Positive behavior support through family-school collaboration for young children with autism. *Topics in Early Childhood Special Education, 21*(1), 22–36.

Buschbacher, P., Fox, L., & Clarke, S. (2004). Recapturing desired family routines: A parent-professional behavioral collaboration. *Research & Practice for Persons With Severe Disabilities, 29*(1), 25–39.

Center for Effective Collaboration and Practice (CECP). (2000). *Creating positive behavioral intervention plans and supports.* Retrieved from http://cecp.air.org/fba/problembehavior3/main3.htm

Cooper, J. O., Heron, T. E., & Heward, W. L. (2007). *Applied behavior analysis* (2nd ed.). Upper Saddle River, NJ: Pearson.

Fein, D., & Dunn, M. A. (2007). *Autism in your classroom: A general educator's guide to students with autism spectrum disorders.* Bethesda, MD: Woodbine House.

Garbacz, S. A., McIntosh, K., Eagle, J. W., Dowd-Eagle, S. E., Hirano, K. A., & Ruppert, T. (2015). Family engagement within school-wide positive behavioral interventions and supports. *Preventing School Failure: Alternative Education for Children and Youth, 60*(1), 60–69.

Johnston, J. M., Foxx, R. M., Jacobson, J. W., Green, G., & Mulick, J. A. (2006). Positive behavior support and applied behavior analysis. *Behavior Analyst, 26*(1), 51–74.

National Research Council. (2001). *Educating children with autism.* Washington, DC: National Academy Press.

Neitzel, J. (2010). Positive behavior supports for children and youth with autism spectrum disorders. *Preventing School Failure, 54*(4), 247–255.

Pierangelo, R., & Giuliani, G. (2008). *Teaching students with autism spectrum disorders: A step-by-step guide for educators.* Thousand Oaks, CA: Corwin.

Preece, D. (2014). Providing training in positive behavioural support and physical interventions for parents of children with autism and related behavioural difficulties. *Support for Learning, 29*(2), 136–153.

Russa, M. B., Matthews, A. L., & Owen-DeSchryver, J. S. (2015). Expanding supports to improve the lives of families of children with autism spectrum disorder. *Journal of Positive Behavior Interventions, 17*(2), 95–104.

Turnbull, A., Edmonson, H., Griggs, P., Wickham, D., Sailor, W., Freeman, R., . . . Warren, J. (2002). A blueprint for schoolwide positive behavior support: Implementation of three components. *TEACHING Exceptional Children, 68*, 377–402.

Environmental Supports

8

"The classroom environment affects everything that happens there. When an environment is chaotic, the people in the environment feel more harried. When an environment is cluttered, the people in the environment feel more disorganized, and valuable time is lost searching for the correct materials or locating needed supplies."

—(ROHRER & SAMSON, 2014, P. 7)

CASE STUDY

Margaret struggles to help Hannah, her 10-year-old daughter with ASD, better manage her time after school. Margaret is frustrated by the daily battle between homework and Hannah's favorite computer activity. To avoid conflict and the resulting challenging behaviors, Margaret gives in and allows Hannah to play on the computer before dinner, which means that homework often suffers.

On a typical day when Hannah comes home from school, she puts her backpack on the floor by the door and goes straight to her computer to play her favorite games. Often during her computer time, Hannah goes back and forth to the kitchen to grab a snack before going back to her computer game.

When it is time for dinner, Margaret usually gives a verbal prompt to Hannah such as, "Time to end computer time and come to dinner." Margaret calls Hannah to come to the table, repeatedly, but Hannah rarely responds. Margaret is growing increasingly frustrated with Hannah's noncompliance. After dinner is equally as difficult for the family. Margaret implements little in the way of routine or

LEARNER OBJECTIVES

After reading this chapter, the learner should be able to do the following:

- Describe the characteristics of ASD that make environmental modifications necessary.

- Discuss a strength that is evident in individuals with ASD and how educators can develop environmental modifications that capitalize on that strength.

- Provide a rationale for how the use of structure— organizing time, space, and sequences—can make learning activities easier to perform for students with ASD.

- Justify the use of visual schedules to help students with ASD better understand the expectations of an activity or of a transition and thereby reduce the likelihood of negative behaviors.

structure for cleaning up after dinner, what the children should do after dinner, or when and how the children should get ready for bed, and so there are many evenings of raised voices and tears. The home environment, from after school to bedtime, is full of stressful experiences for everyone in the family.

Margaret read in a newsletter that finding a way to establish some sort of routine and structure to the home environment might help. The article said that individuals with autism might have difficulties with transitions from one activity or place to the next when instructions are presented verbally (like when Margaret verbally tells Hannah to stop playing a video game and come to dinner or when she gives verbal directions for cleaning up after dinner and getting ready for bed). She learned that her "long strings of verbal information" might be difficult for Hannah to process. "Oh, maybe that's the problem with our afternoon/evening environment," Margaret thought to herself.

....

INTRODUCTION

The idea that "the classroom environment affects everything that happens there" (Rohrer & Samson, 2014, p. 7) should not be underestimated. When students enter the learning environment—the physical and affective climate of the classroom—they want to know that they will be accepted and cared about, that their interests and dreams are valued, and that the people in their environment believe in them (Tomlinson & Moon, 2013). They also want to know that the environment will be structured appropriately for them. Tomlinson and Moon describe the learning environment as the "weather" that affects everything that happens there and the teacher as the weather-maker. They believe that the teacher's aim as the weather-maker should be to make the classroom work for each student who spends time there, being attuned to the students' various needs and responding to ensure that the needs are met (Tomlinson & Moon, 2013). This should be true for all students, regardless of ability.

Students with ASD have deficits in auditory processing, putting them at a disadvantage in the majority of classrooms where information is communicated verbally (Knight, Sartini, & Spriggs, 2015). Students who have auditory processing skills can follow a teacher's verbal instructions and are thus able to move seamlessly from one activity to the next and to engage in the new activity where verbal instructions are the norm. Students with ASD struggle with processing input. They can have problems with transitions from one activity or place to the next when instructions are presented verbally, which can often lead to socially inappropriate behaviors, verbal and physical aggression, and noncompliance (Schneider & Goldstein, 2010).

Autism experts contend that individuals with ASD respond favorably to information that is presented visually (Ganz, 2007). It is, therefore, appropriate that we adopt strategies that capitalize on this visual preference. Visually based strategies such as classroom structuring methods and visual schedules will be examined in this chapter.

If we want to increase the likelihood of success for our students with ASD, we must modify the classroom and help families find ways to modify the home environment, based on the characteristics of the student with ASD. Using visuals in the classroom decreases students' reliance on auditory processing, which is considered a deficit area for students with ASD.

As Meadan, Ostrosky, Triplett, Michna, and Fettig (2011) point out so succinctly, "Most of us use visual supports to navigate our days (calendars, maps, watches, to-do lists—even high-tech versions of these supports), so why not provide similar supports to young children" (p. 28).

This chapter will discuss exactly how we can do that—how we can modify the classroom environment, provide visual supports to encourage routine and structure, and modify the classroom and home to ensure the safety and comfort of individuals with ASD. It makes sense for us to do what we can to provide the best learning opportunities by arranging the physical environment and providing necessary supports so that individuals with ASD have a better chance of academic and social success.

CHALLENGES WITH ASD THAT MAKE MODIFICATIONS NECESSARY

Social Interactions

We know that social interactions are challenging for students with ASD. They might have difficulty with nonverbal behavior (displaying or interpreting), seldom engage in eye-to-eye contact with the teacher or with peers, and show little interest in small-group or collaborative work. Similarly, meaningful social interactions such as taking turns, asking and responding to questions, and understanding nonliteral ideas or actions are challenging. Often, students with ASD will need a lot of prompting and visual cues to achieve successful social interaction in the classroom. We will need to modify some of the ways we interact with our students and the way peers interact with one another if we want to help them be successful in the classroom. Students with ASD might have trouble contributing to a conversation while others can have a single-minded conversational focus and have trouble allowing a conversational partner to get a word in edgewise. Be considerate of this when structuring student pairs or small groups.

Routines and Insistence on Sameness

As you will recall from previous chapters, a core characteristic of ASD is a preoccupation with restricted and repetitive behaviors or a focus on particular objects. Students with ASD may have obsessions, repetitive behaviors, and routines that we should seek to understand and be prepared to intervene appropriately. Even minor changes, such as moving between two activities, can be painful or anxiety producing for some. Unexpected changes are most difficult to deal with. Many times such changes can lead to anxiety or behavioral outbursts.

Sensory Processing Difficulties

We have also discussed in previous chapters that although they are not included in the diagnostic criteria, atypical responses to sensory input are often present in individuals with ASD. Researchers have found a direct link between atypical sensory processing and behavioral and emotional problems (Ashburner, Ziviani, & Rodger, 2008), which can manifest in the classroom. In a study conducted in an inclusive classroom, one where children with ASD were educated with the majority of children who did not have special needs (Ashburner et al., 2008), researchers confirmed that the group of children with ASD was impacted to a significant degree by the stimuli on measures of academic performance and attention to cognitive tasks. In other words, children with ASD, who have difficulty tuning into verbal instructions in the presence of background noise, are more likely to underachieve academically (Ashburner et al., 2008).

Family Voices 8.1

"We know that children with ASD either underreact or overreact to sensory stimuli. Some children might ignore people speaking to them, to the point of appearing deaf, while others seem disturbed by even the slightest of sounds. Sudden noises can be upsetting, and you might see my daughter cover her ears and make repetitive sounds to drown out what's bothering her. Try to find out what sound is upsetting her if you want to know what caused what you believe is a 'meltdown.'"

Strengths

A discussion of areas of weakness would be incomplete if we did not also give attention to the strengths of students who have ASD. Well-implemented instructional strategies for students with ASD capitalize on their strengths, which we know lie in visual-spatial processing, a keen awareness of visual and/or cognitive detail, rote memory, and an attachment to routine that can easily be cultivated to teach meaningful skills (Hume, Plavnick, & Odom, 2012). "Individuals with autism are more likely to perform tasks accurately when instruction is deliberately designed with these strengths in mind"

(Hume et al., 2012, p. 2085). Therefore, the strategies discussed in this designed to capitalize on the visual strengths we know that our students often possess.

Visual processing strengths are apparent in many individuals with ASD.

1. How do you think a weakness in auditory processing could interfere with one's ability to learn at school, where lectures and verbal information are the norm?

2. Imagine that you have been assigned to teach a social studies lesson to a student who has autism. How might you approach this task with a student who had difficulties with auditory processing? What strategies would you include in your lesson that could help?

3. How might you involve the family in making appropriate accommodations in your social studies lesson?

CLASSROOM PHYSICAL STRUCTURE

In this section, we introduce strategies for arranging the physical classroom environment so that individuals with ASD can actively participate in academic and social activities with their peers to the greatest extent possible. Physical structure refers to the way we can set up and organize the physical environment—how we place the furniture and materials in classrooms, the playground, work areas, hallways, locker/cubby areas, and so forth. The physical structure provides environmental organization for students with ASD. It provides clear physical and visual boundaries to help students understand where each area begins and ends, and it helps minimize visual and auditory distractions. The strategies noted here can work well in both general and special education classrooms.

Sensory Considerations

Classroom environments contain an enormous amount of sensory stimulation. The environment is often brightly lit and visually stimulating. Items hang on the wall, and people move about. The physical environment, the visual stimuli, and the activities with movement can affect a student's learning and attention. Classrooms are also noisy, with poor acoustics, which further influences attention, concentration, and academic performance for any student. The sights, sounds, and movements of these highly stimulating classrooms are likely amplified for children with ASD. For students with ASD, the stimuli of the classroom may be overwhelmingly uncomfortable, and they may react to the discomfort with a range of behaviors from avoidance to violent physical aggression (Kuhaneck & Helleher, 2015).

Sensitivities to Light and Sound

For a child with autism, the wrong lighting can be annoying, distracting, or even painful. Not all children with autism will have sensitivity to light, but for those who are affected by light sensitivities, it can sometimes be impossible for them to bear. If you have a child with autism in your class who appears to have sensitivity to light, there are a few things you can do to remove or adjust this stimulus that can be so overwhelming. Fluorescent lighting, the lighting used most often in classrooms, is problematic for many. Try lowering the light level, perhaps by turning off one section of the classroom lights, or replacing older fluorescent lights that flicker with new ones. If it is impossible to turn off some of the lights or replace older ones with newer bulbs, sometimes moving the student's seat can help. It might not be the lights themselves but the reflection of the light on a wall or other surface that causes more of a problem.

In her blog about her sensitivity to light, "Aspiegrrl" (2011) commented, "I'm very sensitive to light, especially fluorescent light, and I can easily be blinded by the sun at the beach or over the snow. With light bulbs, they literally hurt my eyes. They also irritate me to no end with their flickering and humming" (para. 5). The solution for her was to wear sunglasses indoors and out. She said, "Sunglasses are the answer. I wear them anywhere I need them, at night when the headlights are blinding me, in giant over-lit retail stores." (Aspiegrrl, 2011, para. 5).

Researchers say that from 30% to 90% of individuals with autism either ignore or overact to seemingly ordinary sights, sounds, smells, or other sensations, and about 65% are sensitive to noise (Sarris, 2015). They believe that individuals with ASD process information from their senses differently, and many sounds, for example, can be severely distracting or uncomfortable. For individuals with sound sensitivity, noise can become painful and even trigger a panic attack. It becomes almost impossible to pay attention to anything other than the irritating sound.

The constant assault of noise can cause a person's anxiety level to escalate. One mom commented, "When my son was a toddler, he had a panic attack every time our washing machine clicked loudly to change cycles. He developed a phobia of all types of bells. He covered his ears and cried in crowds" (Wang, 2014). For some students with ASD, school air conditioner sounds, the shuffling of feet as others walk by in the hallway, or even the scratching of pencils moving across papers are unpleasant. For others, it's vacuum cleaners, lawn mowers, construction equipment, alarms, beeps, the buzz of fluorescent lights, or noisy crowds that trigger a reaction.

Once you've identified the particular source(s) of irritation for an individual child, there are steps you can take to remove the irritation. Headphones, especially the noise-canceling type, and earplugs may offer comfort and relief from irritating sounds. Relocating a desk to another part of the room might be helpful.

Consider whispering or using a soft voice, especially when the student seems upset. Try to reduce classroom noise by using carpet remnants or attaching cut tennis balls to the legs of noisy chairs. Help prepare the student for a sound you know may be coming (cue the student to be ready, have her put earplugs in, or move away from the sound). Find out if there are sounds that the student finds pleasant or that help him or her relax, and think of ways to incorporate those sounds (e.g., listening to relaxing music through personal earphones or playing soft music to the entire class during a silent reading period).

T.I.P. – Theory Into Practice 8.2

ENVIRONMENTAL SENSITIVITIES

Think of a student you know (from your field-work, your classroom, or someone you know personally) who may have environmental sensitivities. List the ways that you could make the classroom more comfortable for this person.

Classroom Visual Organization

In a well-designed classroom where students with ASD are educated, the needs of the students should be considered when planning the arrangement of classroom furniture and materials—the physical structure of the classroom. Physical structure refers to the way we organize the physical environment for a student—how we place the furniture and materials. Physical structure is essential for a number of reasons. It provides environmental organization and clear physical and visual boundaries to help students know where each area begins and ends, and physical structure minimizes visual and auditory distractions (as we discussed in the previous section).

The classroom that has well-defined spaces appears organized and will help promote a positive learning environment for all students. A physically structured environment should also be extremely organized and free of visual clutter. Room arrangement can help provide a sense of predictability that is so important to students with ASD. Proper arrangement of the physical space allows students with ASD to understand their environment and anticipate what is coming next and helps them be less apprehensive. "Their mental states are more conducive to learning new materials. A decrease in anxiety typically translates into a decrease in misbehavior as well" (Rohrer & Samson, 2014, p. 7). One way to delineate one area from another in the classroom and to reduce visual clutter is by using bookshelves strategically. Bookshelves or other storage units can section off areas for quiet, individual work. They can also be covered with decorative sheets or material to allow easy access to the materials stored there.

Guidelines for Classroom Arrangement

1. Design the student's work area with his or her needs in mind. Some students need more visual cues and boundaries or structure than others.

2. Organize for visual clarity. Designate areas for specific learning tasks and arrange the classroom such that activities are clearly identified in a visual manner.

3. Have clear visual boundaries for each area. Visually clear boundaries can be set by using tape on the floor, rugs to clarify areas in which certain tasks take place, room dividers, and clearing desks of unnecessary materials.

4. Separate independent work areas, and have students complete only tasks that have been mastered there, where they can work without adult supervision. Independent work areas should be visually secluded from the rest of the room, especially when working with students who are easily distracted.

5. Place work areas near shelving so that required materials are within easy reach.

6. Eliminate irrelevant visual material, such as posters or letters of the alphabet, that may distract students with ASD from required tasks. If removal of this type of visual material is not feasible, consider facing the student's desk in the direction opposite the visual "clutter."

7. Consider reorganizing independent work areas as students become more capable. You might be able to decrease some barriers, such as shelving or dividers; move the student closer to peers; and so forth. Gradually decrease the supports you offered initially, and pay close attention to the result of the change you made. If the student has difficulty staying on task as the result of the change, you may decide to reorganize again, going back to the original arrangement for a while.

8. When you notice that a student has difficulty with distractions or with understanding barriers, consider reorganizing the environment. Sometimes, doing so can be a simple solution to an off-task behavior.

TEACCH

TEACCH (Treatment and Education of Autistic and related Communication-handicapped CHildren), established at the University of North Carolina, is an evidence-based intervention based on evidence that individuals with ASD share a number of characteristics (Mesibov & Shea, 2010). The TEACCHing approach capitalizes on the understanding that individuals with ASD have strength and preference for processing visual information, have difficulty with sequencing, are often very distractible, have difficulty with concepts of time, are attached to routines, and have marked sensory preferences and aversions. The approach gives particular importance to the use of structure—organizing time, space, and sequences—to make learning activities easier to perform for students with autism (Mesibov & Shea, 2010).

The TEACCH program recommends four kinds of structure. First is the physical structure (using elements such as furniture arrangement or visual cues that show a student which activities will occur in certain areas), and reducing environmental sources of distraction or overstimulation by not seating a student near a door or window. The second type of structure involves organizing a sequence of events and making the schedule understandable for the child. These schedules can take the form of helping the student make a transition to a new space or new activity. The third type of structure refers to individual tasks, using visual means to show what the student is supposed to do, how long the activity will last, how he can see that he is making progress toward being finished, how he can know when the activity is finished, and what he will do next. The fourth kind of structure involves linking individual tasks into a sequence of activities, which helps increase the time the student spends engaged in productive activities (Mesibov & Shea, 2010).

Individual work systems are a part of TEACCH that we will discuss here. Hume, Plavnick, and Odom (2012) defined *individual work systems* as visually organized spaces where children practice acquired skills. A work system communicates the task the student is supposed to do, how much work is to be completed, how students know they are finished, and what to do when they are finished. Individual work systems also promote students' generalization of skills across settings. That means that students can acquire and practice a skill in one setting with the support of the work system and then use that skill across settings without the support of the system (Hume et al., 2012).

Whereas a picture schedule directs a student where to go, a work system instructs a student what to do once he or she arrives at the designated area. A work system provides required information so that a student can complete a task without adult prompting by teaching the student to attend to visual cues rather than verbal instructions. Work systems can be used with any task or activity, across settings, and for individuals at all levels of functioning.

T.I.P. – Theory Into Practice 8.3

SET UP A WORK SYSTEM

1. Visit the website article, "'I Can Do It Myself!': Using Work Systems to Build Independence in Students With Autism Spectrum Disorders," from Indiana University–Bloomington, available at http://www.iidc.indiana.edu/pages/i-can-do-it-myself-21-using-work-systems-to-build-independence-in-students-with-autism-spectrum-disorders

2. Read about why independence is so challenging for students with ASD and how work systems can be used to increase independence.

3. Read about some sample activities that were created using a work system.

4. Brainstorm an activity for which you could create a work system, and develop the work system.

5. Imagine how the work system would be of benefit to a student with ASD.

VISUAL SUPPORTS

Another group of suitable environmental modifications for individuals with ASD is visual supports. Visual supports, as a category, include organization of materials, visual instructions, and visual cues of any kind. Visual supports involve using pictures or other visual items to help a child with ASD communicate or make sense of a task. (Using visual supports to develop communication skills will be discussed in a subsequent chapter.) Visual supports use photographs, drawings, objects, and written words or lists to depict a sequence of events. They have been used to teach transition behaviors, reduce problem behaviors, and increase on-task behaviors, and also to increase, maintain, and generalize a variety of social skills (Knight et al., 2015).

T.I.P. – Theory Into Practice 8.4

MAKING VISUAL SUPPORTS

1. View this document from Vanderbilt University: "Tips and Ideas for Making Visuals to Support Young Children With Challenging Behavior," available at http://csefel.vanderbilt.edu/modules/module3b/handout2.pdf

2. Use a digital camera or find pictures from the Internet to prepare a visual schedule for someone you know who displays a challenging behavior.

Visual Schedules

Visual activity schedules are a commonly prescribed method of environmental supports for teaching a variety of skills and behaviors to individuals with ASD. Because individuals with ASD sometimes have difficulties learning the order of events, often referred to as sequential processing, certain situations can make them anxious or overwhelmed. In turn, this feeling of anxiety can lead to problem behaviors. The use of visual schedules, which capitalize on visual strengths, can help the individual better understand the expectations of an activity or a transition and can thus reduce the likelihood of negative behaviors.

There is a considerable body of research that supports the use of visual schedules. The literature says that activity schedules are effective with students with ASD in transition behaviors (Banda, Grimmett, & Hart, 2009; Dauphin, Kinney, & Stromer, 2004; Dooley, Wilczenski, & Torem, 2001). They can also be helpful in increasing communication skills (Krantz & McClannahan, 1993), daily living skills (Pierce & Schreibman, 1994; Watanabe & Sturmey, 2003), and academics (Bryan & Gast, 2000; Massey & Wheeler, 2000). Furthermore, they can be beneficial in reducing inappropriate behaviors (Dooley et al., 2001; Dettmer, Simpson, Myles, & Ganz, 2000).

Visual schedules help decrease anxiety for a student with ASD. Some children can become confused or feel anxious and overwhelmed when they don't understand what is being said, which can affect their ability to learn. A visual schedule will help reduce anxiety by making the day more predictable and aiding in transitions for the students with ASD. Visual supports that include photos and/or print can help. When you consider creating a visual schedule, think about making one for daily class schedules, individual student schedules, mini-schedules for parts of the day, or activity schedules for sequencing a task.

Thinking About Visual Schedules

1. You can use visual supports to enhance comprehension of language, to prepare for environmental changes, or to assist with the completion of specific tasks.

2. Visual supports can be used at school, at home, or in the community, and they can be used with large groups, small groups, or individual children.

3. You can use real objects, photographs, line drawings, or words.

4. Break the day, portion of the day, or activity/task into several steps to be represented by pictures or words.

5. Be conscious of every detail of the activity, including even minor steps as needed for the individual child.

6. Determine the best visual format for the individual, based on skills, developmental level, interests, and functionality.

7. Determine how the schedule will be used to show which parts of the activity are completed and which remain to be done (e.g., check off a box, move a picture over one column, etc.).

Creating Visual Schedules

Before you create a visual schedule, it is best to collaborate with parents and any other educators involved with the student to identify the most pressing need. Perhaps it involves transitioning to school from home, or perhaps it transitions from one activity to the next in the classroom, or it might be transitioning to and from recess and lunch that presents the most significant obstacle for a student. Students with ASD may have problems terminating an ongoing activity or beginning a new activity (Banda et al., 2009). Other students may have trouble beginning a new activity, like reading, if they were not able to complete a challenging math worksheet. Some students may become upset when the schedule is changed unexpectedly, as when rain outside requires that recess be held inside.

Next, you want to state the problem behavior in specific, concrete terms, such as, "When Gabriel enters the lunch line in the cafeteria, he screams, 'Me first!' and hits the person at the front of the line." Clearly defining the behavior, along with identifying when the challenging behavior is most likely to occur, are critical first steps.

Next, you should decide the activities that you will depict in the schedule. In the prior case, it was activities involved in the morning routine before arriving at school. Think ahead about the activities that will happen and the order in which they should occur. Find photos or make drawings and/or written words that show the activities you have identified. Consider using a chart on the wall, a typed schedule attached to the student's desk, a laminated page small enough to fit in a backpack or even as small as a wallet, in a file folder, or inside the front sheet of a notebook. You can choose a place to keep larger schedules, such as the refrigerator or on a wall or nearby filing cabinet, and make sure it's in a place always visible to the student.

Family Voices 8.3

"We created a visual schedule for the morning routine at home with four steps: get out of bed, take off dirty clothes, get dressed, and go downstairs and wash up, and we detailed the 'get dressed' part to say what he needs (clean underwear, clean socks, pair of pants, clean T-shirt, and deodorant). This has drastically improved our morning routine. My son's teacher suggested it, and I have to give her an 'A+' for the idea!"

If you decide it is not best to fit the student's entire day onto one schedule or if you know that the student does better when presented with less information at one time, you can put up part of the day or even one task comprising several activities. We are especially fond of "pull-off" schedules, in which you Velcro pictures in the column labeled "To Do," and when the activities are completed, the student can move the picture to the next column labeled "Done," for example. See the example schedule.

Pull-Off Schedule Example	
TO DO	**DONE**
Velcro "Circle Time" image here	
Velcro "Math" image here	
Velcro "Snack Time" image here	
Velcro "Free Play" image here	
Velcro "Art" image here	
Velcro "Writing Time" image here	

Implementing Visual Schedules

The schedule that you design for your students will require teaching. The schedule will not automatically have meaning for your student, so you will have to show your student how to utilize it. You should use enough prompting to ensure the child understands the schedule and completes the sequence of activities and then fade out slowly so he or she goes to the schedule with increasing independence.

Implementing Visual Schedules

1. Give a standard phrase, such as "look at the schedule," to direct the student's attention to the activity schedule.

2. Prompt the student to go to the schedule.

3. Prompt the student to look at or point to the first activity.

4. Prompt the student to go the location of the first activity.

5. When the first activity is over, give the standard phrase again and prompt the student back to the schedule.

6. When he or she returns to the schedule, prompt the student to indicate the first activity is completed (i.e., put a check mark in the appropriate box, move the picture to the "completed" column, or whatever you have set up to indicate completion).

7. Prompt the student to look at or point to the second activity, and complete the steps above until the task, assignment, or period of the day is completed entirely.

Visual Supports to Help With Transitions

Transitions can be especially problematic for the student with ASD, and there are several supports available to help in reducing anxieties or social difficulties associated with the transitions. Problem behaviors during transitions can impact the effectiveness of teacher instruction; it can disrupt other students' activities, and as a result of the behavior problems, students with ASD can be excluded from peer social circles (Banda et al., 2009).

Video modeling and cue cards have been used in education literature to help students with ASD make transitions from one activity to the next. Many problematic behaviors occur during transition periods. Providing a model for expected transition behaviors can contribute to reducing some of those difficult times. McCoy, Mathur, and Czoka (2010) presented a case study that can help us understand this concept.

Students in Ms. Cordova's classroom were expected to go directly to their places upon entering the classroom, avoid interrupting the teacher or others, take out their work packet, and begin working quietly at their places. Ms. Cordova observed that several children arrived to class on time, but they would not start working. They then requested constant attention from her, which took almost 10 minutes before children got settled for work. These behaviors resulted in the loss of valuable instructional time. "Too much time getting to work and staying on-task has been lost" (McCoy, Mathur, & Czoka, 2010, p. 22). Ms. Cordova developed a series of visual supports (video modeling with cue cards) to help increase students' following the expected arrival routine to begin their seatwork.

Family Voices 8.4

"Transitions . . . oh, these are the worst for my son. Without a visual schedule, he'd never be able to walk into the classroom, put his things away, settle down and get down to the business of learning. My son's teacher has helped so much by providing a morning routine schedule. We try it at home with some transitions as well, and it helps there too."

In addition to scheduling things throughout the day, visuals can be used to organize the environment and to represent the places where specific items belong. This was discussed in previous sections of this chapter, and we will provide more specifics here. See the chart, "Ways to Use Visual Supports in the Classroom and at Home" for ideas about ways to use visual supports.

Often, teachers place the classroom rules on the wall as a reminder for the students. Rule reminder cards are an example of a visual support that can be used to visually present expectations for behavior (Meadan et al., 2011). These cards can be formed using line drawings or photographs and are useful for communicating the behaviors that are considered acceptable and unacceptable and what consequences may result from exhibiting unacceptable behavior. Taking photographs of children following the classroom rules is a good way for children to model expected behavior for everyone (Meadan et al., 2011).

Ways to Use Visual Supports in the Classroom and at Home

1. Place laminated photographs of different-sized blocks or toys to organize the center during cleanup, and enable children to put the blocks or toys away in the correct location.

2. Parents can place picture labels on shelves or drawers to help a child clean up by putting each item in its place.

3. A basket for placing completed work can have a photograph of the teacher accepting a student's paper attached to it.

4. Cubbies or hooks where children should place backpacks or other items can have the child's name and a picture of a backpack attached.

Creating Supportive Environments in the General-Education Classroom

Inclusion Tips

CREATING A SUPPORTIVE ENVIRONMENT IN THE GENERAL-EDUCATION CLASSROOM

1. Learn about and adopt the TEACCH approach to organizing the classroom.

2. Consider designing an individual work system for students with ASD (visually organized spaces that communicate what students are supposed to do, how much work is to be completed, how the students know they are finished, and what to do when they are finished).

3. Develop and use visuals for instruction by providing individual visual schedules, highlighting important information in a text, using completed models, color coding relevant information, providing visual directions, making endings obvious by using a "finished work" box or folder, and so forth.

4. Consider soliciting the help of students to create video models of an expected behavior.

5. Consider allowing children with ASD to sit slightly away from groups of their peers, if they prefer it, to eliminate some sensory distractions. (*But be careful to avoid placing a student with ASD "in the corner" or in extreme isolation. Never isolate children with ASD and "ignore" them in your efforts to reduce overstimulation.*)

6. Arrange the physical environment to include close proximity to materials and instruction, limitation of distractions (auditory and visual), development of clear visual boundaries, and making the

(Continued)

(Continued)

key learning centers visually obvious within the classroom by using carpet squares, furniture arrangements, masking tape, and more.

7. Reduce background noise as much as possible during verbal instructions.

8. Visually organize spaces, including those where children practice or perform skills under direct supervision or during independent work time.

9. Make sure the individual work system communicates (1) the tasks the student is supposed to do, (2) how much work there is to be completed, (3) how the student knows when he or she is finished, and (4) what to do when finished (which might include instructions for the next activity in the schedule).

10. Place all required materials near the student to allow completion of work without having to gather tasks and materials.

11. Provide small-group instruction rather than large-group instruction, where directions and classroom instruction can be offered to small groups and one on one as much as possible.

12. Know the student's areas of strengths and interests, and use them to structure curriculum and free-time activities.

13. Educate peers about students with ASD.

14. Provide activities to teach and support social and emotional skills. Social skills development helps students in all aspects of daily life, from childhood through adulthood, and should be actively taught in school environments. This is especially important in inclusive classrooms.

PARTNERING WITH FAMILIES

Environmental Planning and Visual Supports in the Home

A focus of the TEACCH programs is to teach parents how to implement individual supports at home. Clinicians provide parent training for the home TEACCHing model, as parents take on an increasingly active role in teaching their children while under the training and supervision of the clinician, and by the end of the training, parents can conduct sessions independently (Welterlin, Turner-Brown, Harris, Mesibov, & Delmolino, 2011).

Parents can also implement a visual schedule for routines such as the afternoon schedule, bedtime routine, morning routine, preparing to take the bus to school, cleaning the bedroom, getting dressed, getting ready for bed, or getting ready for school, among others, without significant training in the TEACCH approach. Teachers can provide brief instructions that can help parents develop a visual schedule.

Below is a sample of a morning routine that parents can implement at home with little guidance or input from teachers.

It can be relatively easy for parents to create visual schedules by using materials that are readily available. They can take photos with an iPhone or smartphone to use as visual supports, or they can retrieve photos from the Internet. Photos cut out from magazines are another alternative. If it is possible, using photos of the child completing the steps for use in the visual schedule can be meaningful for the child.

Morning Schedule

1. Wash face.

2. Brush teeth.

3. Comb hair.

4. Get dressed.

5. Eat breakfast.

6. Get backpack and jacket.

7. Wait for bus.

Implementing Visual Supports at Home

1. Take digital photos with your iPhone or smartphone to use as visual supports, or use pictures retrieved from the internet to represent activities and routines.

2. Taking photos of your child completing the steps can help the child feel like an important part of the process.

3. Cut out pictures from magazines to represent activities, routines, or rules.

4. Words for visual supports can be handwritten or printed from electronic documents. Pairing print with pictures facilitates learning.

5. Develop a visual schedule for a typical routine at home, such as getting ready for school, cleaning the child's room, or preparing for bed.

6. If you develop a "room cleaning" visual support, you can use images and symbols to represent the specific places where items belong (e.g., clothes in the laundry basket, shoes in the closet, etc.).

SUMMARY STATEMENTS

- Challenges with social interactions, routines and insistence on sameness, and sensory processing difficulties make environmental modifications necessary for students with ASD.

- Classroom environments contain an enormous amount of sensory stimulation—brightly lit rooms, numerous items hung on the wall, people moving about, messy work spaces, and people sitting in close proximity to one another—that can be overwhelming for students with ASD.

- Organizing time, space, and sequences can make learning activities easier to perform and can reduce the likelihood of negative behaviors for students with ASD.

- Creating a visual schedule should start with clearly defining the desired behavior, deciding on the activities to represent on the schedule, and then gathering photographs, drawings, Internet pictures, or magazine clips to depict the sequence of events.

WHAT WOULD YOU DO?

Look back at the case study about Margaret and Hannah presented at the beginning of the chapter. Based on what you have read in this chapter, what you have read in previous chapters, and your own experiences, how would you respond to the following questions?

1. Do you think rules and routines are important for individuals with ASD?
2. If you think specific routines should be established for Hannah, what routines do you feel are important to establish during her after-school time?
3. How would you help Margaret develop a visual schedule for the after-school

routine? What steps would you suggest she implement, how should she present the schedule, and what type should it be (check-off boxes, movable pictures, etc.)?

4. If you were asked to create a visual schedule for after-school and evening, after-dinner time, what would you include?

CHAPTER REFLECTION QUESTIONS

1. How does insistence on sameness and sensory sensitivities contribute to negative behaviors in students with ASD?

2. What strengths evident in individuals with ASD can be used to develop environmental modifications that capitalize on those strengths?

3. What parts of the school environment can be overwhelming for a student with ASD?

4. Why are learning activities easier to perform for a student with ASD when the classroom is organized?

5. What advice would you give to a family member of one of your students who wants to create a visual schedule for getting ready for bed?

RECOMMENDED RESOURCES

Websites

- A blog about sensitivity to light, available at https://aspiegrrl.wordpress.com/tag/light-sensitivity/

- Autism Speaks, "Visual Supports for Students With Autism," available at https://www.autismspeaks.org/docs/sciencedocs/atn/visual_supports.pdf

- Pinterest, "Visual Schedules," available at https://www.pinterest.com/search/pins/?q=visual%20schedule&

rs=typed&0=visual|typed&1=schedule|typed

- "Visual Supports and Autism Spectrum Disorders," available at http://kc.vanderbilt.edu/kennedy_files/VisualSupports-Nov2011.pdf

Articles/Publications

Blagojevic, B., Logue, M. E., Bennett-Armistead, V. S., Taylor, B., & Neal, E. (2011). Take a look! Visual supports for learning. *Teaching Young Children, 4*(5), 10–13.

REFERENCES

Ashburner, J., Ziviani, J., & Rodger, S. (2008). Sensory processing and classroom emotional, behavioral, and educational outcomes in children with autism spectrum disorder. *American Journal of Occupational Therapy*, *62*(5), 564–573.

Aspiegrrl. (2011, December 14). What's it like to have a sensory processing/integration disorder? [Web log post]. Retrieved from https://aspiegrrl.wordpress.com/tag/light-sensitivity

Banda, D. R., Grimmett, E., & Hart, S. L. (2009). Helping students with autism spectrum disorders in general education classrooms manage transition issues. *TEACHING Exceptional Children*, *41*(4), 16–21.

Bryan, L. C., & Gast, D. L. (2000). Teaching on-task and on-schedule behaviors to high-functioning children with autism via picture activity schedules. *Journal of Autism and Developmental Disorders*, *30*, 553–567.

Dauphin, M., Kinney, E. M., & Stromer, R. (2004). Using video-enhanced activity schedules and matrix training to teach sociodramatic play to a child with autism. *Journal of Positive Behavior Interventions*, *6*, 238–250.

Dettmer, S., Simpson, R. L., Myles, B. S., & Ganz, J. B. (2000). The use of visual supports to facilitate transitions of students with autism. *Focus on Autism and Other Developmental Disabilities*, *15*, 163–169.

Dooley, P., Wilczenski, F. L., & Torem, C. (2001). Using an activity schedule to smooth school transitions. *Journal of Positive Behavior Interventions*, *3*, 57–61.

Ganz, J. B. (2007). Classroom structuring methods and strategies for children and youth with autism spectrum disorders. *Exceptionality*, *15*(4), 249–260.

Hume, K., Plavnick, J., & Odom, S. L. (2012). Promoting task accuracy and independence in students with autism across education setting through the use of individual work systems. *Journal of Autism and Developmental Disorders*, *42*, 2084–2099.

Knight, V., Sartini, E., & Spriggs, A. D. (2015). Evaluating visual activity schedules as evidence-based practice for individuals with autism spectrum disorders. *Journal of Autism and Developmental Disorders*, *45*, 157–178.

Krantz, P. J., & McClannahan, L. E. (1993). Teaching children with autism to initiate to peers: Effects of script-fading procedure. *Journal of Applied Behavior Analysis*, *26*, 121–132.

Kuhaneck, H. M., & Helleher, J. (2015). Development of the classroom sensory environment assessment (CSEA). *American Journal of Occupational Therapy*, *69*(6). doi:10.5014/ajot.2015.019430

Massey, N. G., & Wheeler, J. J. (2000). Acquisition and generalization of activity schedules and their effects on task management in a young child with autism in an inclusive pre-school classroom. *Education and Training in Mental Retardation and Developmental Disabilities*, *35*, 326–355.

McCoy, K. M., Mathur, S. R., & Czoka, A. (2010, Spring). Guidelines for creating a transition routine: Changing from one room to another. *Beyond Behavior*, *22*–29.

Meadan, H., Ostrosky, M. M., Triplett, B., Michna, A., & Fettig, A. (2011). Using visual supports with young children with autism spectrum disorder. *TEACHING Exceptional Children*, *43*(6), 28–35.

Mesibov, G. B., & Shea, V. (2010). *Journal of Autism and Development Disorders*, *40*, 570–579.

Pierce, K. L., & Schreibman, L. (1994). Teaching daily living skills to children with autism in unsupervised settings through pictorial self-management. *Journal of Applied Behavior Analysis, 27,* 471–481.

Rohrer, M., & Samson, N. (2014). *10 critical components for success in the special education classroom.* Thousand Oaks, CA: Corwin.

Sarris, M. (2015, June 15). What do we know about noise sensitivity in autism? *Interactive Autism Network.* Retrieved from https://iancommunity.org/print/13787

Schneider, N., & Goldstein, H. (2010). Using Social Stories and visual schedules to improve socially appropriate behaviors in children with autism. *Journal of Positive Behavior Interventions, 12*(3), 149–160.

Tomlinson, C. A., & Moon, T. R. (2013). *Assessment and student success in a differentiated classroom.* Alexandria, VA: ASCD (Association for Supervision and Curriculum Development).

Wang, K. (2014, May 6). Noise control: 11 tips for helping your child with autism deal with noise. *Friendship Circle.* Retrieved from http://www.friendshipcircle.org/blog/2014/05/06/noise-control-11-tips-for-helping-your-child-with-autism-deal-with-noise

Watanabe, M., & Sturmey, P. (2003). The effect of choice-making opportunities during activity schedules on task engagement of adults with autism. *Journal of Autism and Developmental Disorders, 33,* 535–538.

Welterlin, A., Turner-Brown, L. M., Harris, S., Mesibov, G., & Delmolino, L. (2011). The home TEACCHing program for toddlers with autism. *Journal of Autism and Developmental Disorders, 42,* 1827–1835.

Supporting Social Skills Development

LEARNER OBJECTIVES

After reading this chapter, the learner should be able to do the following:

- Identify the types of social skills deficits commonly presented in students with ASD.

- Discuss the Social Stories intervention, including the advantages and how to develop and implement a Social Story.

- Articulate the advantages of using social scripts and how to develop and implement social scripts.

- Discuss the advantages of using video modeling and how to develop and implement a video model to address a social skills deficit.

- Evaluate social skills groups as an intervention for improving social skills.

- Consider the possibilities for partnering with families to implement social skills strategies at home, so that classroom learning continues into natural settings outside the classroom.

CASE STUDY

Anthony is an 8-year-old boy diagnosed with ASD. He attends Mr. Hanson's third-grade general-education classroom for all of his school day. Mr. Hanson reports that Anthony is having difficulty forming relationships, making friends, and getting along with his classmates.

Anthony talks a lot with his peers, always steering the conversation toward his favorite subject, which is automobiles. Anthony is able to read at the third-grade level, according to his teacher, but Mr. Hanson has a hard time getting Anthony to read anything other than books about cars.

Anthony's style of social interaction makes it hard to make friends. He stands or sits very close to peers but rarely initiates conversations, unless it is to talk about cars. When peers ask questions of him, he either does not respond, or he responds in a way unrelated to the question that was asked. Sometimes, he walks away from the conversation before it is finished.

He also appears to have challenges reading his peer's facial expressions and responding appropriately. Anthony speaks fluently, but he rarely talks about anything other than cars, and he does not recognize when his peers appear to be uninterested in further conversation about automobiles. Mr. Hanson believes that Anthony's peers do not want to play or interact with him very often because of this. They are growing frustrated with his singly focused conversations.

He has challenges with joining in activities with others as well. Anthony is often seen wandering around the playground alone at recess, rarely initiating conversations or joining activities with his classmates. Occasionally, he spends time on the equipment, beside his classmates, but rarely does Anthony play "with" his peers. He does not know how to join in what others are doing. He spends most of his time alone.

....

INTRODUCTION

To anyone, social behaviors, situations, and concepts are abstract and complex. By social behaviors, we mean conversational skills (greeting, joining a conversation, verbal turn-taking, listening, being aware of personal space, etc.); play skills (observing, joining play, turn-taking, sharing, coping with "no," coping with losing, ending play, etc.); understanding emotions (reading facial expressions, reading body language, reading voice intonation and pitch, etc.); dealing with conflict (practicing anger management and self-regulation, asking for help, walking away from a stressful situation, being assertive but not aggressive, etc.); and friendship skills (knowing what a friend is, choosing appropriate friends, sharing a friend, dealing with peer pressure, etc.). These types of interactions present problems, especially for a person with ASD.

Individuals with ASD do not seem to naturally develop social skills the same way their peers do. They struggle to understand social nuances and social cues. They *can* learn how to interact in a social situation with instruction that is suited to their needs, ability, and interest level when we plan the intervention carefully. The social skills interventions that are described in this chapter were developed with the intent to help a student with ASD understand the social situation or concept and to apply that knowledge in a social setting. Each of these strategies is designed to capitalize on the child with ASD's strengths in visual processing.

COMMON SOCIAL SKILLS DIFFERENCES

Children who display good social understanding are able to interact positively with peers, teachers, or other adults. They are better able to function successfully in the classroom and in life (Elliott & Gresham, 2013). Children with ASD tend to have impairments in social skills, making interactions with peers or adults challenging. The National Research Council (2001) indicates that while children with autism demonstrate widely differing levels of skills and severity of symptoms, they often demonstrate impairments in their relationships with peers, their nonverbal communicative behaviors in social exchanges, and their use of imitation and symbolic play. They are less often seen imitating other people's actions, movements, and vocalizations (National Research Council, 2001). Social interactions in children with ASD are characterized by low rates of initiation and response and in establishing joint foci of attention. Children with ASD use fewer nonverbal gestures, and they use a more limited range of facial expressions. They also tend to pay less attention to other people's displays of emotion, and they demonstrate fewer acts of empathy or shared emotion.

Infants usually show interest in the world and the people around them. Toddlers try to imitate words, use simple gestures like waving bye-bye, and smile at people, whereas young children with ASD tend to have fewer such interactions with others. For example, they might not imitate actions or gestures like clapping when mom claps and might not show an interest in social games like peek-a-boo (Pierangelo & Giuliani, 2008). They often lack eye contact and have a hard time learning to take turns and share. They have trouble interpreting or understanding other people's feelings and might not want to be held or cuddled. They might have trouble interacting with peers because they often say whatever comes to mind, even if it is inappropriate (Pierangelo & Giuliani, 2008). All of these challenges make it difficult for an individual to engage in social interactions and to make friends.

Children with ASD have difficulty interpreting what others are thinking and feeling. Subtle social cues, like a smile, a wink, or a grimace, can have little meaning to the child with ASD (Pierangelo & Giuliani, 2008). For a child who misses such social cues, a wave to "come here" can mean the same thing in all situations whether the peer is smiling and extending his arms for a hug or frowning and putting his hands on his hips. "Without the ability to interpret gestures and facial expressions, the social world may seem bewildering" (Pierangelo & Giuliani, 2008, p. 12).

Because autism is a spectrum, it makes sense that not all individuals with ASD will demonstrate the same level of social impairment. Reichow, Steiner, and Volkmar (2012) said that on one end of the spectrum, an individual with ASD

> might have strong motivation to interact with their peers and often stay in close proximity to talk to his peers, yet lack the skills to effectively navigate social interactions, for instance by talking incessantly without monitoring others' interest in the topic or participation in the conversation. On the other end of the spectrum, a child might have very little desire to interact with others and avoid social interactions altogether. (p. 10)

However, regardless of degree, difficulties in the social area remain a part of ASD, including those who have average and above average cognitive skills.

We know that children with ASD tend to have strengths in visual processing. Therefore, it makes sense that the lack of visual cues in a social context is what makes social interactions so difficult for someone with ASD. Most social interactions require simultaneous processing and comprehending verbal rather than visual information, making it challenging to glean relevant information from a social context that does not provide visual cues. Therefore, "a visual means of presenting social information would allow children with autism more time to process and comprehend the information" (Laushey, Heflin, Shippen, Alberto, & Fredrick, 2009, p. 1436). Relying on auditory processing or attention is hard for our students with ASD, whereas utilizing visual information in a meaningful way can be less difficult.

Family Voices 9.1

"Does my son want to have friends? Indeed. Does he know how to make friends? Not at all. I am so saddened to know that he desperately wants to have friends and establish meaningful social relationships, but he fails miserably when he tries. Other children just don't have the awareness or understanding about how my son operates socially. This is heartbreaking. Don't all parents want their children to have friends? We're no different."

SOCIAL SKILLS STRATEGIES

Presenting information visually may help individuals with ASD function more effectively in social contexts. Therefore, in this section, we will discuss some social skills interventions that are commonly used to benefit students with ASD. We will look at Social Stories, social scripts, video modeling, and social skills groups, among others. When you try a strategy, always be on the lookout for its effectiveness. If something you try does not have the desired outcome, move on to the next. Never consider the child to be a failure; instead, consider that a new strategy should be implemented that better meets his or her needs. We suggest that strategies shown to be successful through rigorous research be considered before moving toward promising practices that are not yet confirmed through research.

Social Stories

Social Stories are used to support a meaningful exchange of information in social situations (Gray, 2016). They are individualized short stories that help increase appropriate social interactions of children with ASD by teaching them the relevant components of a given social situation. They focus on describing and explaining the social situation, as well as teaching the appropriate responses in that situation. Social Stories are used to provide guidance and directions for responding to various social situations that are unique to the individual for whom you write the story. Usually, Social Stories use words and images to present the situation. Common topics of Social Stories include responding to environmental situations (e.g., fire drills); describing other people's point of view (e.g., some people like to be in a crowd); defining routines (e.g., changing classes or going to school); or describing an upcoming event (e.g., school assembly or field trip).

Advantages of Social Stories

Research tells us that using Social Stories helps increase appropriate behaviors and decrease inappropriate behaviors. Scattone, Wilczynski, Edwards, and Rabine (2002) demonstrated a reduction in inappropriate behaviors in their study with three participants. Lorimer, Simpson, Myles, and Ganz (2002) used Social Stories to decrease a student's tantrum behaviors during attempts to secure attention from adults. Bledsoe, Myles, and Simpson (2003) used Social Stories to target appropriate lunchtime behaviors (decreased spilling of food and drink and increased use of a napkin to wipe the face). Thiemann and Goldstein (2001) combined Social Stories with comic strip conversations and video modeling to increase social communication skills, such as securing attention, initiating comments, and initiating requests. "The advantage of Social Stories seem to be their ability to address social understanding and to provide behavioral solutions to the student in a concrete and portable form" (Denning, 2007, p. 17).

Many different behaviors have been addressed through Social Stories. Research has demonstrated the effectiveness of using Social Stories to address transition behaviors (Schneider & Goldstein, 2010), increase appropriate social interactions (e.g., standing or sitting at reasonable distances from other students and approaching others asking them to play) (Chan & O'Reilly, 2008), raising one's hand in a nondisruptive manner (e.g., vertical rather than horizontal extensions) or making appropriate vocalizations (e.g., comments relevant to classroom activities), and other behaviors.

Family Voices 9.2

"Many of us just take for granted how to operate in social settings, but those with autism need things to be defined. Those unwritten rules of society have to be clearly defined for some children. I like Social Stories. My son's teacher made one for him at school, and she sent it home with the suggestion that we read it for homework, over and over again. These stories are fun for my son, because they are 'his' story!"

Developing and Implementing Social Stories

Gray and Garand (1993) recommend that we describe the situation in which the behavior occurred, describe the perspective of those involved in the situation, and provide guidelines for what the student should do in the future. When writing a Social Story, we want to use a variety of sentences (descriptive, directive, etc.) and provide illustrations, such as drawings, photographs, and children's illustrations, to develop a personalized text (Gray, 2016). A Social Story should be 5 to 10 sentences that describe the skills, appropriate behavior, and others' viewpoints.

Social Stories usually follow a predictable format. They should consist of two to five sentences describing each appropriate behavior: one sentence describing positive and observable appropriate responses, one sentence describing the viewport of others as they react to the situation, one optional sentence describing a commonly shared value or opinions, and one sentence that reminds the child of the appropriate behavior.

Steps in Developing a Social Story	
1. Define	• Define the inappropriate behavior.
2. Define	• Define an alternative positive behavior.
3. Write	• Write the story using the Social Story format.
4. Locate	• Locate pictures to illustrate the Social Story.
5. Read	• Read the Social Story to the child.
6. Practice	• Practice the social skills used in the story.
7. Remind	• Remind the child of the situation where the social skills should be used.
8. Prompt	• Prompt the child to use the social skill at appropriate times throughout the day.
9. Affirm	• Affirm the child when he or she uses the appropriate social behavior.

Usually, Social Stories are written from the student's perspective, in the first person, and are in reassuring language to answer the who, what, when, where, and why of a situation or target behavior. The two main types of sentences used in the stories are descriptive and directive. A descriptive sentence states the facts (e.g., "The teacher is talking") and can include the thoughts and feelings of the selected student and others in the story (e.g., "The teacher likes it when I listen."). A directive sentence identifies possible responses (e.g., "I can tell the teacher when I need to take a break and go to my special place in the classroom") or gently directs behavior (e.g., "I will try to _____."). Gray (2016) suggests that there be two descriptive sentences for every directive sentence.

Descriptive sentences are accurate statements of facts, describing what happens, where the situation occurs, and why. An example of a descriptive sentence is, "Every week we go to art class on Wednesday at 1:30." *Directive* sentences identify a possible response in positive terms that tell the student with ASD what he should do or say. An example of a directive sentence is, "I will try to sit quietly when the teacher is talking to me."

Perspective sentences describe the internal states of other people. This type of sentence provides information about thoughts, feelings, and moods of other people. Sample perspective sentences include, "Many students like to each lunch with their friends," or "Everyone likes it best when each person touches their own food."

Carol Gray recommends that we write two to five descriptive sentences for each directive sentence (which may include perspective sentences). The theory is that stories that follow the ratio can work for a student, whereas stories that do not follow the ratio do not work to improve behavior.

T.I.P. – Theory Into Practice 9.1
IDENTIFY THE SENTENCE TYPE AND RATIO

1. Read the Social Story for greeting someone at school that follows, and correctly identify the type of sentence (i.e., directive, descriptive, affirmative, etc.).

2. Do you see an appropriate ratio between directive and descriptive sentences?

When I see someone I know at school, I will smile and say "hi" or "hello." He or she might say "hi" or "hello" back to me. I can ask someone, "How are you today?" He or she might stop and talk with me.

When I get to school, I can say "good morning" to someone. When it is time to leave school, I can say "goodbye" or "see you tomorrow."

Sometimes, if I am passing someone I know between classes, I can smile or nod my head. Most people like it when I smile at them. Smiling can make others feel good.

Gray (2000) suggests several guidelines for writing Social Stories, which are included in the chart.

Social Stories Guidelines	
1. Decide	• Decide what the story will be about, based on behaviors you have observed.
	• Decide what skill or behavior you want to establish.
	• Decide what you want the student to be able to do.
2. Reasons to Write	• Learn a new routine.
	• Help children cope with and adjust to change.
	• Help advance interpersonal understanding.
	• Aid in the development of appropriate behaviors.
	• Provide insight into what other people are thinking and feeling.
3. Profile	• Know the child's interest in reading.
	• Know the child's reading ability.
	• Know the child's level of understanding language.

Social Stories Guidelines	
4. Task Analysis	• Review the skills being taught, and break it down into small, specific steps the child will need to understand and perform the task.
5. Perspective	• Write a Social Story from the perspective of the person with ASD.
6. Sentence Type	• Use a combination of different types of sentences (descriptive, perspective, directive, etc.).
	• Write according to the formula: two to five descriptive for each directive sentence.
	• Supplement with additional optional types of sentences: affirmative, control, and cooperative.
7. First Person	• Write the Social Story in first-person language (i.e., "I go to lunch everyday at 11:30.").
8. Present Tense	• Stories are usually written in the present tense.

When you share the story with the student, you should read it frequently, and read it in advance of the challenging situation. Read the story to the child or with the child at a consistent time, such as daily before the situation occurs. As the student displays more appropriate behaviors, you can begin to read the story less and less, where eventually the story is no longer needed. After the student masters the story, consider keeping it visible and accessible for reference.

T.I.P. – Theory Into Practice 9.2

DEVELOP AND SHARE A SOCIAL STORY

1. Visit Carol Gray's Social Stories website to view several sample Social Stories at http://carolgraysocialstories.com/social-stories/social-story-sampler

2. View at least 3 of the 16 samples found there.

3. Pick one as a model to follow.

4. Develop a Social Story for a behavior you would like to address. Ideally, make the Social Story appropriate for a student in your fieldwork or someone you know.

5. Make sure to include an appropriate ration of descriptive and directive sentences.

6. Consider sharing your Social Story with another student or with a classmate in your autism course.

7. Ask your professor if you can share or present your story to the class.

8. Consider sharing your Social Story with your fieldwork teacher. You might even get to share it with the student for whom you developed the Social Story.

- The StoryMaker app for iPad and iPhone allows concerned caregivers to create, present, and share Social Stories on a touchscreen smartphone or tablet. Users can import pictures from a built-in library, add them from a camera, or download from the Internet. An unlimited number and variety of stories can be created, presented, and shared with others through printouts and e-mail. Several story templates are provided in the app, and they can be edited and customized for individual needs.

- The app is available at http://kidcompanions.com/new-carol-gray-social-story-app-available

- Purchase the app which you can use in teaching your current and future students, or ask your university to provide access to the app for you.

- Create your own Social Story using the app.

- Share it with a friend or classmate.

SOCIAL SCRIPTING

Social scripts are similar to Social Stories, yet they differ due to their portable nature. Social scripts provide students with specific language they can use in certain social situations, and they may be written for any number of purposes, such as helping to initiate a conversation or responding to common questions. When using this technique, the teacher typically creates a script for the student and has him or her practice reading it until he or she is fairly fluent in delivering it. Then, the student should be given opportunities to practice and improve skills in an authentic context.

Scripting is the practice of using scripts of typical situations and encounters to teach students appropriate social skills and behaviors in an organized way. Social scripts can be used to teach students with ASD how to interact with peers or adults. It may feel awkward at first because the words are scripted, but with practice, students become more comfortable. The ultimate goal of scripting is to help students transfer the skills they learn to other situations.

Family Voices 9.3

"Jamison doesn't naturally have conversation skills. . . . A conversation is something very foreign to him. Writing some scripts for him has allowed him to capitalize on his strengths of memory and doing well with structure and minimizes his weaknesses with language, finding the right words to use, or organizing a sentence. He's working on delivering the script in a more 'natural' voice, but he's working and practicing, and that's what we are hopeful about."

Advantages of social scripts. Scripts can involve conversation starters, the content of a topic, responses to conversations, or ideas that connect conversations. Scripts can help speakers change topics in an appropriate fashion, ask questions, be the speaker, or finish/end conversations. Below is an example of a social script created for a student who was learning how to make small talk with classmates on Monday morning.

> If someone asks, "How was your weekend?" I can say, "My weekend was great. I spent a lot of time playing Wii golf with my cousin, who comes over on the weekends while his mom works. On Sunday, we went to church, and then, we went to lunch at my favorite restaurant." Then, I can ask my conversation partner, "How was your weekend?"

Social scripts are helpful for many students with autism, even very young readers or nonreaders. You can use recorded scripts or pictures when students have limited reading skills or use simple language at the student's reading level.

Developing and implementing social scripts. A typical lesson using social scripts can help the student learn to greet someone or to start a conversation. Making eye contact, listening, and starting and ending a conversation should be a part of the lesson. Scripts should be developed based on the student's needs—observations of social abilities or reports from others who interact with him or her can provide information about which skills need to be practiced. Once students are comfortable practicing the scripts, give them opportunities to practice and enhance their skills. The inclusion of skilled peers can provide opportunities to practice the script.

Most important, scripts should be individualized to take into account a student's current language skills, topics of interest, or interests of friends and family. Scripts can also be individualized by considering situations that a learner needs or wants to participate in but does not yet have the language to be successful. Scripts can be used to teach conversation about any topic, making sure that the script matches the child's needs and takes the child's perspective into consideration. What follows is a script for a student who was learning how to request food in the cafeteria line. His teachers noticed that lunchtime was especially challenging for this student, and so, they developed this script to help.

> When I go to the cafeteria for lunch, I stand in line until it is my time to tell the lady what I want. The lady will ask something like, "What would you like?" I will look at the options, and I will say something like, "I would like the pizza today." She will hand me my plate with the food I requested, and I will say, "Thank you." I will then get my dessert and milk, put them on my tray, and then go sit at my table to eat my lunch.

1. Why do you think a social script could be helpful for someone with ASD?

2. Can you think of anyone who has a need you could address with a social script?

3. Think about a script you could create for one of your own needs that could be a good reminder for how to do an activity (like studying or taking notes for this class).

VIDEO MODELING

Several research studies have used video modeling to address the social skills deficits of children with ASD. Video modeling involves having a child with ASD watch a videotape of a model engaging in a target behavior to be imitated. Watching the videotapes allows the student to memorize and imitate these behaviors in other settings. Video modeling appears to be effective in modifying, changing, or shaping behavior, and it seems to be an appropriate strategy for use at school or home (Malmberg, Charlop, & Gershfeld, 2015; Sansosti & Powell-Smith, 2008).

Advantages of video modeling. Malmberg et al. (2015) compared Social Stories to video modeling in their investigation. The researchers theorized that video modeling is a more effective treatment approach because it minimizes attention and language behaviors and requires the child only to look at a small spatial area (computer, hand-held tablet, etc.) and because the videos allow for spontaneous imitation (Malmberg et al., 2015). Other advantages include the simplicity and ease of creating a video model, as well as the ability to be used repeatedly with the same child or with others who would benefit from the same behavior model (Malberg et al., 2015). Videos have an advantage over printed Social Stories or other printed material, according to Malmberg et al. (2015), because they provide social cues in a relatively realistic context, rather than describing the situation with only words and pictures.

Family Voices 9.4

"Videos? That's all you had to say. Making a video model for a social situation has been the best idea ever for Kirk. He's found his 'calling' as a videographer through this activity. He wants to go to school and become a videographer one day. I love that he has career goals!"

Developing and implementing video models. Consider putting your video together as Sansosti and Powell-Smith (2008) did. They constructed their video model by using a digital camcorder, where similar-aged peers modeled the content of each participant's Social Story. In the videos, peer models engaged in the target behavior in a way that was as natural as possible. Each video was approximately 45 seconds to 1 minute in duration (Sansosti & Powell-Smith, 2008). These researchers and others (e.g., Malmberg et al., 2015) recommend that you first do an assessment to observe the target behavior and to individualize a video that is written intentionally to meet the child's interests and needs.

T.I.P. – Theory Into Practice 9.5

DEVELOP A VIDEO MODEL

1. Use your iPhone or smartphone to develop a short video model (3–5 minutes).

2. Depict yourself or a friend performing a target behavior.

3. Below are just a few examples on YouTube to stimulate ideas for your project:

   - https://youtu.be/8I4KwA5CbqA

   - https://youtu.be/YCBNiSUFOhY

- https://youtu.be/MJYLfekgw2I

- https://youtu.be/DvSk5T_0UfU

- https://youtu.be/3RjRZ9jMfsO

- https://youtu.be/xDYFhrz74ks?list=PLUV-VLbs4zCpnKD2A7-3I_2BvkNuUHm-S

SOCIAL SKILLS GROUPS

Social skills groups are a common intervention used to address difficulties in social interaction for individuals with ASD. They are, in fact, one of the most widely used and recommended treatments for improving the social skills of individuals with ASD (Reichow et al., 2012). Not all studies report significant gains in social skills following the social skills group interventions. Some report less significant gains or limited generalizability to contexts outside the clinical setting (Barry et al., 2003). Even though positive results have been reported in social skills group research, more research is still needed to help determine if social skills group interventions have a long-term positive impact on social functioning (Reichow et al., 2012).

Social skills groups can be formed to teach a variety of skills. For example, some groups have been implemented to teach sharing greetings, exchanging conversation, ending conversation, being a good sport, reading body language, joining in, dealing with anger, or dealing with teasing (Ware, Ohrt, & Swank, 2012). Leaf, Dotson, Oppenheim-Leaf, Sherman, and Sheldon (2012) used social skills groups to teach how to give appropriate greetings, show appreciation, give compliments, change the game when a friend is bored, take turns, play indoor and outdoor games, interrupt appropriately, and so forth.

Advantages of social skills groups. There is some evidence in the research literature that social skills groups improve overall social competence and friendship quality for individuals with ASD (Reichow et al., 2012). Reichow and colleagues reviewed five studies of social skills groups, and they found some indication of improved social competence when compared with those who did not receive treatment. The ability to recognize emotions was measured in some of those studies, and the reviewers discovered no evidence that it was improved by taking part in a social skills group (Reichow et al., 2012). A number of other researchers reported positive outcomes in their participants who were involved in social skills groups (Leaf et al., 2012; Ware et al., 2012; White, Koenig, & Scahill, 2010).

Developing and implementing a social skills group. A social skills group usually involves two to six individuals with ASD who meet once per week for a period of time. Group sessions typically include a structured lesson on a specific skill—modeling of the skills, role-playing or practicing the modeled skill, engaging in discussion, and sharing feedback (Reichow et al., 2012; Ware et al., 2012). As with any intervention, start with an assessment. Meet individually with parents or caregivers to gather information about the child's history and any concerns the parents may have. In those meetings, you can also identify the child's ability to use various social skills, as well as any unknown interests, sensory issues, and health concerns of the child before starting the group. You can then form groups of children based on their developmental level and need.

The groups Ware et al. (2012) researched followed a structured format. Folders were initially created for students to take home after each weekly session. The folders included the skill of the week, steps for using the skill, and ideas for parents to practice the skills with their child. At the beginning of each meeting, children were instructed to give their folders to the group leader and greet each other. Each child would then pick a prize from the box, give it to the leader, and receive a reinforcement chart. The prize was picked before the skills lesson to serve as a motivator for each child to participate in the group. The reinforcement chart contained spaces for stickers, which the leader gave to children when they used a skill or made an effort to participate. If a sticker chart was completely filled at the end of the group, the children got to take their prizes home (Ware et al., 2012).

SOCIAL SKILLS DEVELOPMENT IN INCLUSIVE CLASSROOMS

1. Social Stories. A Social Story is a short, simple story written from the child's perspective that describes a social situation and provides instruction on positive and appropriate social behaviors through text and visual supports. They can be used to encourage positive behavior and increase learning for children with ASD in the inclusive classroom. See the previous discussion for how to develop and implement a Social Story.

2. Social Scripts. Consider developing a short script that your student with ASD can use to interact with his or her peers in your classroom.

3. Video Modeling. You can use your iPhone or smartphone to develop a short video model using peers to model a target behavior. Some target behavior ideas are greeting another student, raising your hand to answer the teacher's question, taking turns speaking in a conversation, taking turns with a toy or other classroom item, going to the cafeteria, communicating the need for a break, and so on.

4. Concept Diagrams. *Concept*: Name the concept or skill that identifies a social abstraction. *Definition*: Provide a definition of the characteristics that are always present in the concept. *Characteristics*: What characteristics are always, sometimes, and never present in

the concept? *Examples and Nonexamples*: Provide examples—characteristics that were named in the "always" category—and nonexamples—explain misconceptions of the concept and what the concept is not. See Laushey et al. (2009) for details.

5. Combinations. You can even combine peer buddies with other interventions for optimum outcomes. Try using social scripts combined with peer buddies. Or use concept diagrams with peer buddies. A combination of interventions may be necessary in some situations, according to some research reports (e.g., Laushey et al., 2009).

6. Social Skills Groups. Incorporating large- and small-group instruction in social skills is beneficial for all students, not just those with disabilities. See examples for how to structure the social skills group instructional time in the "Developing and Implementing a Social Skills Group" section of this chapter.

7. Based on Interest and Abilities. Develop materials based on the interests and abilities of the child with ASD. For example, for the child who likes animals, make a matching game using animal cards, and develop a social script to introduce play initiation and turn-taking skills. High-interest materials help provide motivation.

PARTNERING WITH FAMILIES TO FOSTER SOCIAL SKILLS

There are a variety of interventions that can be implemented at school and at home which are designed to increase appropriate social behaviors and decrease inappropriate ones. Generalization of social skills is advanced when a social skills approach is implemented in naturalistic environments such as the child's home. According to numerous studies, training parents to be cofacilitators in the intervention process can be effective in modifying behavior (Adams, Gouvousis, VanLue, & Waldron, 2004; Ivey, Heflin, & Alberto, 2004; Krantz & McClannahan, 1998; Radley, Jenson, Clark, & O'Neill, 2014; Rogers & Myles, 2001; Smith, 2001; Sofronoff, Leslie, & Brown, 2004).

Social Stories

Some studies have shown positive outcomes for students when parents were involved in implementing Social Stories (Adams et al., 2004; Ivey et al., 2004; Rogers & Myles, 2001; Sofronoff et al., 2004). Dodd, Hupp, Jewell, and Krohn (2007), for example, also involved parents in a Social Stories intervention implemented at home. Social Stories can be individualized for each child.

Social Scripts

In Krantz and McClannahan (1998), the researchers trained parents to implement verbal social scripts at home with three boys. In their research, they first trained parents how to develop a script, practice it with their children, and gradually fade the prompts they gave to their children. Each mother successfully performed the intervention, and all three children were able to initiate a conversation to gain access to their favorite toy set. Unscripted initiations increased for all three boys (Krantz & McClannahan, 1998) following the intervention.

Comic Strip Conversations

Comic strip conversations, which are also similar to Social Stories, have been implemented in home environments. Comic strip conversations rely on the input of the child, who actively constructs the story (Hutchins & Prelock, 2012). Hutchins and Prelock (2012) conducted research involving 17 students with ASD, where they implemented Social Stories and comic strip conversations to increase appropriate behavior and help children understand their own and others' thoughts, feelings, and beliefs. The children were responsible for visually representing the story with their drawing and writing. Parents in this study rated the Social Stories and comic strip conversations as effective over 75% of the time (Hutchins & Prelock, 2012). Results reveal that family-centered practices are effective.

Video Modeling

Researchers have also trained parents to implement video models with a good deal of success. Radley et al. (2014), for example, used a video-modeling strategy for developing social skills in which participants viewed video models of the targeted skills, practiced in role-plays with their peers, played a game that reinforced the skills, and then participated in a homework component. Parents were involved in facilitating the social skills lessons, and the efficacy of the parent-facilitated social skills was clearly demonstrated in Radley et al.'s (2014) research.

Social Skills Groups

Ware and colleagues (2012) worked with parents to implement social skills groups. In their research, the group leader maintained ongoing communication with parents by sending home folders with participants after every group session. The folders contained the skill of the week, steps for using the skill, ideas for parents to practice the skills with their child, and a questionnaire for the parents to complete and return. The questionnaire included questions about the child's level of success in using the skill throughout the week so that the leader could have a better understanding of the child's skill level (Ware et al., 2012). At the end of the series of meetings, the leader invited parents to meet as a group to receive feedback and ask questions.

Strategies Parents Can Implement at Home

1. Social Stories
2. Social scripts
3. Comic strip conversations
4. Video modeling
5. Participation in social skills groups

SUMMARY STATEMENTS

- Children with ASD have strengths in visual processing, and therefore, strategies that capitalize on their visual processing abilities will be the most helpful in developing social skills.

- Social Stories help increase appropriate social interactions by teaching relevant components of a given social situation. They describe and explain the social situation, as well as teach the appropriate responses in that situation.

- Social scripts are similar to Social Stories, but they are written in more of a "portable" format, often as one paragraph.

- Video modeling involves having a student watch a videotape of a model engaging in a target behavior to be imitated. They provide clear models of appropriate behavior in a relatively realistic context, rather than describing the situation with words and pictures.

- Social skills groups can improve overall social competence and friendship quality for individuals with ASD. Several researchers suggest a structured format to follow when forming social skills groups.

- Generalization of social skills is advanced when social skills approaches are presented in naturalistic environments, such as the child's home. Working with parents as cofacilitators in the intervention process has been effective in modifying behavior in several studies.

WHAT WOULD YOU DO?

Look back at the case study about Anthony presented at the beginning of the chapter. Based on what you have read in this chapter, what you have read in previous chapters, and your own experiences, how would you respond to the following questions?

1. Which social interaction deficit do you feel most interferes with Anthony's desire to make friends?

2. Why do you think this deficit is so problematic?

3. Which strategy would you suggest for Mr. Hanson to try that might help increase Anthony's social interaction skills?

4. How do you think that strategy would benefit Anthony?

5. In what ways can Mr. Hanson work with Anthony's family to develop an intervention for use at home that would help Anthony's social interaction skills?

CHAPTER REFLECTION QUESTIONS

1. Why is the Social Stories intervention beneficial for students with ASD?

2. What is a social script, what are the advantages of social scripts, and how can educators develop and implement social scripts?

3. Why would video modeling be preferred over a Social Story or social script?

4. What is your opinion of social skills groups as a way to improve social skills for individuals with ASD?

5. How can educators partner with families to implement social skills strategies at home so that classroom learning continues into natural settings outside the classroom?

RECOMMENDED RESOURCES

Websites

- Autism Classroom Resources. *Video modeling: What is it and why use it?* Available at http://www.autismclassroomresources.com/video-modeling-what-is-it-and-why-use-i

- Autism Speaks. *Social skills and autism.* Available at https://www.autismspeaks.org/family-services/community-connections/social-skills-and-autism

- Carol Gray Social Stories. (2016). *What is a Social Story?* Information and a video presentation, available at http://carolgraysocialstories.com/social-stories/what-is-it

- Gagnon, E. (2014). *Social Stories, social scripts and the power card strategy.* Available at http://www.education.com/reference/article/social-scripts-stories-asperger-ASD

Articles/Publications

- Baker, T. (2012). *Social skills training for children on the autism spectrum: Current research and integration.* Retrieved from http://www.kelbermancenter.org/assets/documents/SocialSkillsTrainingForChildren.pdf

- Reichow, B., Steiner, A. M., & Volkmar, F. (2012). *Social skills groups for people aged 6 to 21 with autism spectrum disorders (ASD).* Retrieved from http://www.kelbermancenter.org/assets/documents/SocialSkillsTrainingForChildren.pdf

- Vanderbilt Kennedy Center. (2014). *How to write a Social Story: Tips and resources for teachers.* Retrieved from https://vkc.mc.vanderbilt.edu/assets/files/tipsheets/socialstoriestips.pdf

REFERENCES

Adams, L., Gouvousis, A., VanLue, M., & Waldron, C. (2004). Social Story intervention: Improving communication skills in a child with an autism spectrum disorder. *Focus on Autism and Other Developmental Disabilities, 19,* 87–94.

Barry, T. D., Klinger, L. G., Lee, J. M., Palardy, N., Gilmore, T., & Bodin, S. D. (2003). Examining the effectiveness of an outpatient clinic-based social skills group for high-functioning children with autism. *Journal of Autism and Developmental Disorders, 33*(6), 685–701. doi:10.1023/b:jadd.0000006004.86556.e0

Bledsoe, R., Myles, B. S., & Simpson, R. L. (2003). Use of a Social Story intervention to improve mealtime skills of an adolescent with Asperger syndrome. *Autism, 7,* 289–295.

Chan, J. M., & O'Reilly, M. F. (2008). A Social Stories intervention package for students with autism in inclusive classroom settings. *Journal of Applied Behavior Analysis, 41,* 405–409.

Denning, C. B. (2007). Social skills interventions for students with Asperger Syndrome and high-functioning autism: Research findings and implications for teachers. *Beyond Behavior, 16*(3), 16–23.

Dodd, S., Hupp, D. A., Jewell, J. D., & Krohn, E. (2007). Using parents and siblings during a Social Story intervention for two children diagnosed with PDD-NOS. *Journal of Developmental and Physical Disabilities, 20,* 217–229.

Elliott, S. N., & Gresham, F. M. (2013). Social skills improvement system. *Encyclopedia of Autism Spectrum Disorders,* 2933–2935. doi:10.1007/978-1-4419-1698-3_509

Gray, C. A. (2000). *Writing Social Stories with Carol Gray, accompanying workbook to video.* Arlington, VA: Future Horizons.

Gray, C. A. (2016). What is a Social Story? In Carol Gray, *Social Stories.* Retrieved March 25, 2016, from http://carolgraysocialstories.com/social-stories/what-is-it

Gray, C. A., & Garand, J. D. (1993). Social Stories: Improving responses of students with autism with accurate social information. *Focus on Autistic Behavior, 8,* 1–10.

Hutchins, T. L., & Prelock, P. A. (2012). Parents' perceptions of their children's social behavior: The social validity of Social Stories and comic strip conversations. *Journal of Positive Behavior Interventions, 15*(3), 156–168.

Ivey, M. L., Heflin, L. J., & Alberto, P. (2004). The use of Social Stories to promote independent behaviors in novel events for children with PDD-NOS. *Focus on Autism and Other Developmental Disabilities, 19,* 164–176.

Krantz, P. J., & McClannahan, L. E. (1998). Social interaction skills for children with autism: A script-fading procedure for beginning readers. *Journal of Applied Behavior Analysis, 31,* 191–202.

Laushey, K. M., Heflin, L. J., Shippen, M., Alberto, P. A., & Fredrick, L. (2009). Concept mastery routines to teach social skills to elementary children with high functioning autism. *Journal of Autism and Developmental Disorders, 39*(10), 1435–1448. doi:10.1007/s10803-009-0757-9

Leaf, J. B., Dotson, W. H., Oppenheim-Leaf, M. L., Sherman, J. A., & Sheldon, J. B. (2012). A programmatic description of a social skills group for young children with autism. *Topics in Early Childhood Special Education, 32*(2), 111–121. doi:10.1177/0271121411405855

Lorimer, P. A., Simpson, R. L., Myles, B. S., & Ganz, J. B. (2002). The use of Social Stories as a preventative behavioral intervention in a home setting with a child with autism. *Journal of Positive Behavioral Interventions, 4*, 53–60.

Malmberg, D. B., Charlop, M., & Gershfeld, S. J. (2015). A two experiment treatment comparison study: Teaching social skills to children with autism spectrum disorder. *Journal of Developmental and Physical Disabilities, 27*(3), 375–392.

National Research Council. (2001). *Educating children with autism.* Committee on Educational Interventions for Children with Autism. Division of Behavioral and Social Sciences and Education. Washington, DC: National Academy Press.

Pierangelo, R., & Giuliani, G. (2008). *Teaching students with autism spectrum disorders: A step-by-step guide for educators.* Thousand Oaks, CA: Corwin.

Radley, K., Jenson, W. R., Clark, E., & O'Neill, R. E. (2014). The feasibility and effects of a parent-facilitated social skills training program on social engagement of children with autism spectrum disorders. *Psychology in the Schools, 51*(3), 241–255.

Reichow, B., Steiner, A. M., & Volkmar, F. (2012). *Social skills groups for people aged 6 to 21 with autism spectrum disorders (ASD).* Retrieved April 1, 2016, from http://www.kelbermancenter.org/assets/documents/SocialSkillsTrainingForChildren.pdf

Rogers, M. F., & Myles, B. S. (2001). Using Social Stories and comic strip conversations to interpret social situations for an adolescent with Asperger syndrome. *Intervention in School and Clinic, 36*, 310–313.

Sansosti, F. J., & Powell-Smith, K. A. (2008). Using computer-presented Social Stories and video models to increase the social communication of children with high-functioning autism spectrum disorders. *Journal of Positive Behavior Interventions, 10*(3), 162–178.

Scattone, D., Wilczynski, S. M., Edwards, R. P., & Rabine, B. (2002). Decreasing disruptive behaviors of children with autism using Social Stories. *Journal of Autism and Developmental Disorders, 32*, 535–543.

Schneider, N., & Goldstein, H. (2010). Using Social Stories and visual schedules to improve socially appropriate behaviors in children with autism. *Journal of Positive Behavior Interventions, 12*(3), 149–160. doi:10.1177/1098300709334198

Smith, C. (2001). Using Social Stories to enhance behavior in children with autism spectrum difficulties. *Educational Psychology in Practice, 17*, 337–345.

Sofronoff, K., Leslie, A., & Brown, W. (2004). Parent management training and Asperger syndrome: A randomized controlled trial to evaluate a parent based intervention. *Autism, 8*, 301–317.

Thiemann, K. S., & Goldstein, H. (2001). Social Stories, written text cues, and video feedback: Effects on social communication of children with autism. *Journal of Applied Behavior Analysis, 34*(4), 425–446.

Ware, J. N., Ohrt, J. H., & Swank, J. M. (2012). A phenomenological exploration of children's experiences in a social skills group. *Journal for Specialists in Group Work, 37*(2), 133–151. doi:10.1080/01933922.2012.663862

White, S. W., Koenig, K., & Scahill, L. (2010). Group social skills instruction for adolescents with high-functioning autism spectrum disorders. *Focus on Autism and Other Developmental Disabilities, 25*(4), 209–219. doi:10.1177/1088357610380595

Building Communication Skills

10

CASE STUDY

Alonzo is an 11-year-old boy who attends public school. When Alonzo was 9 years old, he was referred to the educational psychologist for assessment and then to a neurologist. He received the diagnosis of ASD at the end of his third-grade year. When he reached fourth grade, Alonzo's school set up an intervention plan to help with academic progress. He spends 80% of his day in an inclusive classroom and 20% of his day in a special education classroom. He receives reading instruction from his special education teacher, and for all other subjects, he is educated alongside his typically achieving peers.

The intervention seemed to help with academic skills, but despite this improvement, Alonzo still had significant problems with social communication and establishing friendships with classmates. On most days, Alonzo walks around the schoolyard alone each day. When Alonzo attempts interactions with peers, it is often aggressive or inappropriate in nature. He has been seen grabbing his peers faces to get their attention. And when he tries to speak to his peers, Alonzo often mumbles or screams.

Staff have seen him watch others play basketball during breaks on numerous occasions, so they concluded that he must enjoy playing basketball himself but lacks the skills to initiate conversations or play. Knowing how much he enjoys basketball, they are surprised that Alonzo does not participate in basketball or any other social activities during class breaks.

Until this point, the school has not used any method for developing his social communication skills. In Alonzo's permanent file, staff noted that they have never seen Alonzo smile. Other teachers believe that Alonzo does not like school or any of his peers. Since they always see Alonzo alone and never smiling, they concluded he must not enjoy

LEARNER OBJECTIVES

After reading this chapter, the learner should be able to do the following:

1. Describe *joint attention* and how it impacts communication.

2. Explain how pragmatic language is used in communication.

3. Describe low-tech and high-tech augmentative and alternative communication systems and how they can benefit children with ASD.

4. Describe PECS.

5. Compare the features of ABA and PRT and describe how they can be used to increase communication for students with ASD.

6. Discuss the use of video modeling and script training to develop communication skills.

7. List several ways that inclusive teachers could help children with ASD develop their communication skills.

8. Summarize how we can involve parents in developing communication skills.

being around people. They have not yet determined what reinforcers are motivating for Alonzo.

The school staff would like to see Alonzo respond positively to his peers' initiatives for playing together and to see him take initiative for playing together with peers. Knowing that Alonzo likes basketball, they hope to somehow teach Alonzo to ask others to play this sport with him during class breaks.

School staff hope to teach him to establish eye contact, invite friends to play basketball, participate in playing basketball in an active and friendly manner, demonstrate turn-taking and follow appropriate basketball rules, participate in basketball during break without encouragement, and eventually give positive feedback to the friends he plays with by using appropriate words and gestures.

....

INTRODUCTION

According to the National Institutes of Health (NIH) (2012), the word *autism* has its origin in the Greek word *autos*, which means *self*. "Children with ASD often are self-absorbed and seem to exist in a private world where they are unable to successfully communicate and interact with others" (NIH, 2012, p. 1). Individuals with ASD may have difficulty developing expressive language skills and understanding what others say to them (receptive language). They may also have difficulty communicating nonverbally, such as through facial expressions, eye contact, and hand gestures. Difficulty communicating is a core symptom of ASD.

This chapter will discuss communication deficits commonly exhibited in children with ASD, and it will provide an overview of interventions found to be effective in developing children's communication skills. The chapter will also provide an overview of several interventions designed to develop language skills for children who are either nonverbal or who produce language but have difficulty using it appropriately for social interaction.

CHARACTERISTICS OF COMMUNICATION
IN CHILDREN WITH ASD

The majority of individuals with ASD have difficulty in using language effectively (NIH, 2012). Many have problems understanding the meaning of words, the nuances of vocal tones, and body language. They may demonstrate repetitive or rigid language. Sometimes, they will say things that seem out of context in conversations, such as repeating over and over a word or phrase they've heard (called *echolalia*). A child with autism might show abnormal speech patterns. Their speech has been described as machine-like or monotonic. They might speak in a high-pitched or singsong voice, or they may use robot-like speech. And they may use "stock" phrases they've learned, starting a conversation, for example, by saying, "My name is Jake," even when talking to friends or family (NIH, 2012). Some children with ASD might be completely nonverbal.

By definition, children with ASD show delays and deficits in the acquisition and use of language. Impairments range from almost complete absence of functional communication to adequate linguistic knowledge but impairments in the use of that language in conversation or communication. Their narrow and restricted interests and abilities allow them the capability of delivering "an in-depth monologue about a topic that holds their interest" but may also make them unable to carry on a two-way conversation about the same topic (NIH, 2012, p. 2). They may be able to develop a strong vocabulary in a particular area of interest very quickly and may even be able to read a large number of words before the age of 5 yet not be able to comprehend what they've read. A key diagnostic feature of autism is qualitative impairment in communication.

SOCIAL COMMUNICATION

Individuals with autism show difficulties in social communication and interaction. This is characterized by an unusual approach toward people, including limitations in conversation, and inadequacy in verbal and nonverbal communication (understanding and using body language, gestures, and facial expressions). They have difficulty with imaginary play, sharing, making friends, and developing and maintaining social relations. Individuals with autism also show inadequacy in expressing their inner/emotional states and understanding the feelings of others, apparent indifference and carelessness in looking at the face of others, or reluctance in participating in symbolic play (National Research Council, 2001).

This lack of social skills makes interaction with peers and others very difficult (Akmanoglu, 2015; American Psychiatric Association, 2013; Boyd, Barnett, & More, 2015). Researchers believe that

> impairments in interaction and communication abilities early in life lead to social isolation and difficulty functioning in everyday life in adulthood. By failing to successfully use social skills typically acquired at a young age, adults with ASD often experience mental health problems, poor school achievement, and cognitive deficiencies. (Radley, Jenson, Clark, Hood, & Nicholas, 2014, p. 22)

Impairments in social communication necessitate that effective intervention strategies be used for children with ASD.

Individuals with ASD might have a strong vocabulary and appropriate expressive and receptive language skills yet still experience deficits with social communication. Pragmatic language involves the verbal and nonverbal language skills we use in everyday interactions, often referred to as the "unwritten rules of social communication." Unwritten rules of social communication include things such as making eye contact, nodding one's head in acknowledgement of another person when he or she enters the room, when we speak and what we say, and so forth. Examples of the use of pragmatic language include understanding why a joke is funny; why certain gestures are appropriate in some settings but not others; or understanding what a person means based on his or her body language, gestures, or facial expressions. Most of us are able to make the right decision in a social situation without much thought, but such situations can be painfully difficult for someone with ASD. Individuals with ASD exhibit difficulties with pragmatic language.

JOINT ATTENTION

Joint attention is a pivotal skill in the social-communicative development of infants. A child who can initiate joint attention or follow the joint attention bid of someone else is considered to have "normal development" (Warreyn & Roeyers, 2014). Sharing attention offers the possibility to share experiences and emotions with another person while building and maintaining a relationship with that person. There is evidence in the literature that early joint attention skills are related to later language development (Warreyn & Roeyers, 2014). It is generally accepted that joint attention abilities are impaired or delayed in children with ASD.

Joint attention, or sharing the attention of an object or event with another person, is also an issue for many individuals with ASD. Joint attention, according to the National Research Council (2001) involves coordinating attention between people and objects. Understanding that other people have intentions and attentions that are different from their own and can be shared verbally or nonverbally with their communicative partner is challenging for individuals with ASD. Children with autism have difficulties orienting and attending to a social partner; shifting gaze between people and objects or sharing emotional states with another person; following the gaze and point of another person; and being able to draw another person's attention to objects. "The emergence of joint attention signifies true social understanding and provides the infrastructure for social communication" (Rollins, Campbell, Hoffman, & Self, 2016, p. 2). Joint attention implies an active, shared experience (Boutot & Myles, 2011). Joint attention is difficult for an individual with ASD.

Children who have ASD are often slow to begin talking—or may not learn to talk at all. Others may learn to produce words and sentences but have difficulty using them effectively to accomplish social interactive goals (Paul, 2008). "Because of the centrality of communicative deficits in the expression of ASD, the amelioration of communication problems in children with this syndrome is one of the most important areas of educational service" (Paul, 2008, p. 835). We will now move to discuss several interventions that have been developed to address some of the communication difficulties we see in children with ASD.

ENHANCING COMMUNICATION IN CHILDREN WITH ASD WHO ARE NONVERBAL OR WHO HAVE VERY LIMITED SPEECH

Children who are considered *nonverbal*, or who have not yet developed verbal communication skills, exhibit several key characteristics. These children might show limited attention to others' speech, sometimes failing to respond to their name being spoken; deficits in joint attention; limited range of communicative intentions, such as persuading others to do or not do something for them (requests and protests); failure to point or show for communication; and overall reduced rates of communication (Paul, 2008). Interventions for nonverbal children with ASD are typically grouped into three categories: didactic, naturalistic, and pragmatic.

Didactic methods are based on behaviorist theory and applied techniques, including operant conditioning, shaping, prompting, and more, that we discussed in the applied behavior analysis (ABA) chapter. In didactic approaches, reinforcement is used to shape target behaviors, repetitive periods of drill and practice are utilized, and a trained adult controls all aspects of the interaction (Paul, 2008).

Research has demonstrated that didactic approaches are effective in developing an understanding of language and initiating speech production in children with ASD (Paul, 2008). Intensive instruction uses discrete trials, shaping, prompting, and reinforcement. These approaches rely on interventionists who have a significant level of training to implement. Included in this category is pivotal response training, which we discussed in the ABA chapter, and the TEACCH program (treatment and education of autistic and related communication handicapped children). TEACCH is based on a structured teaching approach, includes parents as cotherapists, uses a communication curriculum, and makes use of behavioral and naturalistic approaches, as well as alternative communication strategies for children who are nonverbal (Paul, 2008).

T.I.P. – Theory Into Practice 10.2

TEACCH

1. Conduct an Internet search to learn about TEACCH.

2. What are the core values of TEACCH?

3. What is structured TEACCHing?

4. What is involved in the TEACCH professional certification program?

Naturalistic methods attempt to incorporate behaviorist principles but in more natural environments using social interactions instead of the typical stimulus–response–reinforcement sequence used in ABA. The aim is to teach skills in informal settings not primarily designed for instruction (Ingersoll, Meyer, Bonter, & Jelinek, 2012). These approaches focus on using intrinsic reinforcers, such as the satisfaction of achieving the desired goal through communication, rather than extrinsic reinforcers, such as a token or a verbal reinforcer. In this approach, for example, the child says, "I want juice," and gets the juice, which is the reinforcer (Paul, 2008). Naturalistic behavioral interventions are based on the application of learning theory, and they use direct prompting and reinforcement within natural contexts to teach social communication skills (Ingersoll et al., 2012).

Finally, the *pragmatic* approach to intervention emphasizes functional communication rather than speech. Functional communication includes the use of gestures, gaze, affect, and vocalizations. In this approach, the adult responds to child initiation by providing rewarding activities as a reinforcer. These approaches strive to develop functional communication. Children are encouraged to use other means of communicating to get their intended message across in the pragmatic approach. This helps them discover the value of communication to regulate others' behavior and control interactions (Paul, 2008). Interventionists follow the child's lead, and they allow the child to choose the course of interaction and the use of materials. The emphasis is on capitalizing on those *teachable moments* that naturally arise during interactions, rather than relying on a predetermined curriculum (Paul, 2008). Social-pragmatic approaches are focused on increasing the adult's responsiveness to the child and establishing balanced turns between the child and the adult (Ingersoll et al., 2012). There is evidence that this type of approach helps increase joint engagement between the parent and child (Ingersoll et al., 2012).

The primary difference between the naturalistic and social-pragmatic approaches is the level of adult prompting used to elicit specific child behaviors (Ingersoll et al., 2012). Naturalistic approaches emphasize direct prompting. Social-pragmatic approaches rely more on adult responsiveness. Ingersoll et al. (2012) investigated the difference in developmental social-pragmatic and naturalistic behavior interventions on elicitation of child language, anticipating that the naturalistic intervention would produce higher rates of overall use of language targets and spontaneous requests than the social-pragmatic approach and that the social-pragmatic approach would produce higher rates of language targets used to comment. All five children in their study increased language targets, used more prompted requests, and showed some improvement in spontaneous requests following the interventions, demonstrating the superiority of the combined condition for increasing expressive language (Ingersoll et al., 2012).

AUGMENTATIVE AND ALTERNATIVE COMMUNICATION STRATEGIES

For children with significantly delayed speech development or for those who can speak but have difficulty with communication competence, alternative methods are introduced that range from low tech to more high tech. Whether they use PECS (Picture Exchange Communication System) or more sophisticated technology like iPads or speech-generating devices, individuals with ASD can be taught other ways to express their intentions or needs. There are a number of options available for supporting communication, social competence, personal independence, academics, and/or transition to work and community. Skype and FaceTime are even useful for allowing service providers to deliver interventions to clients in remote locations (Odom et al., 2015).

Augmentative and alternative communication (AAC) comprises all forms of communication other than oral speech that can be used to express needs, wants, or ideas (Boyd et al., 2015). AAC includes the use of low-tech tools, such as communication boards and graphic symbols, where users can point to what they want or exchange a symbol signifying what they want (PECS), to more high-tech devices, including speech-generating devices, and many things in between. Apple iPads and iPods are gaining popularity, as they are more accessible and affordable, and they are less stigmatizing for the students who use them (Boyd et al., 2015). Some research has shown iPads to be effective in improving social interactions. Several forms of technology are useful for students who are unable to speak and for those who can speak as well.

Generally, technology is appealing to young people. "For many youth with ASD, technology appears to be particularly engaging. Visual presentation of information is a preferred form of learning and support" (Odom et al., 2015, p. 3807). Video presentations can be more effective in conveying information than static presentations for the current generation. A wide variety of options are available for use in clinic, school, and home settings to teach communication skills for verbal children or to assist in communication for those who are unable to speak.

PICTURE EXCHANGE COMMUNICATION SYSTEM (PECS)

PECS is based on the techniques and principles of applied behavior analysis and is considered a "low-tech" option for aiding communication. PECS teaches children to initiate requests by exchanging pictures for desired objects or activities. PECS begins with teaching single-word requests by exchanging a picture for an object and eventually moves to building sentence structure. PECS requires the child to initiate communicative acts by pointing to or handing a picture to an adult to obtain the desired object.

PECS can be easily created in a few minutes. You can use a digital camera or iPhone camera to take pictures of familiar items, or you can find cartoons or pictures from the Internet. To make the pictures more durable, you can laminate them. There are also several commercial PECS solutions that provide an easy way to access pictures for communication. When you make your own, they can be tailored to the child's specific needs, and they are less expensive to create.

T.I.P. – Theory Into Practice 10.3

STOP AND THINK: RESPONSE INHIBITION AND FUNCTIONAL SKILLS

Visit the PECS website at www.pecsusa.com.

1. What are the six phases of PECS?

2. On the website, click the "downloads" tab and then "myths and misconceptions."

3. Imagine that you have been asked to prepare a presentation to your fellow teachers to explain PECS and to discuss the myths and misconceptions commonly associated with PECS. What key points will you make in your presentation?

PECS usually progresses from single words to sentences. When students have learned single-word exchanges, a sentence strip is used to attach pictures to form a sentence. Sentences can be further extended to incorporate additional words, such as verbs, adjectives, and so forth. In the PECS program, a child's expressive communication skills are shaped through the use of reinforcement (Flippin, Reszka, & Watson, 2010). Typically, PECS starts with pictures of desired objects, then moves to pictures with sentence strips (i.e., "I want water"), and finally from pictures to words. PECS can also be used to create visual schedules that provide visual cues about what to do throughout the day.

Using PECS With Eric

Eric is a middle school student who was diagnosed with severe autism. He is able to communicate with a few signs, but he acquires new signs very slowly. The predominant way he communicates is to take the teacher's hand and move it toward the object he wants. Most of his communication appears to serve the function of requesting. A goal for Eric is to learn a different way of communicating.

The team decided to try using PECS with Eric. Since most of his communication at this point involved requesting objects, the team decided to start his PECS lessons utilizing this function of behavior. They also noticed that the objects Eric most often requests are ball, shoe, screwdriver, and water.

The team first removed the objects Eric requests from their original location and replaced each object with a picture. When Eric went to get each of the objects, a teacher would prompt him to hand the picture to her, and she would respond by giving him the object he requested. Once Eric began to exchange the pictures without prompts, the teachers added one

or two other pictures as "distractors" in each location. Eric seemed to have no difficulty selecting the appropriate picture among the choices. The team believed that Eric understood the concepts that a picture represents a specific object.

Once Eric was able to use a picture to request each of the four objects, the pictures were put on a picture board. A few times a day, the pictures were removed from their usual location and placed on the board. When Eric went to the object and could not find it, a teacher would prompt him to get the appropriate picture from his picture board and hand it to the teacher. Eventually these prompts were faded as Eric learned to get the picture from the board and hand it to the teacher to request the desired objects. Eric learned to use the pictures to exchange for objects independently, without any prompts.

To expand Eric's skills, teachers began to add new vocabulary to the picture exchange communication system, focusing on vocabulary that Eric could use in his school and home settings.

T.I.P. – Theory Into Practice 10.4

PECS - TRY IT OUT

Practice using PECS with a friend. Consider recording your "session" on video so you have a record of the process. If your professor has asked you to do so, share your video with him or her.

1. Identify several objects that your friend can request.

2. Remove the objects from their current location, and replace them with a picture of the object.

3. Prompt your friend to hand the picture to you to request the item. Give your friend the object he or she requests.

4. Do this a few more times, gradually fading out the prompts, until your friend can request the items independently with no prompts.

5. Now move the pictures you developed to be placed on a "picture board."

6. Prompt your friend to get the picture from the board and hand it to you to request the desired objects.

7. Gradually fade the prompts until your friend can request items independently.

8. Try to expand your friend's vocabulary by adding new pictures of items he or she can use at home.

TECHNICAL COMMUNICATION AIDS

Children who are nonverbal may benefit from the use of high-tech communication aids. They can be taught to use a computerized voice output communication device to express their needs, request objects, respond to questions, or make comments. For students who are nonverbal or need assistance for communication, specialized speech-generating devices have been developed (Odom et al., 2015). Smartphones, iPod Touches, iPads, and MPS players can help support independent performance of individuals with ASD. There are even virtual reality systems in which people with ASD can participate in social or other activities created with an avatar (Odom et al., 2015).

Researchers have employed a variety of different forms of technology. Traditional technology, such as desktop computers, videotaping performances of participants, and PowerPoint presentations can be useful. Other studies have employed smartphones, electronic tablets, electronic interactive whiteboards, iPad or iPhone applications, and virtual reality to deliver social and communication skills training (Odom et al., 2015).

Speech output devices are a commonly used option with students who are unable to produce speech. There are voice output communication aids (VOCAs) or speech generating devices (SGDs) that enable the user to speak. These types of devices are considered aided systems, and they are portable electronic-aided devices that usually combine digitized or synthesized speech with static visual symbols, such as line drawings, photographs, or abstract symbols (Ganz et al., 2012).

Technology has opened the way to communication for a well-known young lady named Carly Fleishmann. For many years, she was completely unable to speak or to make her needs known. She got a voice output data device, which she says changed her life. You can read more about Carly in a blog, which excerpts her book, found on the Autism Speaks website at https://www.autismspeaks.org/blog/2012/04/09/technology-opens-door-communication-carly. Learn more about her on her website: http://carlysvoice.com/home. She is a young woman with a fascinating story to tell. The power of using voice output devices should not be underestimated.

T.I.P. – Theory Into Practice 10.5

LEARN ABOUT CARLY FLEISHMANN

Learn all you can about Carly Fleishmann, who is a spokesperson for the use of voice output devices.

- See her website and blog mentioned previously: https://www.autismspeaks.org/blog/2012/04/09/technology-opens-door-communication-carly and http://carlysvoice.com/home

- Also visit YouTube to view several videos about Carly, at https://www.youtube.com/user/CarlyFleischmann. We especially recommend this one: https://www.youtube.com/watch?v=KmDGvquzn2k

- Please read and view more than we have suggested here.

After reading and viewing several informational pieces about Carly, reflect on what you've seen and read. Write down your thoughts about using voice output devices. What are the pros, and do you see any cons against such communication? Consider sharing your reflections with your classmates.

- Consider writing a blog about your thoughts and submitting it to a special education blog site, such as www.thespecialedprofessor.com.

ENHANCING COMMUNICATION IN CHILDREN WITH ASD WHO SPEAK

A defining characteristic of ASD is difficulty with communication. Children with ASD may experience delays in the onset of verbal expressive language, or they might never become verbal. While some children with ASD have acquired basic language skills, they may have significant challenges with communicative competence (Paul, 2008). They might use echolalia, which is the imitation of what has been heard, either immediately after it is spoken or at a later time. They may show deficits in prosody, rate, loudness, pitch, quality, or use of stress.

Pragmatics, or the appropriate use of language in social situations, is a prominent aspect of communication deficits found in children with ASD (Paul, 2008).

Children who have ASD are less likely than children with typical development to initiate communication; they show a reduced interest in language spoken to them; and they are less likely to respond to communication bids of peers (Paul, 2008). They might use irrelevant details, make inappropriate topic shifts, perseverate on a particular topic, be unresponsive to partner cues, speak in an excessively formal style, or display discourse that seems scripted. Thus, even if an individual has verbal language, he or she will continue to need instruction in the pragmatic aspects of communication (Boutot & Myles, 2011).

A variety of treatment approaches have been developed to address the communication of children with ASD. The most commonly used treatment options were derived from the field of behavior analysis and are based on theories of learning and operant conditioning (Mohammadzaheri, Koegel, Rezaee, & Rafiee, 2014). In this section, we will discuss ABA, PRT, video modeling, and script training as possible interventions that were developed to teach communication skills to children with ASD.

APPLIED BEHAVIOR ANALYSIS

ABA as an intervention method is useful for children who are vocal. The focus is primarily on the improvement of language, including vocabulary and sentence structure. One example of an ABA approach used to teach language skills is *Teach Me Language* (Freeman & Dake, 1997). The program provides a carefully structured curriculum to target grammar, syntax, and advanced narrative skills. The focus of the program is on repetition, using different examples over and over again with the same structure. Since children with ASD do not learn well through auditory channels, *Teach Me Language* capitalizes on students' visual abilities to teach them oral language (Freeman & Dake, 1997). "It is IMPERATIVE to work on the deficit, which is auditory understanding, while at the same time relying on the strength, which is visual processing" (Freeman & Dake, 1997, p. 9). Slowly, visual cues are faded out so the child comes to rely on auditory processing.

ABA approaches can be effective in producing behavioral changes, but the interventions are not without difficulties. As discussed in another chapter, ABA approaches are highly structured. They define intervention targets, and they address these behaviors through many trials of antecedent–behavior–consequence chains presented repeatedly to promote success (Mohammadzaheri et al., 2014). Drill-based repetition of learning trials is prescribed, requiring as many as 40 hours per week over several months.

There are at least three difficulties with ABA approaches, including extremely slow gains (many trials are often required to teach a single word); gains that are not generalized; and sometimes children are not motivated to be involved in the teaching sessions (Mohammadzaheri et al., 2014). Because ABA is so time consuming and the gains can be so limited, other interventions have been developed that are more child directed. Pivotal response treatment (PRT) is one such approach, based on operant teaching principles to target a wide range of deficits in social skills and communication, but it is carried out in a more natural environment.

PIVOTAL RESPONSE TREATMENT

Pivotal response treatment has been used in the research literature to teach children with autism to increase their social-communication skills. PRT is an effective way to increase functional communication skills, and in most cases, parents are the implementation agents. PRT shares many of the same underpinnings of ABA, but PRT it is most often utilized in the context of everyday routines and natural environments rather than in clinical settings. It is based upon applied behavior analysis, and it focuses on parent involvement in the child's natural contexts. PRT was discussed to a greater extent in another chapter, so we will provide only a brief overview here.

Social initiations, such as asking questions, are important for long-term outcomes for children, but these skills of verbal and nonverbal initiations are often limited in children with autism (Koegel, Bradshaw, Ashbaugh, & Koegel, 2014). Failing to initiate questions may severely impact language development. "This pervasive problem of a lack of question-asking may severely limit verbal learning opportunities and present as pragmatically inappropriate during social interactions" (Koegel et al., 2014, p. 816). Given the importance of question asking, Koegel et al. (2014) explored the use of PRT with students with ASD.

VIDEO MODELING

Video modeling is discussed in more depth in a separate chapter of this textbook; thus, this chapter will provide just an overview. In video modeling, short videos are used to illustrate the use of language in a particular situation, such as asking for a certain food item in the lunch line. The student watches the video with the instructor, discusses the scenario, and then practices by role-playing with the instructor, eventually moving to trying out the newly learned skills in a new setting. A key benefit of video modeling is that it takes advantage of the visual processing strengths common to learners with ASD. Video modeling is a strategy that has been proved effective through several studies (Akmanoglu, 2015; Kikopolous & Keenan, 2004; Özerk and Özerk, 2015; Radley et al., 2014) to be an effective strategy for increasing communication skills.

SCRIPT TRAINING

Another intervention for addressing deficits in communication in children with ASD is script training. Scripts serve as a model of appropriate language tailored for specific situations, and they can be presented in written form, audio recordings, or video models. In script training, children read the scripts and recite them aloud to their communication partners. After improvements in communication are noted, the script is gradually faded to promote independent communication skills (Ledbetter-Cho et al., 2015). Ledbetter-Cho et al. (2015) provided script training to children with ASD to improve peer-to-peer communication during a social activity (playing with toys). They found that all three participants in their study were able to improve their peer-to-peer communication.

Garcia-Albea, Reeve, Reeve, and Brothers (2014) pointed out that many children with autism have difficulty initiating vocal interactions and engaging in spontaneous speech (a verbal response in the absence of verbal stimuli). Spontaneous speech helps naturalize children's speech, permits social interactions, and allows children to obtain information, objects, and attention (Garcia-Albea et al., 2014). Unfortunately, even children with autism who have received intensive language interventions may lack spontaneous speech. They might be able to answer questions and make requests, but they are unlikely to initiate or pursue conversations with others (Garcia-Albea et al., 2014).

TEACHING COMMUNICATION IN THE INCLUSIVE CLASSROOM

More and more children with autism are included in general-education classrooms. Yet many teachers in these classrooms do not have prior training and knowledge to teach children with ASD (Min & Wah, 2011). Many students with ASD require specialized, visually supported instruction to prompt their learning, and they benefit from tangible and concrete reinforcement to motivate them to learn and participate in classroom activities (Min & Wah, 2011). Since speech, language, and communication skills are often impaired in individuals with ASD, and these impairments can impede learning and socialization with others in school, we should strive to find ways to meet their needs in inclusive classrooms and allow them access to the standard curriculum.

1. Thoroughly understand children's characteristics, strengths, and deficits.

2. Prompt children to participate in back-and-forth interactions to develop their joint attention skills (e.g., rolling a ball to each other, taking turns putting puzzles together, taking turns in games on the playground, etc.).

3. Include children in picture-matching games to develop their ability to make symbolic associations.

4. Teach children how to use PECS to request desired objects and activities.

5. Use picture cues as much as possible.

6. Pair gestures with speech as much as possible.

7. Through modeling of verbal interactions provided by adults, children learn to produce speech sounds, imitate the word productions, and link the spoken words to produce sentences. Be intentional about modeling verbal behaviors, and help children participate in verbal interactions to help them develop their speech.

8. Promote social engagement in natural environments: in the classroom, at lunch, and on the playground.

9. Think of prompts you could use to get students to initiate social interactions (e.g., "Ask your friend what he or she will do tonight when he or she gets home." "Ask your friend what he or she did over the weekend." "Ask your friend what he or she had for lunch today."). When students use the prompts, find and use an appropriate reinforcement.

10. Use prompting and reinforcement to increase communication skills.

11. Try video modeling or script training to increase communication skills.

PARTNERING WITH FAMILIES TO TEACH COMMUNICATION

Parents play a pivotal role as interaction partners who are fundamental to the provision of daily communicative learning opportunities. Social engagements between children and their caregivers serve as a central context for learning. It is well established that children with autism demonstrate deficits in joint attention and other social communication skills that impact the child's awareness of others and their ability to coordinate attention between themselves and a partner (Shire et al., 2015). Even though children with ASD may spend limited time jointly engaged, make fewer social initiations, and often reject their parents' bids for attention, it is worth exploring ways that parents can learn to facilitate shared interactions with their children with ASD.

Because of the importance of involving parents as intervention agents, a number of promising programs have been designed for parents to implement at home to support their child's development. Shire et al. (2015) worked with 61 children and their families to implement an intervention designed to increase joint attention, symbolic play, and social engagement. Following a brief training period, parents were able to implement a range of interventions at home, and their children's mean time jointly engaged increased as a result of the intervention, as did play diversity and flexibility (Shire et al., 2015).

Stadnick, Stahmer, and Brookman-Frazee (2015) also investigated a parent-mediated intervention targeting social communication that was implemented in a community-based setting. They saw significant improvements in child communication skills following their 12-week intervention. Stadnick et al. (2015) used the Project ImPACT intervention, which focuses on reciprocity, social engagement, and shared affect and follows a prescribed set of naturalistic teaching strategies used throughout daily activities and routines. Project ImPACT is a parent-mediated intervention that can be used throughout their child's day, increasing the intensity of the intervention and promoting generalization (Ingersoll & Wainer, 2013).

The most striking aspect of Project ImPACT is its collaborative nature. Parents and trainers engage in collaborative goal setting to identify treatment targets. Trainers present new intervention techniques, discuss how the treatments can be useful for addressing the child's specific language goals, model the techniques with the child while the parent watches, and allow parents to practice with positive and corrective feedback. At the end of each training session, parents and trainers develop a homework plan for the parent to carry out between sessions (Ingersoll & Wainer, 2013).

A study worth mentioning here is the Gengoux et al. (2015) study using PRT as a parent-mediated intervention. Since PRT usually requires significant child–clinician interaction, which can be time-consuming and costly, Gengoux and colleagues trained parents to implement PRT. Results of their study indicated that children whose parents received PRT training had gains in communication at the end of the treatment, and these gains were maintained in a 3-month follow-up (Gengoux et al., 2015). Since "parents spend significant time with their children and therefore have ample opportunities to implement PRT throughout the day," programs in which parents are trained to implement PRT deserve our attention (Gengoux et al., 2015, p. 2894).

SUMMARY STATEMENTS

- Difficulty communicating is a core symptom of ASD.

- Individuals with ASD exhibit difficulties with pragmatic language.

- Children with autism have difficulties orienting and attending to a social partner; shifting gaze between people and objects or sharing emotional states with another person; following the gaze and point of another person; and being able to draw another person's attention to objects.

- For children with significantly delayed speech development or for those who can speak but have difficulty with communication competence, alternative methods are introduced that range from low tech to more high tech.

- PECS focuses on teaching children to initiate requests by exchanging pictures for desired objects or activities.

- Children who are nonverbal may benefit from the use of high-tech communication aids. They can be taught to use a computerized voice output communication device to express their needs, request objects, respond to questions, or make comments.

- ABA, as an intervention method, is useful for children who are able to speak. The focus is primarily on the improvement of language, including vocabulary and sentence structure.

- PRT shares many of the same underpinnings of ABA; however, it is most often utilized in the context of everyday routines and natural environments rather than in clinical settings, and it usually focuses on parent involvement in the child's natural contexts.

- In video modeling, the student watches the video with the instructor, discusses the scenario, and then practices by role-playing with the instructor, eventually moving to trying out the newly learned skills in a new setting.

- Because of the importance of involving parents as intervention agents, a number of promising programs have been designed for parents to implement at home to support their child's development.

WHAT WOULD YOU DO?

Look back at the case study about Alonzo presented at the beginning of the chapter. Based on what you have read in this chapter, what you have read in previous chapters, and your own experiences, how would you respond to the following questions?

1. What strategy or approach would you recommend for Alonzo to help him initiate play or conversations with his peers, and why?

2. Do you agree with the staff that Alonzo likes basketball and that it would be a good appropriate reinforcer or instructional activity? Why, or why not?

3. How would you determine what kind of activities or objects are the best reinforcers for Alonzo?

4. What kinds of reinforcers would you use with Alonzo?

5. How would you respond to Alonzo's general-education teacher, who is asking about how to help with his communication skills?

6. How would you involve Alonzo's parents in implementing an intervention to help Alonzo develop his communication skills?

CHAPTER REFLECTION QUESTIONS

1. What is *joint attention*, and how does it impact communication?

2. How would you define pragmatic language and describe how it is used in communication?

3. What are some low-tech and high-tech augmentative and alternative communication systems? Which one are you most likely to try with a student in the future?

4. How does one implement PECS?

5. What is the difference between ABA and PRT, and how they can be used to increase communication for students with ASD?

6. If a parent asked you to try video modeling or script training to help with her child's communication skills, how would you respond?

7. What strategies would you suggest to a general-education teacher who wants to develop communication skills in her students with ASD?

8. How can we involve parents in developing communication skills for children with ASD?

RECOMMENDED RESOURCES

Websites

- The Art of Autism. The value of art therapy for those on the autism spectrum. Available at http://the-art-of-autism.com/the-value-of-art-therapy-for-those-on-the-autism-spectrum

- Ed Web.net. *Project ImPACT (Improving Parents as Communication Teachers) for children with autism.* Available at http://home.edweb.net/project-impact-for-children-with-autism

- Teaching.monster.com. *22 tips for teaching students with autism spectrum disorders.* Available at http://teaching.monster.com/benefits/articles/8761-22-tips-for-teaching-students-with-autism-spectrum-disorders

Articles/Publications

Eisenberg, B. (2015). *5 ways to encourage communication with a nonverbal child diagnosed with autism.* Retrieved from http://www.friendshipcircle.org/blog/2015/04/21/5-ways-to-encourage-communication-with-a-non-verbal-child-diagnosed-with-autism

Freeman, S., & Dake, L. (1997). *Teach me language: A language manual for children with autism, Asperger's syndrome and related developmental disorders.* Canada: SKF Books.

REFERENCES

Akmanoglu, N. (2015). Effectiveness of teaching naming facial expression to children with autism via video modeling. *Educational Sciences Theory and Practice, 15*(2), 519–537.

American Psychiatric Association. (2013). *Diagnostic and statistical manual of mental disorders* (5th ed.). Washington, DC: Author.

Boutot, E. A., & Myles, B. S. (2011). *Autism spectrum disorders: Foundations, characteristics, and effective strategies.* Upper Saddle River, NJ: Pearson Education.

Boyd, T. K., Barnett, J. E. H., & More, C. (2015). Evaluating iPad technology for enhancing communication skills of children with autism spectrum disorders. *Intervention in School and Clinic, 51*(1), 19–27.

Flippin, M., Reszka, S., & Watson, L. R. (2010). Effectiveness of the Picture Exchange Communication System (PECS) on communication and speech for children with autism spectrum disorders: A meta-analysis. *American Journal of Speech-Language Pathology, 19*(2), 178. doi:10.1044/1058-0360(2010/09-0022)

Freeman, S., & Dake, L. (1997). *Teach me language: A language manual for children with* autism, Asperger's syndrome and related developmental disorders. Canada: SKF Books.

Ganz, J. B., Earles-Vollrath, T. L., Heath, A. K., Parker, R. I., Rispoli, M. J., & Duran, J. B. (2012). A meta-analysis of single case research studies on aided augmentative and alternative communication systems with individuals with autism spectrum disorders. *Journal of Autism and Developmental Disorders, 42,* 60–74.

Garcia-Albea, E., Reeve, S. A., Reeve, K. F., & Brothers, J. (2014). Using audio script fading and multiple-exemplar training to increase vocal interactions in children with autism. *Journal of Applied Behavior Analysis, 47,* 325–343.

Gengoux, G. W., Berquist, K. L, Salzman, E., Schapp, S., Phillips, J. M., Frazier, T. W., ...Hardan, A. Y. (2015). Pivotal response treatment parent training for autism: Findings from a 3-month follow-up evaluation. *Journal of Autism and Developmental Disorders, 45,* 2889–2898.

Ingersoll, B., Meyer, K., Bonter, N., & Jelinek, S. (2012). A comparison of developmental social-pragmatic and naturalistic behavioral interventions on language use and social engagement in children with autism. *Journal of Speech, Language, and Hearing Research, 55,* 1301–1313.

Ingersoll, B., & Wainer, A. (2013). Initial efficacy of project ImPACT: A parent-mediated social communication intervention for young children with ASD. *Journal of Autism and Developmental Disorders, 43,* 2943–2952.

Kikopolous, C. K., & Keenan, M. K. (2004). Effects of video modeling on social initiations by children with autism. *Journal of Applied Behavior Analysis, 37*(1), 93–96.

Koegel, R. L., Bradshaw, J. L., Ashbaugh, K., & Koegel, L. K. (2014). Improving question-asking initiations in young children with autism using pivotal response treatment. *Journal of Autism and Developmental Disorders, 44,* 816–827.

Ledbetter-Cho, K., Lang, R., Davenport, K., Moore, M., Lee, A., Howell, A.,... O'Reilly, M. (2015). Effects of script training on the peer-to-peer communication of children with autism spectrum disorder. *Journal of Applied Behavior Analysis, 48,* 785–799.

Min, L. H., & Wah, L. L. (2011). Teaching of speech, language, and communication skills for young children with severe autism disorders: What do educators need to know? *New Horizons in Education, 59*(3), 16–27.

Mohammadzaheri, F., Koegel, L. K., Rezaee, M., & Rafiee, S. M. (2014). A randomized clinical trial comparison between pivotal response treatment (PRT) and structured applied behavior analysis intervention for children with autism. *Journal of Autism and Developmental Disorders, 44,* 2769–2777.

National Institutes of Health (NIH), U.S. Department of Health and Human Services, & National Institute on Deafness and Other Communication Disorders. (2012). *Communication problems in children with autism spectrum disorders.* Retrieved July 25, 2016, from https://www.nidcd.nih.gov/sites/default/files/Documents/health/voice/NIDCD-Communication-Problems-in-Children-with-Autism-FS_0.pdf

National Research Council (U.S.), National Academy of Sciences, & U.S. Department of Education. (2001). *Educating children with autism.* Washington, DC: National Academy Press.

Odom, S. L., Thompson, J. L., Hedges, S., Boyd, B. A., Dykstra, J. R., Duda, M. A.,... Bord, A. (2015). Technology-aided interventions and instruction for adolescents with autism spectrum disorder. *Journal of Autism and Developmental Disorders, 45,* 3805–3819.

Özerk, M., & Özerk, K. (2015). A bilingual child learns social communication skills through video modeling—A single case study in a Norwegian school setting. *International Journal of Elementary Education, 8*(1), 551–566.

Paul, R. (2008). Interventions to improve communication in autism. *Child and Adolescent Psychiatric Clinics of North America, 17*, 835–856.

Radley, K. C., Jenson, W., Clark, E., Hood, J., & Nicholas, P. (2014). Using a multimedia social skills intervention to increase social engagement of young children with autism spectrum disorder. *Intervention in School and Clinic, 50*, 22–28.

Rollins, P. R., Campbell, M., Hoffman, R. T., & Self, K. (2016). A community-based early intervention program for toddlers with autism spectrum disorders. *Autism, 20*(2), 219–232.

Shire, S. Y., Goods, K., Shih, W., Distefano, C., Kaiser, A., Wright, C., . . . Kasari, C. (2015). Parents' adoption of social communication intervention strategies: Families including children with autism spectrum disorder who are minimally verbal. *Journal of Autism and Developmental Disorders, 45*, 1712–1724.

Stadnick, N. A., Stahmer, A., & Brookman-Frazee, L. (2015). Preliminary effectiveness of Project ImPACT: A parent-mediated intervention for children with autism spectrum disorder delivered in a community program. *Journal of Autism and Developmental Disorders, 45*, 2092–2104.

Warreyn, P., & Roeyers, H. (2014). See what I see, do as I do: Promoting joint attention and imitation in preschoolers with autism spectrum disorder. *Autism, 18*(6), 658–671.

Building Academic Skills: Instructional Approaches

11

CASE STUDY

Christian is a 12-year-old student diagnosed with ASD. He is very interested in the Civil War, and he knows many facts about the battles, weapons used, transportation, and uniforms. He has watched every Civil War movie or documentary he can find. He has also read a great deal about the Civil War, and his comprehension of what he reads on this topic is very high. He has difficulty with comprehension when he reads about other topics in his language arts class, especially fiction. Christian does especially well with tasks related to nonfiction texts. When he reads fiction material, especially on his own during silent reading, he has difficulty understanding story lines and character motivation. He understands the literal meaning of events in a text, but he has difficulty interpreting events or making inferences.

Christian receives instruction in general-education classrooms for most of the day, with the exception of math. He receives special education instruction for math. Christian's teachers report that he does very well with small-group instruction, but when left on his own for silent reading, he has difficulty attending to the task and working independently.

Christian is very sociable, and he has made a few friends at school, yet he struggles to find friends who are as interested in the Civil War to the extent that he is. He is happiest when he is reading about the Civil War, watching a movie or documentary about it, or when he is discussing anything about it.

Christian has begun falling behind in language arts. His teacher is not aware of any strategies to use to increase comprehension and the many other components to

LEARNER OBJECTIVES

After reading this chapter, the learner should be able to do the following:

1. Describe the necessary instructional components for students with ASD.

2. Explain why reading comprehension and writing can be difficult for students with ASD, and describe several strategies to aid in developing these skills.

3. Explain why mathematics can be challenging for students with ASD, and describe several strategies for developing math skills.

4. Explain how graphic organizers are useful as instructional strategies for students with ASD.

5. Explain the rationale for involving parents in instruction for students with ASD, and describe one way to facilitate parent involvement.

language arts. Christian's school has adopted the Common Core State Standards, and his teachers are at a loss as to how to help him meet the high expectations of critical thinking and problem solving inherent in the standards. Writing is also a particular challenge for Christian. Organizing his thoughts and getting them onto paper for an assignment is one of Christian's areas of difficulty.

....

INTRODUCTION

Students with ASD may display a number of characteristics that make it challenging for teachers to address their academic needs. Many students with ASD have difficulty with verbal or auditory information that has been read or heard, and therefore, visual supports are often necessary. Others have challenges with explaining the main idea of a text or drawing inferences, for example, and would require some level of support. Young students with ASD may have difficulty imitating others, which presents challenges to learning to produce words by blending sounds, for example, and would again require instructional supports. Difficulty with social interactions might make participation in group work settings a challenge, and therefore, the teacher should make adaptations and modifications for this type of instruction, if necessary.

Supporting the academic skills of students with ASD is important, given the expectation that they be given access to the general-education curriculum and are expected to succeed in various content areas (Spencer, Evmenova, Boon, & Hayes-Harris, 2014). Of course, no single instructional approach for teaching students with ASD is successful for all students. There are approaches to instruction that have proved to be successful for students with ASD that we can suggest you try. In general, instruction for students with ASD should be systematic, it should include much use of visual supports, and it should include appropriate modifications and adaptations.

EFFECTIVE COMPONENTS OF INSTRUCTIONAL PRACTICES

Instruction for students with ASD should be systematic, intensive, follow a specific instructional format, promote generalization, and include appropriate modifications and accommodations (Carnahan, Williamson, & Christman, 2011; Iovannone, Dunlap, Huber, & Kincaid, 2003). Also remember that students with ASD have difficulty understanding and remembering lengthy verbal instructions. Keep verbal instructions brief, and consider pairing verbal instructions with visual supports as well. Keep your language simple and concrete. Most important, make sure the work environment is organized.

INDIVIDUALIZED SUPPORTS AND SERVICES

The IEP determines the appropriate level of support, and choices about the curriculum can be made from those determinations. Some students require minimal modifications and adaptations while others require more significant supports. Determining the most appropriate intensity and level of instruction should be based on a consideration of family preferences, the child's preferences and special interests, and a focus on the child's strengths and areas of need (Iovannone et al., 2003).

Strategies for supporting high rates of engagement for students with ASD are important. Engagement, or the time that students attend to and interact with the environment, is one of the best predictors of positive student outcomes (Iovannone et al., 2003). Engagement may require deliberate and careful planning, systematic use of materials, and capitalizing on student interest, and it may be possible to occur in one-on-one instruction, independent work time, or during group instruction (Iovannone et al., 2003). Ways to support active engagement include PRT (which we detailed in another chapter) and using preferred objects and natural reinforcers to increase motivation. Incorporating the child's unique interests into instructional activities is also an effective method to enhance engagement in activities.

SYSTEMATIC INSTRUCTION

Another critical component of instruction for students with ASD involves providing systematic instruction, which is carefully planned and orchestrated in ways that meet the needs of students with ASD and promotes high levels of engagement. Strain, Schwartz, and Barton (2011) had this to say about systematic instruction:

> Systematic and effective instruction does not just mean that educators have toolboxes full of strategies that have been identified as evidence based by a national panel. It requires that educators know how to identify the instructional needs of their students, develop instructional plans to address those needs, and then match the needs of their students with the instructional strategies they have at their disposal. (p. 324)

Once the plan is developed and instruction is implemented, teachers then collect data to show evidence of progress or lack thereof. If the current strategy is not yielding the desired outcome, based on the data analysis, then changes should be made (Strain et al., 2011).

STRUCTURED LEARNING ENVIRONMENTS

Highly structured learning environments and materials are essential for students with ASD (Carnahan et al., 2011; Iovannone et al., 2003). The structured environment permits a student to predict what is currently happening in the learning process and to anticipate what will occur next as well as upcoming transitions. Visual schedules to organize sequences of time and activities and to facilitate transitions are especially helpful, as is the use of labels and arrangement of physical boundaries (Iovannone et al., 2003).

To create a structured environment, make sure to build visual boundaries to define the work area. Help students understand the rules and routines, schedules, and activities during the school day. When activities are clearly organized, with designated beginnings and endings, we enable students to stay focused and organized (Carnahan et al., 2011). Consider color-coding and using to-do and finished boxes, binders, or folders and checklists to help promote organization. Creating visual cues, such as helping students identify what to do when they need help, helps students know what to do. A more thorough discussion of classroom organization is provided in a separate chapter of this text.

INDIVIDUAL VERSUS SMALL- OR LARGE-GROUP INSTRUCTION

Using multiple formats of instruction will facilitate greater learning. Recognize that some students will be better served in a group setting while others will benefit from quiet, one-on-one instruction where they are removed from noise and/or distractions. The student's learning style should determine the appropriate format for instruction. Because children with ASD have difficulties with social and communicative skills, many researchers recommend that initial skill development is best accomplished through individual instruction. Still others find success in small-group formats for children with ASD.

Carnahan, Musti-Rao, and Bailey (2009) pointed out that because many children with ASD have difficulty engaging in social communication interactions with others, initiating and maintaining attention to activities, and processing information from the environment, teachers tend to excluded them from group instruction. While students benefit greatly from one-on-one individualized instruction, it is costly for staff, in terms of the time commitment and significant training required of the teacher (Carnahan, Musti-Rao, & Bailey, 2009; Ledford & Wehby, 2015). Strategies that require less intensive staffing, such as small-group instruction, warrant our consideration (Carnahan, Musti-Rao, & Bailey, 2009).

GENERALIZATION

Students with ASD have difficulty with generalization, or applying the skills they learned to new or novel situations. Finding ways to perform newly learned skills in natural environments should be a priority when instructing students with ASD. Skills should be generalized across time, settings, material, and persons. By *time*, we mean maintenance of the skills over time, even after instruction has concluded. Across *settings* means students have the ability to apply the skill to an environment outside the one in which it was acquired. For example, a student who learned to initiate a social interaction in the classroom should be able to utilize that skill on the playground or in the community. Generalization across *materials* means the student can transfer the skill to other examples of the same item. Finally, generalization across *persons* means the student can apply the skill regardless of who is in the environment and with whom the student is interacting.

MODIFICATIONS AND ACCOMMODATIONS

Modifications and accommodations allow children with ASD equal access to instruction and assessment and provide necessary supports for learning.

A *modification* refers to a change in what is being taught or expected from the student. One example of a modification is asking students with ASD to produce a different level of work than other students, according to his or her abilities. An *accommodation* is a change that helps a student work around the disability. It is a support or alteration that allows the student to demonstrate his or her knowledge in an alternate fashion. Allowing a student who has challenges with writing things down to give his answers orally is one example of an accommodation. The student is still expected to know the same material, but he can show his knowledge of the information in a different way.

ASSISTIVE TECHNOLOGY

We've seen in previous chapters how assistive technology can be used to develop communication and social skills in students with ASD. Assistive technology (AT) refers to any item, piece of equipment, product, or anything that is modified or customized that is used to increase or improve functional capabilities of a person with a disability. In addition to communication and social skills, AT can be used to teach writing, spelling, reading, mathematics, study/organizational skills, listening, behavior, and various functional skills (i.e., dressing, toileting, eating, etc.). The chart below shows several low-tech and high-tech options for teaching academic and writing skills.

Assistive Technology for Academic Skills	
No-Tech	✓ Pictures
	✓ Break card
	✓ Highlighters
	✓ File folders
	✓ Writing grips
	✓ Scribe
	✓ Schedule
	✓ Workstation
	✓ Checklist
	✓ Self-assessment scale
Low-Tech	✓ One-message voice output
	✓ Multiple-message voice output
	✓ Communication aid (e.g., Go Talk)

Assistive Technology for Academic Skills	
	✓ Tape recorder
	✓ Timer
	✓ Electronic reminder
	✓ Watch
	✓ Speaking speller
High-Tech	✓ Voice output communication aid with dynamic display
	✓ Talking word processor programs
	✓ Video camera
	✓ Computer
	✓ Software
	✓ Websites
	✓ Adaptive hardware
	✓ Scanner
	✓ Smartphone

VISUAL APPROACHES

We strongly recommend that using visual aids be the first thing you try with a student with ASD for instruction in any content area. Written or picture cues can help students with ASD to learn many different skills, from academic to social, behavioral, and self-management. Information presented orally may pose problems for students with ASD. It can be difficult for them to process oral language, and it may be difficult for the student to attend to relevant information and block out background stimulation. Using visual supports helps the individual with ASD focus on the message. Visual aids can range from simple to abstract. You can use real objects or situations, copies, color photographs, color pictures, black-and-white pictures, line drawings, or written language.

Visual supports can be used to accomplish a variety of things in the classroom. They can be used to organize the student's activity through daily schedules, activity checklists, calendars, or choice boards. They can be used to provide directions or instructions for the student through things such as visual displays of assignments, file cards with directions for specific activities or tasks, or written instructions for learning new information. They can also be used to label objects, charts, containers, lists, or message centers. The use of visual supports allows students to better understand instruction.

1. In this chapter and in others, we've discussed how beneficial visual supports can be for our students with ASD.

2. Interview your fieldwork teacher to find out what types of visual supports he or she uses regularly. Ask why he or she chose these particular strategies.

3. On your own, observe the visual supports in the classroom as students make use of them. In your opinion, do you think they are helpful? What student behaviors can you notice that indicate such visual supports are helpful?

4. What other strategies might be helpful for these particular students in your fieldwork class?

COMMON CORE STATE STANDARDS

No discussion of educating students with ASD would be complete without addressing the topic of the Common Core State Standards (CCSS). The CCSS were developed for the purpose of regulating educational standards across states so that all students would be adequately prepared to meet the demands of colleges and businesses of the future (Marsh, 2015). These standards were drafted by teachers and educational experts to provide consistent guidelines about what every K–12 student should master in English language arts and mathematics, with a focus on critical thinking, problem solving, and analytical skills. While not every state uses CCSS, we would still like to give some attention to the CCSS and the difficulty that students with ASD have with reaching the expectations of the CCSS.

Students with ASD "should not be denied access to the same skills sets; however, how and at what rate and level they acquire these skills must be individualized" (Marsh, 2015, p. 67). To address the CCSS, we must also be attentive to strategies for helping our students with ASD meet these standard expectations. Students with disabilities are still expected to follow grade-appropriate standards, but they are permitted to respond at their ability-appropriate standard (Marsh, 2015). This means that a fifth-grade student with ASD might be expected to follow the standard that is worded as follows: "Determine the meaning of words and phrases as they are used in a text, including figurative language such as metaphors and similes." Responding at their ability level may be more closely aligned with the kindergarten standard that asks students to "ask and answer questions about unknown words in a text."

The teacher in the prior situation might use developmentally appropriate literature to introduce the concepts, with clear illustrations, to address the standard interpreted from earlier levels of the same standard, which are better suited to the student's abilities (Marsh, 2015). Teachers of students with disabilities could use a variety of instructional supports to present the standards in multiple ways. Teachers can be flexible in both their presentation of learning opportunities and in the ways students are allowed to demonstrate their knowledge, depending on the student's individual learning style and academic or social needs (Marsh, 2015).

Family Voices 11.1

"Common Core . . . who invented this craziness? I get that teachers have to adhere to the standards. But it seems that they are forced to ignore the unique strengths that my child has, and they can't accommodate for the areas of weakness under Common Core."

Extensive use of visual cues, such as pictures from the story, can be very helpful for helping students with ASD meet expectations for the CCSS. Strategies can be modified for older students or for those requiring fewer supports, for example, by providing multiple-choice written answers on cards projected in a slideshow instead of pictures (Marsh, 2015). Older students may also enjoy learning opportunities in the form of popular television quiz shows (e.g., "calling a friend," as in the show, "Who Wants to Be a Millionaire?"). Another helpful strategy for addressing the CCSS—or any content for that matter—is to use the student's unique interests or preoccupations. When students have an intense interest in a topic, such as computers or trains or weather, it may be difficult for them to stop thinking about these things long enough to focus on a lesson that does not relate to their interest (Marsh, 2015).

T.I.P. – Theory Into Practice 11.3

COMMON CORE STATE STANDARDS

1. In addition to what you've read in this chapter about the Common Core State Standards, conduct an Internet search to find all you can that will add to your understanding of the concept. (Try using "Common Core State Standards for students with ASD" as your search term, for example.)

2. What additional ways can you find about how we can help our students with ASD meet the standards?

3. Develop a PowerPoint presentation to keep for future reference. Consider sharing the presentation with your peers or even your fieldwork teacher or other teachers at the school.

TEACHING IN THE CONTENT AREAS

There are several approaches to supporting a student with ASD in the content areas. Finding an approach that is helpful first requires us to understand that each student has a unique learning style, and we should therefore tailor the approach to that particular student's needs. Observe your students to notice their strengths and areas of needs, and seek to capitalize on those strengths when approaching any intervention.

TEACHING READING

Students with ASD may demonstrate sufficient print awareness and decoding skills, but they may not meet grade-level expectations in word recognition and reading comprehension (Carnahan, Williamson, & Haydon, 2009; Spector & Cavanaugh, 2015; Spencer et al., 2014; Whalon & Hart, 2011b). Deficits in reading achievement may be linked, in part, to the cognitive, behavioral, and verbal limitations associated with ASD, although several researchers believe it may "reflect insufficient access to the instructional conditions that are essential to success in beginning reading" (Spector & Cavanaugh, 2015, p. 337).

Spector and Cavanaugh (2015) believe that students at risk for reading difficulties should receive instruction from teachers who have significant preparation and knowledge to work with students with ASD, first and foremost. "Teaching reading is rocket science," Spector and Cavanaugh (2015, p. 337) asserted, and those charged with the responsibility of teaching reading should have a deep knowledge of what they are teaching, they must know their students well, and they must be able to alter instruction when a particular approach is not working.

Secondly, reading instruction should be of sufficient intensity to support progress. Recommendations for beginning reading programs include a dedicated instructional block of 90–120 minutes for all students (Spector & Cavanaugh, 2015). Students who are below grade level should receive more intensive instruction. Thirdly, beginning reading instruction should be comprehensive so that all essential components of reading are addressed (Spector & Cavanaugh, 2015). To say, "all components of reading," refers to phonological awareness, phonics, fluency, vocabulary, and comprehension.

> ## Family Voices 11.2
>
> "Teach my child to read? Yes, please. Reading is so hard for him when you move beyond factual text. He just doesn't get the implications or anything else that isn't literal. What can I do to help at home?"

Carnahan, Williamson, and Haydon (2009) suggested several strategies for facilitating comprehension skills. They believe that literacy instruction should include work in all components of reading, such as word work, reading, and writing. They also recommend using topics or themes of interest to promote engagement. Overall, they suggest that teachers provide daily, ample opportunities for reading; use highly motivating topics; provide clear directions using visuals; provide opportunities for word work (decoding, vocabulary, etc.); apply specific strategies; and link reading and writing activities (Carnahan et al., 2011).

Guided reading. Guided reading occurs in a small-group setting to allow for interaction between the teacher and readers. In guided reading, teachers vary each lesson dependent upon the reader's different strengths and needs by selecting the appropriate level of reading text for each group. Groups can participate in mini-lessons tailored to their strengths and needs to build background knowledge and develop skills before interacting with the reading material. After a guided reading lesson is complete in the small group, students typically rotate to another "station" to complete activities related to the story. Based on student needs and abilities, following the story, students can either write a reflective statement of the story, draw a picture of something they remember from the story, or brainstorm words they learned from the story, for example.

Question-generating strategies. Question-generating strategies teach students how to generate and respond to questions about the text they are reading. Whalon and Hart (2011a) suggested that students with ASD would benefit from question-and-answer relationships (QAR) as a strategy for increasing comprehension. QAR instruction is a question-generating strategy in which students are taught to ask questions about whether the information is "in my head" or "in the book." They adopted QAR instruction for use with students with ASD by presenting characters that assume specific roles in the question-generating process, such as "Fran the Fact Finder" who asks "right there" questions, to serve as a prompt to help students generate questions (Whalon & Hart, 2011a).

Graphic organizers. Graphic organizers can be extremely helpful for addressing comprehension difficulties. Picture walks are one type of graphic organizer. A traditional picture walk involves surveying the illustrations of a story, making predictions about the story, and confirming the predictions. It helps children form expectations about what might occur in the story. "Focusing children with ASD on pictures satisfies their tendency to learn visually and is more effective than simply talking or reading a summary of the book jacket" (Gately, 2008, p. 42). When there are no pictures available, using visual maps is an alternative.

Story maps are another type of graphic organizer. Stringfield, Luscre, and Gast (2011) found story maps to be an effective and efficient strategy for students with autism who have problems with planning and working memory. The maps provided a framed outline of basic story elements, which eliminated the need for students to hold each story element in memory while considering how they related to one another to respond to story questions (Stringfield et al., 2011). Graphic organizers can help students with disabilities recall story information and organize story grammar (Stringfield et al., 2011).

Teaching Reading to Students With ASD:
Considerations and Strategies

Students with ASD may have sufficient print awareness and decoding skills but might not meet grade-level expectations in word recognition and reading comprehension.

Teachers responsible for reading instruction should have confidence in their abilities to teach children with ASD and make gains in student reading achievement.

Reading instruction should be of sufficient intensity to support progress.

Literacy instruction should:

- Include all components of reading (word work, reading, and writing)

- Use topics of interest to promote engagement

- Provide clear directions using visuals

- Link reading and writing activities

- Activate background knowledge

- Involve explicit instruction to build comprehension

Beneficial strategies include:

- The use of graphic organizers

- Cooperative learning groups

- Guided reading

- Question-generating techniques

- Picture walks and visual maps

- Think-alouds and reciprocal teaching

- Cartoon bubbles

TEACHING WRITING

Writing is an area where students with ASD have particular difficulty. Cognitive characteristics, such as highly literal thinking, difficulty understanding abstract concepts, lack of imagination, and difficulty imagining possible future events and scenarios make writing a very challenging process for students with ASD (Asaro-Saddler, 2014). Deficits in theory of mind make it difficult to take another's perspective in writing a piece. And students with ASD typically lack organizational skills, working memory, and story recall ability that makes planning writing through the use of notes and translating the notes into a story difficult, which hinders the act of writing (Asaro-Saddler, 2014). The writing process requires skills in language, organization, motor control and planning, and sensory processing—four areas in which students with ASD have difficulty (Oehler, 2013).

Family Voices 11.3

"The day my daughter's teacher used a graphic organizer to help her write an essay is the day the light came on. Why hadn't any other teacher before provided such a miraculous aid to writing?"

Some students with ASD have sufficient skills in printing and handwriting while others may have difficulty with written tasks because of problems with fine motor skills. Technology can be used in many ways to compensate for the limitations students may have in their writing skills. The use of keyboards, word processors, and writing software may facilitate the writing process for some students. For many students with ASD, using a computer is a highly preferred activity, and you may find this to be highly motivating for students who struggle with writing.

Graphic organizers. Other ways to facilitate writing for students with ASD include visuals or graphic organizers to gather their thoughts. Students with ASD have difficulty organizing and sequencing thoughts, especially in writing. They may be able to visualize well-developed ideas, but getting the idea onto paper is much like translating something into a different language (Oehler, 2013). One strategy Oehler recommends is the use of visual strategies facilitated by an adult. For example, the teacher can ask a student what he knows about the topic, and as the student talks, the adult draws simple pictures or writes keywords to represent student ideas along a straight line, or "timeline." At the end of this exercise, the student "reads" the assignment to the adult, using the pictures or keywords as prompts. This verbal exercise helps the student hear the logical flow of language and can help the student complete the writing assignment using the "timeline" as visual support.

Self-regulated strategy development. Self-regulated strategy development (SRSD) is a well-researched writing intervention for students with or without disabilities. SRSD includes multiple strategies to support student writing, such as explicit instruction, mnemonics, and prewriting strategies like graphic organizers (Evmenova et al., 2016). SRSD combines instruction in specific content (such as story planning) with training in self-regulation strategies (such as self-monitoring and self-reinforcement) (Asaro-Saddler, 2014). SRSD helps students with ASD develop their areas of challenge, including the development of writing ideas and audience awareness, development of monitoring their use of writing strategies while writing, and forming positive attitudes about themselves as writers (Asaro-Saddler, 2014).

Studies have shown the benefits of SRSD strategies for developing writing skills in students with ASD. In one study, the researchers taught students with ASD a mnemonic guide for the writing process and planning a story, and they saw significant improvement in students' story writing ability (Asaro-Saddler & Saddler, 2010). In a follow-up study, they found that students increase the number of story elements included in their stories, the number of words, and the overall quality following the SRSD intervention (Asaro-Saddler, 2014). Moreover, after the intervention, each student in the study engaged in some type of planning prior to writing (Asaro-Saddler, 2014). Results of these studies indicate that SRSD approaches can effectively improve the planning and story writing skills of students with ASD. The researchers also discovered that special education teachers could easily implement SRSD strategies with a minimal time investment (Asaro-Saddler, 2014).

Teaching Writing to Students With ASD:
Considerations and Strategies

Cognitive characteristics, such as highly literal thinking, difficulty understanding abstract concepts, lack of imagination, and difficulty imagining possible future events and scenarios, make writing a very challenging process for students with ASD.

Students with ASD typically lack organizational skills, working memory, and story recall ability that make planning writing through the use of notes and translating the notes into a story difficult.

Some students may have difficulty with written tasks due to fine motor skills impairments.

Beneficial strategies include:

- Fill in the blank

- Multiple-choice questions

- Use of keyboards or word processors

- Writing software

- Graphic organizers

- Self-regulated strategy development (SRSD)

TEACHING MATHEMATICS

The abstract nature of math provides challenges to learning for students with ASD. Rote memorization of facts may come somewhat easily for students with ASD in the early grades. Those same students may struggle when math content becomes more abstract and cognitively complex and emphasizes problem solving and higher-level thinking and reasoning (Barnett & Cleary, 2015). Working with fractions presents particular challenges because it requires a strong number sense, knowing the rules and when to apply them, multiple procedural steps, finding common denominators when necessary, and so on (Yakubova, Hughes, & Hornberger, 2015).

Several instructional methods have been shown to be effective for improving math performance, including systematic and explicit instruction, peer tutoring, and visual representation. Also, many teachers have effectively used technology to supplement instruction, and researchers say it may increase student achievement (O'Malley, Lewis, Donehower, & Stone, 2014). Since more than 25% of students with ASD contend with a math disability (Barnett & Cleary, 2015), effective strategies for helping students acquire math skills and increase math achievement should be implemented.

Using visuals. Given the visual strengths often apparent in students with ASD, anytime we can incorporate visual aspects into math instruction will provide benefit to our students. Visual representations in mathematics include manipulatives, pictures, number lines, and graphs (Barnett & Cleary, 2015). Visual approaches to problem solving include pictures or diagrams and objects that assist in understanding abstract mathematical concepts. Some studies have evaluated the use of the "touch-point" technique to teach math skills, in which students use dot positions for numbers (Barnett & Cleary, 2015). The use of iPads and video self-modeling are visual approaches that use technology, which we will discuss next.

Video-based interventions. Technology can provide an opportunity for students with disabilities to access the core curriculum and achieve improved learning outcomes (Burton, Anderson, Prater, & Dyches, 2013). Video self-modeling, in which learners view themselves performing a task at a more advanced level than they typically perform the skill, has been used in some investigations. For example, Burton et al. (2013) used video self-modeling with junior high students to show them successfully completing five math story problems related to the Common Core math standards via an iPad. O'Malley et al. (2014) used an iPad application to increase independent task completion and teach basic math skills to students with ASD, suggesting that iPads may be an effective instructional tool to enhance learning. The use of iPads as an instructional tool can make learning portable, mobile, and accessible and offer opportunities for innovative instructional interventions (O'Malley et al., 2014).

Interventions that incorporate video technology have become increasingly popular. "Incorporating video technology into teaching can be an equalizer for students with disabilities and enable students to engage in learning at an individual pace with opportunities for repeated practice" (Yakubova et al., 2015, p. 2867). One particular strategy called *point-of-view video modeling* shows promise. Point-of-view video modeling involves video recording of a target skill with step-by-step instructions, showing the model's hand performing the task and providing instruction. The student views the video clip multiple times, as many as necessary, and then completes the target task until he or she achieves mastery.

INSTRUCTIONAL APPROACHES FOR THE INCLUSIVE CLASSROOM

We suggest that you provide the most subtle form of support possible in the inclusive classroom—don't call attention to yourself or to the student with ASD. Provide support that is so unobtrusive that in many cases, no one knows you are providing support at that moment. As the role model for the students and staff who observe you, demonstrate the way you want everyone to treat this child.

Carter et al. (2015) are strong advocates of strategies that use peer support as an alternative to an exclusive reliance on assistance from special education staff. Recruiting and equipping peers to provide academic support to their classmates as they work together on activities designed by the classroom teacher is a promising alternative

(Carter et al., 2015). "Conceptually, paraprofessionals and peers work in tandem to enable the focus student to learn relevant content from the classroom teacher. In other words, support from these individuals should supplement, rather than supplant, instruction provide by a highly qualified professional" (Carter et al., 2015, p. 210).

Inclusion Tips

INSTRUCTIONAL CONSIDERATIONS FOR CHILDREN WITH ASD

1. Allow for short breaks between teaching sessions, providing time for the student to be alone if needed.

2. Students with ASD may have difficulty maintaining eye contact. Consider other ways the student can demonstrate that he or she is listening.

3. You may need to adjust the number of items the student must complete. (For example, require the student to complete only the even numbers on a math worksheet.) This helps maintain the student's attention without overwhelming him or her while giving the teacher enough information to know the student has mastered the skill.

4. Consider allowing extra time for completing assignments if needed.

5. Modify the environment so the student can learn successfully. The desk should be close to the teacher, facing the front of the room to remove distractions. A quiet zone is also helpful when the student becomes overloaded with stimuli and needs a break.

6. Implement visuals as much as possible (visual activity and time schedules, visual boundaries for work areas, etc.).

7. Keep your language simple and concrete. Avoid sarcasm or idioms.

8. Provide warnings for any impending change of routine or switch of activity.

9. Provide very clear structure and set a daily routine. Communicate clear beginning and ending points of activities and lessons.

10. Find ways to link work to the student's particular interest.

11. Watch for signs of high anxiety or difficulties the student may be having with sensory overload (e.g., students may put their hands over their ears, plug their ears, rock back and forth, etc.). Show them a self-selected self-calm area, such as a special chair or quiet area where they can go when they are feeling stressed.

12. Try guided reading or QAR as strategies to increase comprehension.

13. Find creative ways to increase peer awareness of ASD, such as using quality children's literature that directly or indirectly addresses the characteristics of ASD.

14. Use peer-support networks (as suggested by Carter et al., 2015) to

    - assist with completing class assignments;

    - motivate/encourage the student;

    - redirect when the student is off task;

    - help student participate in group activities;

    - assist in taking notes or sharing notes;

    - paraphrase lectures or discussions; or

    - write down answers given orally.

FAMILY INVOLVEMENT IN INSTRUCTION

We know that schools are required by IDEA to include parents in the IEP process. Beyond legal requirements, involving parents as active partners in instructional approaches helps generalize behaviors learned in one setting or with one person to others. A collaborative partnership with the family can contribute to the overall effectiveness of interventions and educational programming (Iovannone et al., 2003). To the greatest extent possible, teach parents to implement the strategies used at school. "Education practices and strategies have a better chance of being effective if they are implemented across all settings, including the home and community" (Iovannone et al., 2003, p. 162).

Parents can be effective in delivering a variety of interventions, especially in routines like homework. Homework provides a bridge between home and school environments, and it "provides students with opportunities to practice skills learned in school while developing work habits and study skills beneficial later in life" (Hampshire, Butera, & Bellini, 2016, p. 23). Typically, when parents help with homework, they might provide the student with multiple prompts to ensure completion. This can be helpful, but it might create learned helplessness, where students will wait for parental prompting before moving to the next step of an assignment rather than working independently (Hampshire et al., 2016). Therefore, Hampshire et al. (2016) provided instruction to parents about prompt-fading procedures and self-management strategies to target task independence.

For students with ASD who may lack independence and self-organization, display task-avoidant or attention-seeking behaviors, have anxiety about homework, or are easily distracted, teaching self-management and independence are critical. Parents in Hampshire et al.'s (2016) research learned to provide their child with self-management training while completing math homework. The combination of self-management strategies and parents as interventionists improved independent behavior during homework for all participants in their study (Hampshire et al., 2016). Overall, parents rated the intervention as beneficial to their child and easy to implement, and they felt that their child was more successful and independent after the intervention. Teachers also felt the intervention improved overall performance for their student (Hampshire et al., 2016).

T.I.P. – Theory Into Practice 11.6

FAMILY INVOLVEMENT IN INSTRUCTION

1. Interview your fieldwork teacher, asking questions about how he or she works with parents to implement academic interventions at home (i.e., homework completion, independence, etc.).

2. Reflect on the strategies he or she uses, and think about which ones you might try in the future.

3. Write out a brief plan for how you will involve parents in developing academic skills for their child with ASD.

SUMMARY STATEMENTS

- Students with ASD may display a number of characteristics that make it challenging for teachers to address their academic needs.

- Instruction for students with ASD should be systematic, intensive, follow a specific instructional format, promote generalization, and include appropriate modifications and accommodations.

- Determining the most appropriate intensity and level of instruction should be based on a consideration of family preferences, the child's preferences and special interests, and a focus on the child's strengths and areas of need.

- Systematic instruction means that teachers provide a structured teaching plan that also incorporates strategies designed to promote high levels of engagement and that include data collection to monitor progress.

- The structured environment permits a student to predict what is currently happening in the learning process and to anticipate what will occur next, as well as upcoming transitions.

- A *modification* refers to a change in what is being taught or expected from the student. One example of a modification is requiring a different level of work than other students.

- An *accommodation* is a change that helps a student work around the disability. It is a support or alteration that allows the student to demonstrate his or her knowledge in an alternate fashion.

- The Common Core State Standards include rigorous expectations for students at each grade level. What deserves our attention, however, is the difficulty that students with ASD have with reaching the expectations of the CCSS.

- Supporting reading comprehension is important for teachers of students with ASD. Graphic organizers can be extremely helpful for addressing comprehension difficulties.

- The abstract nature of math provides challenges to learning for students with ASD. Rote memorization of facts may come somewhat easily for students with ASD in the early grades; however, the same students may struggle when math content becomes more abstract and cognitively complex and emphasizes problem solving and higher-level thinking and reasoning.

- A collaborative partnership with the family can contribute to the overall effectiveness of interventions and educational programming.

WHAT WOULD YOU DO?

Look back at the case study about Christian presented at the beginning of the chapter. Based on what you have read in this chapter, what you have read in previous chapters, and your own experiences, how would you respond to the following questions?

1. Why do you think Christian has difficulty when reading fiction but has little trouble reading and comprehending nonfiction?

2. What strategies would you recommend to help Christian with his reading comprehension with fiction material?

(Continued)

(Continued)

3. Explain your reasons for choosing these strategies.

4. How would you organize Christian's learning environment in ways that might help him use independent work time more effectively?

5. How would you respond to a parent who insists that you refrain from

requiring Christian to do work that is too difficult for him?

6. How would you involve Christian's parents in implementing an intervention to help him develop his academic skills?

CHAPTER REFLECTION QUESTIONS

1. Which of the instructional approaches that were mentioned in this chapter are the most surprising to you?

2. How has technology influenced interventions for students with ASD in the content areas?

3. List the important instructional components that are helpful for students with ASD?

4. How can group instruction be beneficial for students with ASD?

5. What is the difference between a *modification* and an *adaptation*?

6. Why do you think graphic organizers are so beneficial to students with ASD?

7. What makes math so challenging for many students with ASD?

RECOMMENDED RESOURCES

Websites

- Autism Speaks. *Five tips for helping nonverbal children with autism learn to read.* Available at https://www.autismspeaks.org/blog/2015/11/06/five-tips-helping-nonverbal-children-autism-learn-read

- The Art of Autism. *Autism and writing: How to teach your child to write.* Available at http://the-art-of-autism.com/autism-and-writing-how-to-teach-your-child-to-write

- Special Education Support Service. *Practical teaching strategies for students with ASDs.* Available at http://www.sess.ie/categories/autismautistic-spectrum-disorders/aspergers/practical-teaching-strategies-students-asds

Articles/Publications

- Marsh, W. W. (2015). Common Core and the uncommon learner: How autism affects acquisition of Common Core State Standards. *Contemporary School Psychology, 19,* 66–76.

- Oehler, K. (2013, January). Please don't make me write! *Autism Asperger's Digest*. Retrieved August 20, 2016, from http://www.edu.gov.on.ca/eng/general/elemsec/speced/autismSpecDis.pdf

- Ontario Ministry of Education. (2007). *Effective educational practices for students with autism spectrum disorders: A resource guide.* Toronto, Canada: Author. Retrieved from http://www.edu.gov.on.ca/eng/general/elemsec/speced/autismSpecDis.pdf

REFERENCES

Asaro-Saddler, K. (2014). Self-regulated strategy development: Effects on writers with autism spectrum disorders. *Education and Training in Autism and Developmental Disabilities, 49*(1), 78–91.

Asaro-Saddler, K., & Saddler, B. (2010). The effects of planning and self-regulation training on the writing performance of young writers with autism spectrum disorders. *TEACHING Exceptional Children, 77*, 107–124.

Barnett, J. E. H., & Cleary, S. (2015). Review of evidence-based mathematics interventions for students with autism spectrum disorders. *Education and Training in Autism and Developmental Disabilities, 59*(2), 172–185.

Burton, C. E., Anderson, D. H., Prater, M. A., & Dyches, T. T. (2013). Video self-modeling on an iPad to teach functional math skills to adolescents with autism and intellectual disability. *Focus on Autism and Other Developmental Disabilities, 28*(2), 67–77.

Carnahan, C., Musti-Rao, S., & Bailey, J. (2009). Promoting active engagement in small group learning experiences for students with autism and significant learning needs. *Education and Treatment of Children, 32*(1), 37–61.

Carnahan, C. R., Williamson, P. S., & Christman, J. (2011). Linking cognition and literacy in students with autism spectrum disorder. *TEACHING Exceptional Children, 43*(6), 54–62.

Carnahan, C. R., Williamson, P., & Haydon, T. (2009). Matching literacy profiles with instruction for students on the spectrum: Making reading instruction meaningful. *Beyond Behavior, 19*(1), 10–16.

Carter, E. W., Asmus, J., Moss, C. K., Biggs, E. E., Bolt, D. M., Born, T. L., . . . Weir, K. (2015). Randomized evaluation of peer support arrangements to support the inclusion of high school students with severe disabilities. *TEACHING Exceptional Children, 82*(2), 209–233.

Evmenova, A. S., Regan, K., Boykin, A., Good, K., Hughes, M., MacVittie, N., . . . Chirinos, D. (2016). Emphasizing planning for essay writing with a computer-based graphic organizer. *TEACHING Exceptional Children, 82*(2), 170–191.

Gately, S. E. (2008). Facilitating reading comprehension for students on the autism spectrum. *TEACHING Exceptional Children, 49*(3), 40–45.

Hampshire, P. K., Butera, G. D., & Bellini, S. (2016). Self-management and parents as interventionists to improve homework independence in students with autism spectrum disorders. *Preventing School Failure, 69*(1), 22–34.

Iovannone, R., Dunlap, G., Huber, H., & Kincaid, D. (2003). Effective educational practices for students with autism spectrum disorders. *Focus on Autism and Other Developmental Disabilities, 18*(3), 150–165.

Ledford, J. R., & Wehby, J. H. (2015). Teaching children with autism in small groups with students who are at-risk for academic problems: Effects on academic and social behaviors.

Journal of Autism and Developmental Disorders, *45*, 1624–1635.

Marsh, W. W. (2015). Common core and the uncommon learner: How autism affects acquisition of common core state standards. *Contemporary School Psychology*, *19*, 66–76.

Oehler, K. (2013, January/February). Please don't make me write! *Autism Asperger's Digest*. Retrieved August 20, 2016, from http://www.edu.gov.on.ca/eng/general/elemsec/speced/autismSpecDis.pdf

O'Malley, P., Lewis, M. E. B., Donehower, C., & Stone, D. (2014). Effectiveness of using iPads to increase academic task completion by students with autism. *Universal Journal of Educational Research*, *2*(1), 90–97.

Spector, J. E., & Cavanaugh, B. J. (2015). The conditions of beginning reading instruction for students with autism spectrum disorder. *Remedial and Special Education*, *36*(6), 337–346.

Spencer, V. G., Evmenova, A. S., Boon, R. T., & Hayes-Harris, L. (2014). Review of research-based interventions for students with autism spectrum disorders in content area instruction: Implications and considerations. *Education and Training in Autism and Developmental Disabilities*, *49*(3), 331–353.

Strain, P. S., Schwartz, I. S., & Barton, E. E. (2011). *Journal of Early Intervention*, *33*(4), 321–332.

Stringfield, S. G., Luscre, D., & Gast, D. L. (2011). Effects of a story map on accelerated reader postreading test scores in students with high-functioning autism. *Focus on Autism and Other Developmental Disabilities*, *26*(4), 218–229.

Whalon, K. J., & Hart, J. E. (2011a). Adapting an evidence-based reading comprehension strategy for learners with autism spectrum disorder. *Intervention in School and Clinic*, *46*(4), 195–203.

Whalon, K. J., & Hart, J. E. (2011b). Children with autism spectrum disorder and literacy instruction: An exploratory study of elementary inclusive settings. *Remedial and Special Education*, *32*(3), 243–255.

Yakubova, G., Hughes, E. M., & Hornberger, E. (2015). Video-based intervention in teaching fraction problem-solving to students with autism spectrum disorder. *Journal of Autism and Developmental Disorders*, *45*, 2865–2875.

Understanding and Addressing Functional Skills

"The essential implication for all who support individuals with ASD is to first recognize the importance of independence as a curricular area. 'Teaching for independence should become the focus of every activity.'"

—(HUME, BOYD, HAMM, & KUCHARCZYK, 2014, P. 108)

CASE STUDY

Sarah is a second-grade student in Mrs. Daniels's class. Her teachers have been working on her basic academic skills, including reading words and sentences, adding and subtracting single-digit numbers, and printing her name and address. Sarah is making progress in each of these goals, but her mother, Mrs. Avery, also has concerns about her level of interaction with her peers on the playground. Sarah wants to play games during recess with her peers but does not know how. Mrs. Avery requested an IEP meeting to discuss adding a functional goal to Sarah's IEP regarding learning to play the recess games popular at Sarah's school. The team would like to develop goals for Sarah to participate in playground activities with her peers.

According to her teacher, Sarah is highly dependent on verbal prompts for task completion across many areas. Because of Sarah's dependence on adult prompting, they are unsure how to increase her independence for engaging in playground activities.

Teachers and playground staff have observed Sarah's attempts at peer interactions at recess. It seems that Sarah has difficulty understanding nonverbal language, understanding emotions and social cues of her peers, and

LEARNER OBJECTIVES

After reading this chapter, the learner should be able to do the following:

1. Define functional skills and describe their impact on individuals with ASD.

2. Describe executive functioning and how it affects individuals with ASD.

3. Explain how task analysis can be used to teach functional skills.

4. Describe several interventions designed to teach functional skills.

5. Describe what we should consider when designing functional goals for an IEP.

obeying the rules of playground games. Sarah's peers are frustrated with her behavior, and they do not invite her to join in any activities when they are at recess. Initiating and planning activities are a weak point for Sarah as well.

School staff feels that Sarah is cognitively and physically capable of performing many actions, but when she is on the swings and the bell rings, with several teachers telling everyone to get up and come back to class, Sarah is very slow to respond.

The IEP team agrees that teaching Sarah how to play games at recess, like Foursquare and Duck-Duck-Goose, could help develop her peer interaction skills, so they have developed a goal with short-term objectives related to teaching Sarah how to participate in playground games. The desire is that Sarah would develop socially appropriate behaviors, such as taking turns, and learn to follow playground game rules and that she would gradually increase independence in these activities.

....

INTRODUCTION

This chapter will focus primarily on functional skills, or the nonacademic/daily living skills. In addition, we will briefly touch on executive function (the skills that help the brain organize and act on information) and how difficulties with executive function can impact one's ability to learn functional skills.

Functional skills, in the special education context, refer to those skills related to nonacademic areas, also called daily living skills. We can think of it as preparing children how to "function" in the world. They are necessary skills for everyday functioning, including the ability to care for oneself, communication skills, and social skills. They are the practical skills that individuals with ASD may need to learn to use in their daily lives. Functional skills that we will discuss in this chapter include those related to self-care, communication, self-direction, social skills, home and school living, community life (e.g., shopping and using transportation), and health and safety. Functional skills are those skills that a student needs in order to live as independently as possible.

Executive function (EF) is a term used to describe the cognitive skills necessary for working memory, impulse control, inhibition, organizing, and sustaining attention (Cui, Gao, Chen, Zou, & Wang, 2010; Hume, Boyd, Hamm, & Kucharczyk, 2014; van den Bergh, Sheeren, Begeer, Koot, & Guerts, 2014). Executive functions help the brain organize and act on information. Such skills enable people to plan, prioritize, organize, remember things, pay attention, and get started on tasks. Some—but not all—individuals with ASD demonstrate impairments in executive functioning (de Vries, Prins, Schmand, & Geurts, 2015; Hume et al., 2014; van den Bergh et al., 2014; Wertz, 2012). Executive functioning can directly impact an individual with

ASD's ability to independently complete daily living or functional skills. Let us look more in depth into functional skills and executive functioning and how the two are intertwined.

FUNCTIONAL SKILLS

Functional skills are those skills that assist us in managing and living a better quality of life. These are the skills that help us achieve our dreams, live to our full potential, and exist as contributing members of our communities. Functional skills are those skills that you teach to the child that are intended to be practical, useful, or helpful in a variety of situations. They should be age-appropriate skills relevant to the child and the people in his or her life. Functional skills are usually very specific to the particular individual.

There is no definitive list of functional life skills. A generally accepted list of important life skills include the following:

- Getting along with all kinds of people, including those whose backgrounds and experiences are different from our own

- Developing and maintaining friendships and meaningful relationships

- Working collaboratively with others

- Identifying, learning, and practicing interests and talents to make important decisions such as career choice and hobbies

- Showing up on time and being prepared for whatever is required

- Communicating thoughts, ideas, opinions, and feelings in ways that are clearly understood

- Displaying socially appropriate behaviors

- Following rules, routines, or schedules as necessary

- Safety skills (i.e., crossing the street safely, stranger danger, bullying, swim safety, etc.)

- Basic living skills like feeding, toilet training, dressing, brushing teeth, tying shoes, personal hygiene, food preparation, laundry, shopping, ordering at a restaurant, making one's bed, and so on

- Skills needed later in life, such as getting and keeping a job, using an ATM or credit card, managing a checking account, cooking, and the like

Functional skills focus on daily living skills, interpersonal skills, and some occupational skills. Depending on their cognitive level, some of our students might need to learn how to count money or make purchases; basic safety; planning meals, purchasing food, preparing meals, and cleaning up; demonstrating appropriate responses to frustrations; identifying how personal behavior affects others and showing respect for others and their property; setting personal goals; responding to authority and supervision; and working cooperatively with others.

Family Voices 12.1

"What do our children with ASD need to be successful in the world? I ask what does ANY child need to be successful in the world? I don't want my kid to have a 'fill in the bubble' mentality . . . that won't help him be successful. He needs out-of-the-box thinking . . . to solve problems not yet imagined. . . . Kids with ASD have that! He also needs critical thinking, self-directed learning, how to take perspective, self-control . . . aren't these the 'functional' skills you talk about?"

THE ROLE OF EXECUTIVE FUNCTION

Executive functions help the brain organize and act on information and enable people to plan, prioritize, organize, remember things, pay attention, and get started on tasks. Difficulties in EF can manifest themselves in a variety of ways. Planning a multistep sequence of events (e.g., steps needed to complete a homework project) and demonstrating mental flexibility (e.g., shifting quickly from one idea or plan to another) may be difficult for individuals with ASD. Other difficulties include dealing with new situations or processing complex information (Hume et al., 2014). Some students with ASD pay attention to minor details but fail to see how those details fit into the bigger picture. Others have difficulty with the complex thinking that requires holding more than one train of thought simultaneously. Others find it difficult to maintain their attention or organize their thoughts and actions. Executive functioning can also be associated with poor impulse control.

Impairments in EF contribute to difficulties in independent daily functioning for people with ASD. A wide range of executive function deficits found in children with ASD may explain their social and nonsocial problems, such as repetitive behaviors and restricted interests (Cui et al., 2010). Children who seem disorganized, inflexible, or impulsive or who struggle with planning and problem solving may have difficulties with EF. They might also find it difficult to achieve in school, follow through with responsibilities, or interact with others appropriately in school or community settings.

Symptoms of Executive Functioning Issues		
A student who struggles with executive functioning issues might display some of the following behaviors:		
What It Is	**What It Does**	**How It Looks**
Impulse Control (Inhibition)	Helps people think before acting	• Blurt out inappropriate things • Engage in risky behavior
Emotional Control	Helps people keep their feelings in check; bringing rational thought to bear on feelings	• Overreacting • Trouble dealing with criticism/ feedback when something goes wrong
Flexible Thinking (Cognitive Shift)	Allows people to adjust to the unexpected	• Trouble "rolling with the punches" • Frustrated when asked to think of something from a different angle • Loses interest in a task or project, leaving it unfinished, if interrupted • Trouble switching gears, especially when learning a new skill or task • Panic when rules and routines are changed
Working Memory	Helps people keep key information in mind for the purpose of completing a task	• Trouble remembering directions (even if they've taken notes or if you've repeated it several times)
Self-Monitoring	Allows people to evaluate how they're doing; monitor one's performance against some standard of what is needed or expected	• Surprised by a bad grade or negative feedback
Planning and Prioritization	Helps people decide on a goal and plan to meet it	• May not know which parts of a project are most important • Trouble figuring out how much time a task requires • Trouble seeing the big picture • Trouble understanding which details to focus on
		(Continued)

Symptoms of Executive Functioning Issues		
A student who struggles with executive functioning issues might display some of the following behaviors:		
What It Is	**What It Does**	**How It Looks**
Task Initiation	Helps people take action or get started	• Difficulty getting started on a task • May freeze up because they have no idea where to begin • Difficulty generating ideas, response, or problem-solving strategies
Organization	Helps people keep track of things physically and mentally; manage task demands	• Loses train of thought, especially when interrupted • Loses items, like phone, homework, work materials, etc. • Mixes up assignments • Doesn't bring handouts or materials necessary for homework or task completion • Desk appears messy, full of crumpled papers; folders are unorganized

FOUR KEY DOMAINS OF EXECUTIVE FUNCTION

Researchers have outlined four key executive functions of the brain that can help us understand why children with ASD do not engage in some behaviors successfully. The four executive functions that are most important for completing daily routines successfully include response inhibition, working memory, cognitive flexibility, and planning (Adams & Jarrold, 2011; Johnston, Madden, Bramham, & Russell, 2010; van den Bergh et al., 2014; von Hahn & Bentley, 2013).

Response inhibition. Inhibition refers to the ability to voluntarily and deliberately suppress irrelevant or interfering information or impulses (van den Bergh et al., 2014). Inhibition is the part of executive function that allows individuals to withhold inappropriate or irrelevant responses or ignore distracting stimuli to give appropriate responses (Adams & Jarrold, 2011). The ability to suppress the activation, processing, or expression of information that would otherwise interfere with goal attainment (or response inhibition) is impaired in students with ASD (Johnston et al., 2010).

Response inhibition can impact social situations and classroom functioning for students with ASD. In social situations, we might see the urge to perform an action considered inappropriate for a specific situation. "Intact inhibition is vital for withholding those urges in order to perform socially appropriate, and therefore acceptable, behaviors" (Adams & Jarrold, 2011, p. 1052).

Inhibiting the response to speak before his or her turn and ignoring irrelevant information (i.e., trying to listen to the teacher but hearing other children speak) are two types of inhibition important for classroom functioning. Understanding when previously learned information becomes irrelevant and interferes with new information, such as when a teacher tries to learn the names of her new students to replace the names of students in former classrooms, is another type (van den Bergh et al., 2014).

Weak inhibition can interfere with reaching a goal for the child with ASD. Inhibition is needed for sustained attention and for delayed gratification (the capacity to wait until later before engaging in a preferred activity or receiving a reward). Concepts such as waiting your turn in an activity or putting your toys away before watching TV require inhibition. For example, midway through the cleanup routine, they might get distracted and start to play with their toys (von Hahn & Bentley, 2013).

Response Inhibition

A student who has working inhibition difficulties might display some of the following behaviors:

- Impulsivity
- Emotional explosiveness/cries easily
- Laughs hysterically with little provocation
- Generally neglects to "look before leaping"
- High level of physical activity and motion
- Inappropriate physical response to others
- Tendency to interrupt
- Tendency to disrupt group activities

T.I.P. – Theory Into Practice 12.1

STOP AND THINK

Response inhibition is one domain of executive functioning.

1. How does response inhibition affect individuals with ASD?

2. How do you think response inhibition could interfere with one's ability to learn daily living or functional skills?

3. Imagine that you have been assigned to teach a student a daily living skill, such as taking one's turn when playing a board game. How might you approach this task with a student who had difficulties with response inhibition?

4. How might you involve the family in implementing your strategy at home?

Cognitive flexibility. Another domain of executive function is cognitive flexibility, which refers to the ability to think about one activity and then shift thinking to another activity or how you are thinking about that activity. It is like "switching mental gears." Flexible thinking allows individuals to switch gears and look at something differently, it allows the ability to unlearn old ways of doing things that might not be working, and flexible thinking plays a role in most types of learning (academic or functional skills).

"Inflexible adherence to specific routines, resistance to change, difficulty in transitions between different locations or events, or circumscribed interests and inordinate preoccupation with particular objects or activities" reflects impairments in cognitive flexibility (Leung & Zakzanis, 2014, p. 2628). Recess is usually held outside, for example, but when bad weather makes it necessary to move recess indoors, the child with ASD might have a meltdown because the rules aren't being followed (von Hahn & Bentley, 2013).

Inflexible behaviors also include repeating the same approach to solving a problem even if it isn't working or failing to incorporate or accept new methods to solving a problem (Yerys, Wolff, Moody, Pennington, & Hepburn, 2012). They seem to prefer that tasks be completed in the same way each and every time. For example, if mom is usually the one to make eggs for breakfast every morning but on one particular day mom has to leave for work early and dad agrees to make breakfast instead, this could present a challenge for a student with ASD. Or a child who has learned how to use the toilet in one environment (at home, in a private restroom with one toilet) might have difficulties learning to use the toilet in a different environment (such as at school, with multiple toilets in a larger, public setting). Inflexible thinking may cause children to get frustrated each time the learning environment changes. Considering new information and adjusting one's behavior when presented with new information can be challenging for those with inflexible thinking.

Cognitive Flexibility

A student who has difficulty with cognitive flexibility might display some of the following behaviors:

- Perseverative behavior/unable to drop topics of interest

- Difficulty with transitions

- Rigid and inflexible

- Requires consistent routines

- Unable to move beyond a disappointment

- Lack of creativity/flexibility in problem solving

- Tendency to apply same incorrect responses even with negative feedback

- Difficulty maintaining new responses and a heightened tendency to revert to old preferences

- Difficulty generating new approaches to solve a problem

- Difficulty responding to the needs or interests of friends

- Difficulty accepting different viewpoints

Working memory. Working memory refers to the ability to maintain and manipulate incoming information received through visual or verbal channels (Cui et al., 2010; van den Bergh et al., 2014). It is a temporary storage system that is necessary for processing complex thoughts. The processes involved in working memory include conserving information for short periods of time and context-relevant updating of information (Barendse et al., 2013; Williams, Goldstein, & Minshew, 2006). Working memory plays an important role not only in processing complex cognitive information, but it is also essential to social cognition and interpersonal interactions (Barendse et al., 2013).

Working memory involves remembering all of the steps needed to reach a goal. For example, the task of getting ready for school requires that a child remembers all of the steps in the morning routine, such as dressing, eating, brushing teeth, getting the backpack together, and more. Many children with ASD have difficulty getting ready for school independently. Impairment in working memory is one reason why they might have trouble with such independence (von Hahn & Bentley, 2013).

Family Voices 12.2

"A teacher once told me that children with ASD don't have any difficulties with global memory. They can store large amounts of information in long-term memory and retrieve it easily. But demands on short-term working memory must be kept low if we want success."

Working memory is also required to successfully navigate one's social world. In a social interaction, one must learn how to interpret salient social cues and adapt their behavior to rapidly changing social environments (Barendse et al., 2013). Visual working memory makes it possible to read body language and other social cues so one can respond accordingly. A student with ASD may struggle with processing the nonverbal communication from peers, which results in the social complications they often experience. Compared with control groups, individuals with autism do not perform as well on tasks involving the interpretation of social stimuli (Williams et al., 2006).

Working Memory

A student who has working memory difficulties might display some of the following behaviors:

- Trouble remembering facts and procedures, such as new vocabulary words or mathematical procedures

- Exhibit slow retrieval of information

- Difficulty following instructions despite repeated instructions

- Demonstrate poor attention to detail, such as beginning to write a sentence and then struggling to remember all of the words in the sentence, skipping words within sentences, and writing shorter sentences

- Make place-keeping errors, such as losing track of steps completed or steps yet to be completed; may repeat steps needlessly or constantly have to start over

- Difficulty starting work

- Difficulty staying on task; may abandon tasks frequently

- Losing track of belongings

- Struggles with mental manipulation tasks

- Frequent off-task behavior/inattention

Self-Regulation. Self-monitoring occurs when a student assesses his or her own behavior to determine whether the desired behavior occurred (Bouck, Savage, Meyer, Taber-Doughty, & Hunley, 2014). It is the ability to stop, think, and then make a choice before acting in a situation. It is self-regulation that enables an individual to become more aware of whether he or she is performing a specific task (Finn, Ramasamy, Dukes, & Scott, 2014). Such skills are important to performing many things in daily life, such as time management, acquiring and comprehending new information, meeting deadlines or due dates, and performing multistep tasks (Finn et al., 2014).

Difficulties with self-regulation show up in a number of ways in individuals with ASD. For example, writing is especially difficult when self-regulation is impaired. The ability to self-regulate in writing involves monitoring, assessing, and reinforcing writing behaviors without depending on prompts from adults, and students with ASD exhibit poor self-regulatory abilities (Asaro-Saddler & Saddler, 2010). Children who demonstrate self-regulation are able to stop and ask for what they want, instead of having a tantrum; they take turns when playing a game with friends; they wait in line when it is required; they follow directions. Increasing self-monitoring can increase independence and decrease over-reliance on external sources of monitoring (i.e., teacher or another adult), increase instructional time, and improve overall quality of life (Bouck et al., 2014).

Self-Regulation

A student who has self-regulation difficulties might display some of the following behaviors:

- Rushes through tasks

- Makes seemingly careless errors

- Often skips steps of a task

- Doesn't seem to check work or final result

- Neglects to monitor progress toward goals

- Seems not to exhibit pride in goal attainment

- Does not track effect of behavior on others

- Does not adjust or alter behavior if ineffective or offensive

- Difficulty with the writing process

- May have difficulties playing games with friends (e.g., taking turns)

T.I.P. – Theory Into Practice 12.3

STOP AND THINK: SELF-REGULATION AND FUNCTIONAL SKILLS

Self-regulation is one domain of executive functioning.

1. How does self-regulation affect individuals with ASD?

2. How do you think self-regulation could interfere with one's ability to learn daily living or functional skills?

3. Imagine that you have been assigned to teach a student a daily living skill: looking both ways before crossing the street and waiting until the cars have cleared before crossing. How might you approach this task with a student who has difficulties with self-regulation?

4. How might you involve the family in implementing your strategy at home?

Planning/Organization. Planning refers to the ability to order one's steps in a logical sequence so that a goal can be reached. Usually, children can set a goal, such as drawing a picture of a house, and then successfully carry out the plan, whereas the same is not necessarily true for children with ASD. Planning and reaching a goal involves setting the goal, understanding the steps needed to reach the goal, ordering the steps logically, and staying on task to ultimately reach the goal. This task can be difficult for an individual with ASD.

Children with ASD often have less developed planning skills, and they prefer to adhere to scripts or carry out tasks the same way every time. Scripts or routines are appropriate for morning routines, for example, but play behaviors might not always be carried out the same way and require more flexibility (von Hahn & Bentley, 2013). Organization is the child's ability to keep track of information and things; students with organizational issues often lose or misplace things, and children with ASD can appear to have trouble getting organized even when there are negative consequences to being disorganized.

Planning and Organization

A student who has planning or organization difficulties might display some of the following behaviors:

- Difficulty initiating tasks without direction

- Seems to approach tasks in a haphazardly fashion

- Gets caught up in the details and misses the main idea

- Becomes overwhelmed by large amounts of information

- Difficulty obtaining correct tools or materials in advance

- Difficulty breaking down tasks or using strategies to problem solve

- Difficulty maintaining order in environment

Now that we have fully explored functional skills and how executive functioning can impact functional skills, let us now move to ways that educators can support independent functioning.

SUPPORTING INDEPENDENT FUNCTIONING

Some researchers have identified evidence-based practices useful for supporting independent functioning in students with ASD (Hume et al., 2014). Strategies for teaching functional skills include reinforcement, task analysis, visual supports, and prompting and chaining.

Reinforcement

We discussed reinforcement in other chapters of this text. As a reminder, reinforcement is the delivery of a reward following an action that increases the chances the behavior will occur again. We can think of reinforcement as a "paycheck." It is not a bribe; it helps create an eager learner. Reinforcement lets the child know he or she has done a good job.

Let us look at the example of a mother teaching a child to make a peanut butter and jelly sandwich to see how reinforcement develops functional independence. She prepares the teaching setting in advance by gathering all of the necessary materials (bread, peanut butter, jelly, and spreading knife). She is careful to remove any distracting items or sensory issues from the counter. The mother conducted her task analysis (as we will discuss in more detail below), she planned appropriate teaching times, she determined appropriate reinforcement, set all the materials in place, and she prompted and faded the prompts as appropriate.

It is best to make sure the reward is something your student wants. Rewards or reinforcements can be edible, tangible, social, and activity or a token in nature. Once you have created the primary reward, you can make it a visual experience. Use a picture of the reward, and consider using visual schedules of the task. Also, it is important to reward immediately on skill completion (or partial completion as you deem appropriate). Ideal timing is 1 to 3 seconds following the desired action.

Task Analysis

A helpful approach for teaching functional skills is through task analysis. Task analysis involves breaking down complex tasks into more manageable steps and putting the steps in order for the student. It involves taking a closer look at a given task and determining what skills, knowledge, and adaptations would be necessary for the student to be successful. Our goal for students with ASD is independence.

A task analysis promotes independence by providing a checklist of steps required to complete the task. A student can use a task analysis independently, without intensive adult prompting that is sometimes required in the absence of such a checklist. Task analysis can be used to teach functional activities like washing hands, motor tasks like using scissors, academic tasks like writing letters, and social skills like sitting quietly and participating appropriately during circle time.

Task analysis has been used in several studies to teach functional skills and verbal interactions to students with ASD. Parker and Kamps (2011), for example, designed a cooking activity, where students chose a recipe written on a piece of construction paper that gave step-by-step instructions on how to make the food, and they used toy appliances to bake the food items. In a restaurant activity, some participants were given two dollars to independently order a small drink and a side order using the overhead menus from restaurants. A task analysis that outlined the steps needed to complete an activity was created for each of the cooking and restaurant activities.

Figure 12.1 shows a sample task analysis schedule, in the form of a visual schedule, used for hand washing, which we helped a family create for implementing at home with their daughter.

Prompting and Chaining

Prompting is any additional cue or assistance needed to get your child to produce the desired behavior. We can use prompts, but we should not do the task *for* the child.

FIGURE 12.1

Handwashing task analysis

1. Turn faucet on	**2. Get soap**

3. Scrub hands	**4. Rinse hands**

5. Turn faucet off	**6. Dry hands**

Prompts can be gestural, modeling, verbal, or positional. Gestural prompts involve the use of gestures to nudge your child to perform the appropriate behavior, like pointing to the spreading knife to prompt the child to pick it up and begin the task. Modeling is when you demonstrate or show your child what you want him to do, like spreading the peanut butter on the bread. Verbal prompting, the most common form of prompting, involves telling the child what to do. "Pick up the knife and spread the peanut butter," for example. Positional prompting is placing the needed item closer to the student.

Chaining is the way in which behaviors are linked together in a sequence. Each small skill is linked or "chained" together for a routine or whole task to be completed. Consider the steps for washing hands. The child should reach for the faucet, grasp the faucet, turn the faucet on, reach for the soap, push soap dispenser, and so on. Each behavior in the chain will serve as the cue for the next response. Chaining is teaching one of the tasks to independence before moving to the next task in the sequence.

Let us consider the hand-washing task analysis we created earlier. Imagine that in your task analysis, you determined that the following steps are required: turn on water; get soap; rub hands together; rinse hands; turn off water; dry hands (using visuals/pictures to represent each step of the task). In chaining, you could tell the child to go wash her hands (the prompt) and wait to see if she walks to the sink. If she doesn't go, you could point to the sink (a gestural prompt). When she begins to go to the sink independently, then you could tell her to turn on the water, using prompting as necessary. When she goes to the sink on her own and she turns on the water, you would go through the same prompting to guide her through the rest of the steps (i.e., getting soap, rubbing hands together, etc.). You keep doing this as she masters each step in the correct order until she can complete the whole task independently.

Visual Supports

Video modeling and other visual supports (e.g., visual schedules like the hand-washing example used earlier in this chapter) are used to provide instruction that can help decrease the students' over-reliance on adults to provide verbal reminders of what is expected (Hume et al., 2014). Using visual supports helps build upon the strengths of individuals with ASD. Brain-imaging studies have shown that students with ASD have enhanced visual mental imagery, or visual thinking, compared with typically developing individuals (Hume et al., 2014). The use of visual supports can facilitate independence while capitalizing on our students' strengths (Hume et al., 2014).

One visual support (graphic organizer) we've grown fond of is the recipe for making a hamburger paragraph we created to help with writing, as shown in Figure 12.2.

Counting and using money are functional skills that many teachers use in classroom instruction. It would be a fun activity for students, as they are learning, to display pictures of grocery produce items. Students could select a picture, take it to the pretend cash register, and make a purchase. Or better yet, the teacher could use plastic or toy fruit or food items that students can "purchase." You could have students make a grocery list and figure out how much money they need to shop. You could ask students to find the items on their list and write the prices down on the list. You could have one student serve as a clerk, so he or she has to make change when students make purchases. These kinds of activities will capitalize on students' visual strengths and make learning fun.

FIGURE 12.2

Hamburger Paragraph Recipe

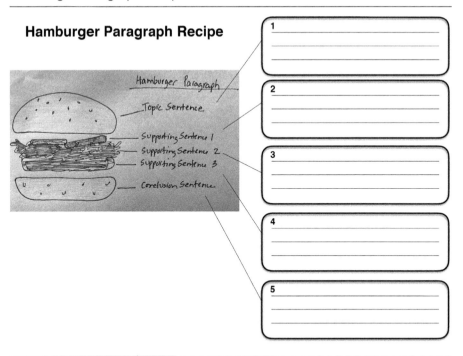

Hamburger Paragraph Recipe

Hamburger Paragraph

Topic Sentence

Supporting Sentence 1
Supporting Sentence 2
Supporting Sentence 3

Conclusion Sentence

1

2

3

4

5

T.I.P. – Theory Into Practice 12.4

TEACHING FUNCTIONAL SKILLS

1. Search on Pinterest for "autism functional skills."

2. Take some time to view the many "pins" you find there.

3. Select three of your favorites.

4. Take note of the approach used (i.e., reinforcement, task analysis, visual supports, or prompting and chaining).

5. Consider sharing a description and "how to" with your peers or fellow teachers.

6. As an "extension" activity, try to develop a strategy (i.e., task analysis, prompting and chaining, visual supports, reinforcement, etc.) for teaching some behavior (e.g., ordering lunch in the cafeteria).

7. Consider how you could involve the family in implementing your strategy at home.

STRATEGIES FOR TEACHING FUNCTIONAL SKILLS

Video Modeling

Video-based interventions can provide increased opportunity for students with disabilities to acquire important functional skills. Video modeling (VM) is an instructional technique that involves the students watching a video of a model engaging in target behaviors or skills and performing the same set of skills (Burton, Anderson, Prater, & Dyches, 2013). Video self-modeling (VSM) is a specific application of VM in which the student observes himself or herself performing the target behavior. Although research shows the benefits of peers serving as models on the video, giving the student an opportunity to view himself or herself performing well in a particular task may have positive outcomes as well (Buggey, 2007). "Direct video evidence is provided that the child can succeed. This positive visual imagery thus becomes part of the viewer's memory" (Buggey, 2007, p. 151).

Researchers have utilized mobile devices such as iPhones and iPads to teach functional skills to individuals with ASD (Ayres, Smith, Mechling, & Smith, 2013). Specifically, Ayres et al. (2013) studied the effectiveness and efficiency of narration in their video models with promising results. They crafted videos of an adult model performing the target task, overlaying narration onto each video, and compared the intervention with videos that had the volume muted (no narration). Participants in their research preferred the video models with narration, and results indicated that video modeling is an effective tool for teaching functional skills (Ayres et al., 2013).

The efficacy of VSM has been verified in a wide range of studies. VSM has produced results that show increased competence in targeted skills that can be generalized across situations, persons, and environments (Buggey, 2007). Buggey (2007) suggested using iMovie on a Macintosh computer to capture students role-playing specific situations. Recording the role-playing activities would provide a record of the students successfully performing the behavior, adding a self-observation component to strengthen the effect. Buggey has found VSM to be especially effective with students with mild ASD. "Most of the time, these students cooperate enthusiastically in the role-playing activity, can participate in the planning stages of videotaping, and view their movies with excitement" (Buggey, 2007, p. 153).

In another study, Buggey (2007) used VSM with a student who rarely finished his lunch. This student was very distractible and needed frequent prompts to attend to his lunch; he engaged in laughing aloud for no apparent reason and self-stimulating by twirling his silverware. This student achieved the most dramatic results. He watched the film on a Thursday afternoon, and by the following Tuesday, he finished his lunch with minimal prompting, cleaned up his space, and had several minutes of free time. The student watched the videotape several times during the week, and his self-stimulating behavior virtually ceased (Buggey, 2007).

OTHER STRATEGIES FOR TEACHING FUNCTIONAL SKILLS

Another instructional intervention worth mentioning here involves using peers to deliver interventions. Brady, Honsberger, Cadette, and Honsberger (2016) taught peer partners to deliver a story involving making a peanut butter and jelly sandwich with adolescents with autism to teach daily skills and facilitate their ability to successfully enter postschool roles and environments. The researchers first performed a task analysis to determine 14 steps necessary in making the sandwich, and they constructed an eight-page storybook depicting how they built the sandwich. Each page consisted of one to two photographs of a student performing the steps, and the bottom of each page contained a sentence or phrase describing what the student in the picture was doing. During the intervention, trained peers read the story to the student; once all of the pages were completed, the peer asked the student to make the sandwich as the peer stood nearby to prompt if necessary. Following the intervention, all research participants improved their accurate and independent performance substantially (Brady et al., 2016).

Family Voices 12.3

"Now that Simone is in high school, I hope that she can learn life skills like shopping, maintaining a clean wardrobe, budgeting, preparing meals, cleaning, using public transportation, basic household maintenance. We work on teaching these at home, but I'd love to partner with her teacher to think of ways we can do this at school . . . perhaps in some peer interactions . . . yes, that would be helpful. I think peer models can be good tutors."

SELECTING FUNCTIONAL GOALS FOR THE IEP

It is critical that IEP teams write goals and objectives in the IEP that address deficits in executive functions and increase independence. This may involve writing a goal related to a process rather than a product, such as how to break down an assignment into smaller steps (process), rather than identifying a correct answer (product). Include goals related to self-management to support independence (Hume et al., 2014).

Some functional skills appropriate to be included in an IEP are as follows:

- Communication: making needs and wants known through language, pictures, and signs

- Choice making: choosing a preferred item or activity

- Purchasing items at a store

- Safety, how to call 911 in an emergency, and what to do in case of an accident

- Using a public restroom

- Self-care: toileting skills, such as wiping, bathing, or other hygiene issues

- Doing laundry

- Crossing a street safely

- Personal space: what it is and how to respect it

- Personal hygiene skills, such as applying deodorant

Without careful consideration of the person's age, family values, or respecting the dignity of the individual, it is possible for functional skills to be taught incorrectly, or they are not considered "functional" for the child. For example, consider the case of the toddler who had the IEP goal to "use a fork." Teachers spent week after week teaching the child how to use a fork because an assessment revealed that he did not have the skill. In his home environment, the child rarely used utensils, as the family ate mostly finger foods like tortillas and such. Since the school did not communicate well with the family, teachers did not know that the skill of using a fork was not necessarily functional for this child.

WRITING MEASURABLE FUNCTIONAL GOALS IN THE IEP

Critical elements of the IEP include the child's present level of performance, goals, and a statement of the special education services intended to move the child from the present level to the goal. The IEP should contain measurable goals and objectives, benchmarks, and progress markers.

The following example represents the critical components of an IEP, with examples:

- Present Levels of Performance: Julie does not tell time.

- Objectives:

  1. Given pictures of clock faces with the short hand pointing to an hour, Julie will state the hour and demonstrate that she can count to 60 by fives in 9 out of 10 trials.

  2. Given pictures of clock faces with the long hand pointing to the half hour, Julie will state the time by saying the hour and the word "thirty" (e.g., nine-thirty) in 9 out of 10 trials.

3. Given pictures of clock faces with the long hand pointing to the quarter hour, Julie will state the time by saying the hour and the words "fifteen" or "forty-five" (e.g., nine-fifteen or ten forty-five) in 9 out of 10 trials.

- Goal: Given pictures of clock faces with the hands in any position, Julie will state the correct time in "minutes after," accurate to the nearest 5 minutes in 9 out of 10 trials.

Notice how the above IEP verbiage states the present level of performance, objectives, and goals for Julie in measurable terms. Keep in mind that what a student does can be measured in terms of frequency (e.g., 9 out of 10 trials), duration (e.g., for 20 minutes), distance (e.g., 15 feet), or accuracy (e.g., 90% accuracy).

T.I.P. – Theory Into Practice 12.5

WRITING IEP GOALS

1. Go to the website, Results Matter Video Library–Just Being Kids, from the Colorado Department of Education, to view several videos related to functional skills for students: http://www.cde.state.co.us/resultsmatter/RMVideoSeries_JustBeingKids.htm#top

2. Pick one of the scenarios to describe to your peers.

3. Consider writing several IEP goals for a student you've observed in your fieldwork or in your own personal experience.

Inclusion Tips

EXECUTIVE FUNCTION SUPPORTS

1. Use visual supports whenever possible.

2. Make checklists.

3. Use task analysis to promote independence.

4. Use planners and calendars.

5. Give one task at a time to reduce working memory load.

6. Reduce the amount of material the student is expected to complete.

7. Provide written directions for reference.

8. Provide information in multiple ways (speak it, show it, and provide multiple opportunities to work with it).

9. Try to incorporate iPad/iPhone apps that support task completion, organization, reminders, and so forth.

10. Find ways to encourage self-monitoring.

FAMILY INVOLVEMENT IN TEACHING EXECUTIVE FUNCTION SKILLS

Parents and caregivers can play an important role in helping students become more independent, and educators are critical to providing the education and support that parents need to implement such strategies.

T.I.P. – Theory Into Practice 12.6

PARENT EDUCATION

1. View the "Autism Distance Education Parent Training (ADEPT)" program from UC Davis Mind Institute at http://media .mindinstitute.org/education/ADEPT/ Module1Menu.html

2. Specifically, go through the module, "Lesson 1: The ABCs of Teaching Skills," an annotated 30-slide presentation, where you will learn how to define *antecedents*, *behaviors*, and *consequences* and how to reinforce appropriate behaviors effectively.

3. After viewing this lesson, ask yourself, In what ways do you consider this parent training useful?

4. How do you think you could incorporate this training with your students' parents?

5. Consider how you can use the information here to conduct your own parent training session(s) for your students' families.

Involving Families to Teach Functional Skills	
Video Self-Modeling	✓ At school, develop a video of the student performing a targeted behavior appropriately, and encourage parents to show it as often as possible at home.
Work Systems	✓ Teach families how to set up work systems in the home setting (visual information informing a student what to do in a work situation) to promote the student's ability to complete tasks without the need for continued adult monitoring and support.

SUMMARY STATEMENTS

- Functional skills are those skills that are necessary for functioning daily, including the ability to care for oneself, communication skills, and social skills.

- Skills that allow children to function independently in a classroom, in special or general education, include complying with adult requests; taking turns; listening to directions;

sitting quietly during activities; raising one's hand; walking in line; picking up toys or work materials; and communicating about basic needs.

- Impairments in executive functioning contribute to difficulties in independent daily functioning for people with ASD.

- Overall approaches to developing functional skills include reinforcement, task analysis, visual supports, and prompting and chaining.

- Functional skills should be included in the student's IEP.

WHAT WOULD YOU DO?

Look back at the case study about Sarah presented at the beginning of the chapter. Based on what you have read in this chapter, what you have read in previous chapters, and your own experiences, how would you respond to the following questions?

1. Why might Sarah appear unmotivated to follow directions when she is asked to get up from the swings and come back inside the class when recess is over?

2. What role does working memory play in Sarah's social interactions?

3. What IEP goals would you suggest for Sarah?

4. How would you work with playground staff to get Sarah to follow directions more quickly?

5. How would you respond to Sarah's mother, who has read a few things on the Internet about executive function and who thinks that Sarah might have such difficulties?

6. How would you involve Sarah's parents in implementing an intervention to help her develop her functional skills?

CHAPTER REFLECTION QUESTIONS

1. Given what you have just read in this chapter, what was the most powerful insight you have acquired, and what are the implications for your teaching?

2. What is executive functioning, and how does it impact one's ability to learn functional skills?

3. Imagine that the local school district is recommending that all staff incorporate functional skills into the school curriculum. How will you respond?

4. Which approaches to teaching functional skills resonate the most with you?

5. In what ways can you work with families and caregivers to implement some of the strategies from this chapter at home?

RECOMMENDED RESOURCES

Websites

- Autism Classroom Resources. *Functional curriculum.* Available at http://www.autismclassroomresources.com/functional-curriculum-are-these-4-right-for-your-special-education-students/

- Autism Speaks. *Executive functioning and theory of mind.* Available at https://www.autismspeaks.org/family-services/tool-kits/asperger-syndrome-and-high-functioning-autism-tool-kit/executive-functioni

- Musings of an Aspie. *Executive function.* Available at https://musingsofanaspie.com/executive-function-series/

Articles/Publications

- Cannon, L., Kenworthy, L., Alexander, K. C., Werner, M. A., & Anthony, L. (2011). *Unstuck and on target!: An executive function curriculum to improve flexibility for children with autism spectrum disorders.* Baltimore, MD: Paul H. Brookes.

- UC Davis Mind Institute. *Autism Distance Education Parent Training (ADEPT).* Retrieved from http://media.mindinstitute.org/education/ADEPT/Module1Menu.html

REFERENCES

Adams, N. C., & Jarrold, C. (2011). Inhibition in autism: Children with autism have difficulty inhibiting irrelevant distractors but not prepotent responses. *Journal of Autism and Developmental Disorders, 43,* 1052–1063.

Asaro-Saddler, K., & Saddler, B. (2010). Planning instruction and self-regulation training: Effects on writers with autism spectrum disorders. *TEACHING Exceptional Children, 77*(1), 107–124.

Ayres, K., Smith, M., Mechling, L., & Smith, K. (2013). Comparison of the effects of video modeling with narration vs. video modeling on the functional skills acquisition of adolescents with autism. *Education and Training in Autism and Developmental Disabilities, 48*(2), 164–178.

Barendse, E. M., Hendriks, M. P. H., Jansen, J. F. A., Backes, W. H., Hofman, P. A. M., . . . Aldenkamp, A. P. (2013). Working memory deficits in high-functioning adolescents with autism spectrum disorders: Neuropsychological and neuroimaging correlates. *Journal of Neurodevelopmental Disorders, 5,* 14. http://dx.doi.org/10.1186/1866-1955-5-14

Bouck, E. C., Savage, M., Meyer, N. K., Taber-Doughty, T., & Hunley, M. (2014). High-tech or low-tech? Comparing self-monitoring systems to increase task independence for students with autism. *Focus on Autism and Other Developmental Disabilities, 29*(3), 156–167. doi:10.1177/1088357614528797

Brady, M. P., Honsberger, C., Cadette, J., & Honsberger, T. (2016). Effects of a peer-mediated literacy based behavioral intervention on the acquisition and maintenance of daily living skills in adolescents with autism. *Educating and Training in Autism and Developmental Disabilities, 51*(2), 122–131.

Buggey, T. (2007). A picture is worth. . . . Video self-modeling applications at school and home.

Journal of Positive Behavior Interventions, *9*(3), 151–158.

Burton, C. E., Anderson, D. H., Prater, M. A., & Dyches, T. T. (2013). Video self-modeling on an iPad to teach functional math skills to adolescents with autism and intellectual disability. *Focus on Autism and Other Developmental Disabilities*, *28*(2), 67–77. doi:10.1177/1088357613478829

Cui, J., Gao, D., Chen, Y., Zou, X., & Wang, Y. (2010). Working memory in early-school-age children with Asperger's syndrome. *Journal of Autism and Developmental Disorders*, *40*, 958–967.

de Vries, M., Prins, P. J. M., Schmand, B. A., & Guerts, H. M. (2015). Working memory and cognitive flexibility-training for children with an autism spectrum disorder: A randomized controlled trial. *Journal of Child Psychology and Psychiatry*, *56*(5), 566–576.

Finn, L., Ramasamy, R., Dukes, C., & Scott, J. (2014). Using WatchMinder to increase the on-task behavior of students with autism spectrum disorder. *Journal of Autism and Developmental Disorders*, *45*(5), 1408–1418. doi:10.1007/s10803-014-2300-x

Hume, K., Boyd, B. A., Hamm, J. V., & Kucharczyk, S. (2014). Supporting independence in adolescents on the autism spectrum. *Remedial and Special Education*, *35*(2), 102–113.

Individuals with Disabilities Education Act, 20 U.S.C. § 1400 (2004).

Johnston, K., Madden, A. K., Bramham, J., & Russell, A. J. (2010). Response inhibition in adults with autism spectrum disorder compared to attention deficit/hyperactivity disorder. *Journal of Autism and Developmental*

Disorders, *41*(7), 903–912. doi:10.1007/s10803-010-1113-9

Leung, R. C., & Zakzanis, K. K. (2014). Brief report: Cognitive flexibility in autism spectrum disorders: A quantitative review. *Journal of Autism and Developmental Disorders*, *44*, 2628–2645.

Parker, D., & Kamps, D. (2011). Effects of task analysis and self-monitoring for children with autism in multiple social settings. *Focus on Autism and Other Developmental Disabilities*, *26*(3), 131–142.

van den Bergh, S. F. W. M., Sheeren, A. M., Begeer, S., Koot, H. M., & Guerts, H. M. (2014). Age related differences of executive functioning problems in everyday life of children and adolescents in the autism spectrum. *Journal of Autism and Developmental Disorders*, *44*, 1959–1979.

von Hahn, E., & Bentley, B. M. (2013). Executive functions in children with ASDs. *Autism Consortium*. Retrieved from http://www.autismconsortium.org/blog/detail/executive-functions-in-children-with-asds

Wertz, S. R. (2012). Improving executive function in children with autism spectrum disorders. *Growing Minds*. Retrieved from http://www.autism-programs.com/articles-on-autism/improving-executive-function.htm

Williams, D. L., Goldstein, G., & Minshew, N. J. (2006). The profile of memory function in children with autism. *Neuropsychology*, *20*(1), 21–29.

Yerys, B. E., Wolff, B. C., Moody, E., Pennington, B. F., & Hepburn, S. L. (2012). Brief report: Impaired flexible item selection task (FIST) in school-age children with autism spectrum disorders. *Journal of Autism and Developmental Disorders*, *42*, 2013–2020.

Early Interventions: Effective Practices for Young Children (Ages 3–5) With ASD

13

CASE STUDY

Vincent is a child with ASD enrolled in an inclusive preschool classroom with one lead teacher and two assistant teachers. Vincent communicates using one- and two-word phrases. He seldom initiates interactions with his classmates and usually does not respond to their invitations to join in. Vincent is usually engaged primarily in solitary play, although he is able to play alongside other children. He engages in repetitive play with a few selected toys, especially toy cars, and he does not take turns with his peers or share toys readily.

Rarely does Vincent ask for a preferred item. His requests are usually something like, "car, car," as he looks at the toys. Vincent often does not respond to questions, from the teachers or from peers.

Vincent participates in circle time and small-group play inconsistently. Sometimes, he interacts with his peers or the teachers, but he usually plays alone and does not respond to questions asked of students during circle time. There are two boys in the class that seem to want a friendship with Vincent, and they frequently ask Vincent to join them, but Vincent rarely responds. When it is snack time, the teacher has been showing students how to request a snack (i.e., choose crackers or fruit cups), but Vincent has been unable to make a verbal request so far.

Vincent loves to play with the toy cars. When it is time to put the cars away, Vincent cries and screams. Vincent's mother and his teacher worry about how to teach Vincent to communicate his wants and needs.

Vincent's teacher, Miss Jennifer, would like to incorporate strategies that could help Vincent develop communication

LEARNER OBJECTIVES

After reading this chapter, the learner should be able to do the following:

- Describe the early signs of ASD and how a diagnosis is made.

- Describe how we can modify the classroom environment effectively to help children with ASD function more independently.

- Discuss how we can develop appropriate social skills in young children with ASD.

- Discuss milieu teaching and discuss its use for developing communication skills in young children with ASD.

- Suggest ways that we can support children with ASD in early childhood environments.

- Explain the important considerations for working with families of young children with ASD.

and exhibit prosocial behavior, but she feels ill-equipped to try any new techniques. She wants to help Vincent communicate and interact with others, but she is not aware of any interventions or how to implement strategies that might benefit Vincent.

Vincent's behavior has been a source of frustration for his mother as well. Michelle, Vincent's mother, would like to implement some strategies at home to help with his behavior and communication, but she has no idea how to get started. Both Michelle and Miss Jennifer are hoping to learn techniques that support the development of Vincent's communication skills.

....

INTRODUCTION

Children with ASD are less likely than typically developing children to efficiently encode social information, to positively construct and evaluate competent responses, and to exhibit prosocial behaviors (Ziv, Hadad, & Khateeb, 2014). Young children with ASD may have difficulty engaging in typical activities of childhood, such as daily living, social participation, play, and education (O'Donnell, Deitz, Kartin, Nalty, & Dawson, 2012). Young children with ASD tend to process social information in less competent ways than typically developing children, and research shows these difficulties are related to maladjusted behavior (Ziv et al., 2014).

Children with ASD are also more likely to attribute hostile intentions to others in benign social situations, to construct more aggressive responses, to construct more avoidant responses, and to display more externalizing behaviors (Ziv et al., 2014). Accurately processing social interactions; understanding the intents, feelings, and thoughts of others; and selecting appropriate social responses are challenging for young children with ASD (Ziv et al., 2014).

Many children with ASD are integrated into preschools and early childhood settings where engaging in positive social interactions with their peers is a common developmental objective (Katz & Girolametto, 2013). Evidence-based social interaction interventions that address socialization deficits in children will, therefore, form the bulk of this chapter. Strategies for developing goals, designing an effective classroom environment, and implementing instruction that is individualized will be described in this chapter.

Before we discuss possible interventions, we will first consider some early signs and symptoms of autism, as well as early screening tools. The American Academy of Pediatrics (Johnson & Myers, 2007) recommends that all children receive autism-specific screening at 18 and 24 months of age, and the Modified Checklist for Autism in Toddlers, Revised with Follow-Up (M-CHAT-R/F; Robins, Casagrande, Barton, Chen, Dumont-Mathieu, & Fein, 2014) is the screening tool used to identify children 16 to 30 months of age and can be administered in well-child visits (National Autism Association, n.d.). The M-CHAT-R/F is designed to identify children who may benefit from a more thorough developmental and autism evaluation (Robins et al., 2014).

EARLY AUTISM SCREENING

The American Academy of Pediatrics suggests that pediatricians be able to recognize the signs and symptoms of ASD and have a strategy for assessing them systematically (Johnson & Myers, 2007). One assessment tool is the M-CHAT-R/F. The M-CHAT-R/F can be administered to parents or guardians in the context of regular pediatrician well-child visits. It is designed to serve as an initial screening tool to identify children 16 to 30 months of age who should receive a more thorough assessment for possible early signs of ASD. The M-CHAT-R/F was tested for reliability and validity in a 2014 study (Robins et al., 2014).

The Autism Speaks website indicates that appropriate screening can determine whether a child is at risk for autism as young as 1 year old. Studies show that early interventions improve learning, communication, and social skills in young children, so the earlier the diagnosis, the better chance of receiving early interventions that can make a big difference (Autism Speaks, n.d.). Some of the "red flags" that may indicate a child is at risk for an autism spectrum disorder, according to Autism Speaks, are as follows:

- No big smiles or warm expressions by 6 months or thereafter

- No back-and-forth sharing of sounds, smiles, or other facial expressions by 9 months

- No babbling by 12 months

- No back-and-forth gestures such as pointing, showing, or reaching by 12 months

- No words by 16 months

- No meaningful, two-word phrases by 24 months

- Any loss of speech or social skills at any age

A young person at risk for ASD might not respond to his or her name, point at objects or things of interest, or play "pretend" games. He or she might also avoid eye contact, prefer to be alone, have difficulty understanding other people's feelings, or have no speech or delayed speech. In addition, young children with ASD might repeat words or phrases over and over (echolalia), get upset by minor changes, flap their hands, have obsessive interests, avoid or resist physical contact, or give unrelated answers to questions (National Autism Association, n.d.). Other symptoms include impulsivity, short attention span, aggression, meltdowns, unusual sleeping and eating habits, or unusual mood or emotional reactions (National Autism Association, n.d.).

Family Voices 13.1

"What do I feel about getting a diagnosis? It didn't change my child . . . he always had autism . . . now there is just a name for what we've seen. The official label changed nothing about who my child is and will be."

Once a diagnosis has been received, there are a number of effective early interventions that we will discuss in this chapter. Before implementing interventions, we should first gather information from a variety of sources and use that information to develop appropriate goals. To help children reach those goals, there are a number of environmental modifications we can make in our general teaching approaches and in specific interventions that can address communication and social skills development. We will also discuss how to address behavioral challenges in this chapter.

T.I.P. – Theory Into Practice 13.1

STOP AND THINK

1. Why do you think it could be so difficult for a parent to learn of his or her child's autism diagnosis?

2. Give some thought to how you would interact sensitively with a parent who had just received this news.

GOAL DEVELOPMENT

The first step in designing appropriate interventions for young children with autism is to gather information from a number of formal and informal assessments, which can then be used to develop individualized goals (Barton, Lawrence, & Duerloo, 2012). The goals should focus on addressing their core deficits (i.e., communication, social skills, and restricted and repetitive behaviors). And goals should have a specific focus on (a) the ability to attend to relevant environmental cues; (b) imitation of peers and adults; (c) the ability to understand language and communicate; (d) functional and pretend play with toys; and (e) social interactions (Barton et al., 2012).

We must be careful to establish goals in collaboration with families. Families are most likely in the best position to provide information about the child's daily routines, strengths, and areas of need that we can address through appropriate interventions. Some families may be hesitant to express their opinion on these issues, especially early in the child's educational career, so we might need to take initiative on gathering such information through formal or informal interviews or family-centered planning tools. Family members may still be learning about their child's special needs, the supports available to them, and the professionals and systems that provide them, and they may be unclear about their own roles and responsibilities (Woods & Lindeman, 2008). Engaging the family, supporting their continued participation, and effectively gathering integral information may take some intentional effort on the part of the teacher.

Some guidelines to support reciprocal and respectful communication exchanges are detailed in Figure 13.1, based on information provided by Woods and Lindeman (2008). These strategies provide sufficient ways for engaging family members and supporting their continued involvement in the interventions process. The authors promote a reciprocal approach, giving "families information (e.g., the relevance of teaching and learning opportunities within daily routines, their child's abilities) while gathering information (e.g., the family members' concerns and priorities, the child's interests, and the places and activities of their daily life available for teaching and learning)" (Woods & Lindeman, 2008, p. 273). Five strategies that facilitate a reciprocal approach to exchanging information, according to Woods and Lindeman (2008), are listed in Figure 13.1.

Family Voices 13.2

"When you receive the diagnosis . . . the 'A' word . . . go ahead and express whatever emotions you feel. Don't think it's a reflection on you. You didn't exercise bad parenting. Surround yourself with other families in the same boat . . . they will become good friends and a support to your family. And find out what supports and services are available in your area. Hopefully your child's preschool teacher can help with that, but mine didn't. Don't be afraid to ask questions."

CLASSROOM ENVIRONMENTAL CONSIDERATIONS

Most children with autism benefit from highly structured and organized environments. Such structure and organization helps children identify relevant environmental cues, predict activities and routines, and understand behavioral expectations (Barton et al., 2012).

FIGURE 13.1

Five ways to exchange information

Source: adapted from Woods, J. J., & Lindeman, D. P. (2008). Gathering and giving information with families. *Infants and Young Children, 21*(4), 272–284

SENSORY STIMULATION

Research suggests that more than 80% of children with ASD respond negatively to sensory stimuli such as sounds, touch, or movement (Case-Smith, Weaver, & Fristad, 2015). Their responses can include distress or avoidance, and some children exhibit sensory-seeking behaviors (Case-Smith et al., 2015; O'Donnell et al., 2012). Students may exhibit challenging behaviors because of these sensory symptoms, or they may limit participation in certain activities or situations. Researchers believe that sensory processing issues for children with ASD are an underlying factor related to behaviors such as stereotypic or repetitive behaviors or repetitive movements such as rocking, twirling, or spinning, and they may influence a child's functional performance in daily activities such as eating and sleeping (Case-Smith et al., 2015). Sensory processing difficulties have also been linked to anxiety.

Sensory Issues

"These kids experience too much or too little stimulation through their senses and have trouble integrating the information they're getting. As a result, it's difficult, if not impossible, for them to feel comfortable and secure, function effectively, and be open to learning and socialization" (Beth Arky, n.d., Child Mind Institute).

Sensory-based interventions (SBIs) can be implemented in the classroom as part of the child's daily routine to improve behaviors associated with sensory reactivity. Sensory input, such as deep touch and rocking, brushing, swinging, bouncing on a therapy ball, weighted blankets, or wearing a weighted vest, has been used in the research literature with positive outcomes. These techniques have been used to promote calming, enhance self-regulation, or improve social interaction, increase purposeful play, and reduce hyper-reactivity in young children (Case-Smith et al., 2015). Teachers can incorporate sensory integration materials into the classroom, but they should consider the children's sensory needs, as well as their sensory aversions, when planning their learning environment (Deris & Di Carlo, 2013).

Classroom modifications can be valuable for facilitating success in the classroom for children with ASD. Two of the most critical aspects of the classroom include classroom arrangement and arrangement of materials. For example, Deris and Di Carlo (2013) suggest that teachers label classroom centers with pictures and words to give children the opportunity to communicate by requesting or refusing to play in a particular area. They also suggest creating quiet areas in the classroom where children can take a break or escape an overwhelming situation or eliminating distracting sensory stimuli, such as noise level, temperature, smells, or tactile and visual stimuli that might be anxiety producing. Creating well-organized workspaces, providing cues when transitions or changes to the schedule are forthcoming, and creating a daily schedule that provides routine and structure to the day are other suggestions (Deris & Di Carlo, 2013).

VISUAL SUPPORTS

We have already established through other chapters of this text that visual supports are highly recommended as effective practices for children with autism. In many preschool classrooms, teachers already make use of visual schedules, and they refer to them throughout the day to help children transition from one activity to the next (Barton et al., 2012). Visual schedules can be used with children with ASD to increase their independence in following directions, following daily routines, managing transitions, increasing task completion, and reducing challenging behaviors (Barton et al., 2012). These practices that are already in place in preschool classrooms have great value for children with autism as well.

There are many helpful kinds of visual supports that early childhood educators can use in the classroom every day. Of course, we should first assess the child before deciding which type of visual representations would be best. You can use real objects, photographs, line drawings, or words on the visual supports you choose.

Visual schedules can be used to illustrate what activity is taking place, specify what activity will occur next, indicate when an activity is finished, or identify any changes that might occur in the regular schedule. Visuals can also be used to structure the environment to help children with ASD function more independently. You can use images, symbols, and words to represent specific places where items belong, or you can put labels on shelves and drawers to help with cleanup. Visual schedules provide structure, predictability, and orderliness in the environment, and they can help provide a sense of stability for children with ASD (Meadan, Ostrosky, Triplett, Michna, & Fettig, 2011).

Visual scripts are another form of visual supports that are effective with young children with ASD. Visual scripts are written scenarios or examples that young children can use to initiate conversations or interactions with others. Also, visual reminder cards (e.g., visually representing classroom expectations on a poster board with photographs or drawings) can help children learn acceptable and unacceptable behaviors. Finally, a visual task analysis can provide step-by-step support to help children with ASD complete tasks independently (e.g., brushing teeth) and can be especially helpful for children who forget or confuse the order of a multistep process or who become easily distracted (Meadan et al., 2011).

WORK SYSTEMS

Many children with autism may benefit from structured work systems to help them learn self-management. Work systems are visually structured tasks that are arranged so that students know exactly what is expected of them, how to know the task is finished, what the reinforcement will be, and what activity will come next (Barton et al., 2012). There should be a clear beginning and end to each task that is organized through a work system. Work systems can provide directions for completing a task, such as hanging up one's coat and backpack or retrieving materials for an art project, for example.

T.I.P. – Theory Into Practice 13.2

GOALS FOR VINCENT

1. Review the case study for Vincent presented at the beginning of the chapter.

2. Write one to three goals for Vincent

to address skills you think should be developed.

REINFORCEMENT

An organized schedule or reinforcement is important for young children with autism. Reinforcement is a consequence for a behavior that increases the probability that the behavior will continue, and it is crucial to the effectiveness of interventions for children with ASD (Barton et al., 2012). Recall from previous chapters that reinforcement can take several forms, including tangible objects or activities; natural reinforcers, such as receiving something one has asked for; and social reinforcers, such as a smile or praise (Barton et al., 2012). Carefully observe what tends to provide motivation for an individual child, and use those things as reinforcers. Also, make sure that when a student performs the target behavior, reinforcement occurs immediately.

MODELING

Modeling can take many forms, and it can be easily embedded into daily routines (Barton et al., 2012). Peer and adult modeling can be used to show a child how to use a picture schedule, participate during circle time, or exchange appropriate social interactions (Barton et al., 2012). Video modeling can be an effective teaching tool. In video modeling, a peer of the child himself performs the target behavior, which is recorded on video. The video can be shown to the student as often as necessary to demonstrate activities such as social skills, play skills, requesting a snack, gathering materials, or many others.

NATURALISTIC TEACHING

Naturalistic teaching approaches use naturally occurring antecedents and consequences, they follow the child's interest, they are embedded into daily routines and activities, and they provide structured teaching across a variety of materials, routines, and people (Barton et al., 2012). One naturalistic teaching approach is called *incidental teaching*. This approach focuses on following the student's lead and waiting for him or her to request or indicate interest in something. In this approach, the teacher arranges the learning environment with preferred materials so that the student initiates interest in something. When the child looks, reaches for, or points to something of interest, the teacher models the target behavior (i.e., say the name of the object, point and look, make a verbal request, etc.). If the student imitates the target behavior, give the student access to the object (Barton et al., 2012).

T.I.P. – Theory Into Practice 13.3

ENVIRONMENTAL CONSIDERATIONS

1. Evaluate your fieldwork—or ideally, an early childhood classroom—to determine which of these environmental considerations are in place in that classroom and which represent areas for improvement.

2. Consider sharing your findings with your peers in the autism class, if your professor allows.

INSTRUCTIONAL APPROACHES

Developing Social Skills

Another evidence-based strategy for educating young children with ASD to teach social and communication skills is through peer-mediated interventions, which help provide opportunities to interact with socially competent peers. In this approach, the teacher first demonstrates to the typically achieving peers how to initiate social interactions, engage in organized play, or assist another student when he or she needs help. The peers practice these strategies with the teacher or adult and then use their skills to interact with the children with ASD (Barton et al., 2012). Peer-mediated interventions typically use routine activities to promote the development of age-appropriate social interactions with peers rather than with educators. Studies have suggested that interventions that systematically teach peers to engage children with ASD in positive play activities may have substantial positive effects on their social skills (Katz & Girolametto, 2013).

Family Voices 13.3

"As parents, we are our child's first teacher. In the course of normal development, we can support language, social, and academic development. A partnership with our preschool teacher was invaluable in knowing what kinds of things we could do at home to support development in all areas."

Katz and Girolametto (2013) trained educators who then worked with peer interventionists to engage in 20-minute play sessions that were supervised by teachers. During the play sessions, adults prompted children to use a specific strategy (e.g., "Johnny, do you want a block? What can you say?") whenever there was a period of 30 seconds with no joint interaction (Katz & Girolametto, 2013). Their intervention improved the social engagement of the children with ASD in their study, and they were able to maintain those gains in a maintenance text 4 to 5 weeks after the intervention was completed.

Ganz and Flores (2010) combined visual supports, such as scripts and instruction cards, in playgroups with typically achieving peers to improve social and communication skills in children with ASD. Visual cues, in this example, are cards with drawings and short phrases that give children suggestions for interacting in playgroups. Scripts are cards with pictures and short phrases that can be used during play or other social activities that provide cues about appropriate things to say. Choosing a theme for the dramatic play sessions, such as interacting in a bakery, with a baker, cashier, and customer, can be fun for children, too. Other possible themes include baby care, cooking lunch, barbershop, birthday party, camping, circus, farm, grocery shopping, pet shop, restaurant, or video store.

Peer-mediated support is recommended by the U.S. Department of Health and Human Services (2013). Teaching children specific social skills through peer-mediated support helps encourage friendships. It is suggested adults help children with peer-mediated support by teaching social skills during circle time, for example (U.S. Dept. of Health & Human Services, 2013). Social skills that can be taught during this time include getting a peer's attention, sharing an object, asking for an object, and giving compliments. Encourage children to use these newly learned skills with each other during daily activities, free play, outdoor play, mealtime, and transitions (U.S. Department of Health & Human Services, 2013). Remember to reinforce children when you find them practicing their skills.

DEVELOPING COMMUNICATION SKILLS

Expressive communication provides children a means to share wants and interests with peers, caregivers, teachers, and other adults. Young children with ASD often demonstrate delays in expressive communication, and therefore, naturalistic language intervention, or milieu teaching, is an important area of investigation (Lane, Shepley, & Lieberman-Betz, 2016).

There are several research studies demonstrating the effectiveness of early interventions such as milieu teaching to improve communication skills for young children with ASD. Christensen-Sandfort and Whinnery (2013), for example, implemented milieu teaching, emphasizing child initiation in the natural environment, as well as specialized instruction. "Unstructured activities, characterized by child-directed experiences, provide opportunities for skills practice in natural settings, taking advantage of a child's interests and motivation" (Christensen-Sandfort & Whinnery, 2013, p. 212). Christensen-Sandfort and Whinnery (2013) combined structured activities that were carefully planned and teacher directed, for intensive practice, with unstructured activities that were child directed for opportunities to practice the skills in natural settings. Improvements in spontaneous communication among the children in their study demonstrated the effectiveness of milieu strategies with young children with ASD (Christensen-Sandfort & Whinnery, 2013). Julien and Reichle (2015) also advocated for milieu teaching for the development of target vocabulary words through pretend play scenes (e.g., playing with animals and cooking and food toys).

MILIEU TEACHING

Milieu teaching involves adult–child interactions that occur during natural, unstructured times to help develop communication skills. Routine activities, such as playing, eating, and dressing, provide the perfect opportunity to embed learning activities into early childhood settings. When we embed learning opportunities into everyday routines and environments, we call them *naturalistic interventions*. Such techniques are based on the principles of applied behavior analysis, used to increase language through guided support (i.e., prompting) and reinforcement (using favored items to increase the desired behavior) in everyday environments that follow the child's lead (Ingersoll, 2011).

Milieu teaching is considered a naturalistic model that uses child interest as opportunities to model and prompt language in everyday contexts (Kaiser & Roberts, 2013). It involves arranging the environment in ways that increase the likelihood that the child will communicate; selecting and teaching specific skills that are appropriate to the child's developmental level; responding to the child's initiations with prompts for elaborated language; and reinforcing the child's communicative attempts by providing access to requested objects, with continued adult interaction and feedback (Kaiser & Roberts, 2013). There is evidence that this kind of teaching increases the use of social communicative language in children with disabilities.

There are four major teaching procedures in milieu teaching: modeling, mand-modeling, delay, and incidental teaching. In modeling, the teacher notices opportunities to model a response, waits for the child to respond, and provides prompts as she gauges the child's interest in a particular item. Mand-modeling builds upon the modeling procedure by providing a directive, such as, "Tell me what you want." The teacher also waits for a response in this procedure, provides prompts, and gauges the child's continued interest. The delay procedure is most often used for responses that a child has acquired but does not use consistently or frequently. Finally, incidental teaching involves using one of the three procedures mentioned here in an "unplanned" opportunity. We will discuss the model procedure, the mand-model procedure, and incidental teaching here.

Family Voices 13.4

"My son's teacher taught us how to use milieu teaching strategies at home. She showed us how to model a behavior or some form of language in small ways at home. I think this has been invaluable for Mia's language development."

Modeling. To implement milieu teaching, we first arrange the learning environment to ensure that two or three of the child's favorite items or toys are within reach. Begin implementing a milieu teaching strategy once the child begins to show interest or engages in the toy. One strategy involves modeling. In modeling, we would hold up the desired item and say the name of the toy aloud (i.e., "car"). If the child imitates the word, give the toy to the child and provide praise (i.e., "Yes, car," enthusiastically). If the child does not imitate, provide the model again, and look for the child to imitate. If by the third model, the child does not imitate, this time, give the item to the child.

Mand-modeling (asking a question). A similar technique uses questions to encourage communication. In this strategy, you would hold up the desired item and ask the child, "What do you want?" If the child responds appropriately, provide the item and follow with praise ("Car! You want to play with the car!"). If the child does not respond, ask the question again. If the child still does not respond, provide a verbal model (i.e., "car").

Incidental teaching. Incidental teaching involves using unplanned occasions to use milieu teaching strategies. When a child makes an attempt to communicate in any context, provide one of the strategies, such as modeling or mand-modeling. For example, before going to bed, the child might look around for her favorite stuffed bunny. You could hold up the bunny at that time and provide a model or mand-model. The focus of incidental teaching is to look for opportunities for language interventions that aren't necessarily planned in advance. Many times in teaching, we often call this a *teachable moment.*

Inclusion Tips

EARLY CHILDHOOD SUPPORTS

1. Provide visual supports (scripts, visual schedules, work systems, etc.).

2. Provide reinforcement.

3. Incorporate peer-mediated strategies.

4. Seek to understand the communicative function of behavior, to replace them with more appropriate behaviors that serve the same function.

5. Promote generalization of learned skills by providing multiple opportunities to practice in different settings, with different people, and with different materials.

6. Organize opportunities to participate in structured playgroups, combining children with ASD and typically achieving peers, around themes to teach social skills.

7. Look for opportunities to provide modeling or mand-modeling interventions. Plan these interventions, or look for incidental teaching opportunities.

8. Arrange the environment carefully.

FAMILY INVOLVEMENT IN EARLY INTERVENTION

In early childhood settings, we can observe developmental differences that may be indicators of ASD in children, and we may be called upon to refer families for screening, assessment, and intervention services (Nuner & Griffith, 2011). Behaviors such as differences in socialization, unresponsiveness or over-responsiveness to excitement in the environment, fixation on certain toys or parts of objects, dependence on rituals or routines, sensitivities to sensory inputs, difficulties with language used in socialization or having their needs met or language delays, and other such behaviors could be possible early signs of ASD that teachers in early childhood settings may notice. Early childhood educators should be knowledgeable of potential early signs of ASD, how families might respond when informed, and how to outline steps for intervention in ways that maintain a level of sensitivity to family needs (Nuner & Griffith, 2011). "When teachers of young children discuss such sensitive issues with families, it is important to express care and concern for the well being and health of the family without attaching diagnostic labels" (Nuner & Griffith, 2011, p. 13).

Early childhood educators are responsible for noticing atypical development, documenting areas of concern, and communicating with families any specific concerns about development (Nuner & Griffith, 2011). Early childhood educators may also assist with the screening or assessment process. Nuner and Griffith admonish early childhood educators to communicate frequently with families as they seek to find answers about their child's development (2011). What is most important is that we provide ongoing support to families through the process, ensuring that we never place diagnostic labels—it is not our place as educators to diagnose.

Families can experience a myriad of feelings when coming to grips with an ASD diagnosis. They might "feel disconnected and sometimes even misled by well-meaning professionals" (Nuner & Griffith, 2011, p. 17). Families might feel a lack of support from professionals, feel that some professionals are unhelpful or unqualified, or report "cold indifference and a lack of respect on the part of the professionals in understanding the family's experiences" (Nuner & Griffith, 2011, p. 17). Interactions with families should be handled by caring, informed, and empathetic professionals, and Nuner and Griffith (2011) suggest the following steps to better support families as they learn about their child's diagnosis and navigate the intervention system:

1. **Determine the parents' level of knowledge and comfort with an ASD diagnosis**. Do not assume that families understand everything. Gently lead parents to realize the challenges their child will face while continually celebrating the child's unique strengths and abilities. Have conversations with families often.

2. **Gently facilitate acceptance**. Understand that families might experience high levels of stress as they learn about a diagnosis, or they might feel rejected by family, friends, or strangers in the community, which can be isolating or overwhelming. Early childhood educators can help alleviate some of this stress by handling communication with parents with sensitivity and caring.

3. **Assist with referrals**. Help find programs available at the county or community level, depending on age and need, that can involve behavioral interventions, cognitive interventions, speech therapy, physical therapy, occupational therapy, family education, or assistive technology, for example. Work closely with families to ensure they are aware of local services that are available.

4. **Assist with intervention services**. Teachers might participate in IEP development, implement assistive technology in the classroom, involve therapists to work with individual children, or work with children in the classroom.

Above all, understand that "families are learning to maneuver through a new system of personnel and procedures whose existence they were probably unaware of prior to the referral" (Nuner & Griffith, 2011, p. 19). As such, families may need the knowledge, support, and reassurance of an early education team with whom they have a trusting relationships (Nuner & Griffith, 2011).

We can collaborate with families to implement interventions designed to address disruptive behaviors in young children with ASD. Bearss, Johnson, Handen, Smith, and Scahill (2013), for example, indicated that behaviors such as tantrums, aggression, noncompliance with routine demands, and recklessness (behaviors that interfere with the acquisition and performance of daily living skills and can also interfere with family quality of life) can be addressed through parent training. We can teach parents to use strategies such as visual schedules, environmental manipulations, reinforcement, and various techniques for delivering instructions to increase the child's compliance. Bearss et al. (2013) developed a parent training manual using the ABC (antecedent, behavior, and consequence) model to assess possible functions and motivations of disruptive behaviors, to utilize strategies that support antecedent management and reinforcement, and to implement strategies for teaching new skills. They felt that their parent training program not only produced reductions in disruptive behaviors and gains in adaptive functioning but also represented "an important step toward developing a service delivery model that can be implemented more efficiently and on a larger scale than existing interventions" (Bearss et al., 2013, p. 836).

Involving Families in Early Intervention

- Know the early signs of ASD.

- Document concerning behaviors objectively, communicate clearly, listen empathetically, and understand the family's feelings when learning of an ASD diagnosis.

- Refer families to available services, depending on the child's needs.

- Teach parents to use the ABC model (antecedent, behavior, and consequence) to understand the function of challenging behaviors and teach replacement behaviors.

- Collaborate with parents to use visual schedules at home.

- Show families how to manipulate the environment in ways that meet student needs.

SUMMARY STATEMENTS

- Young children with ASD exhibit challenging behaviors because of sensory issues, and they may limit participation in certain activities or situations.

- Research shows that visual supports, such as scripts, visual schedules, and the like, can improve children's social and communication skills as they participate in classroom and recreational activities and can help increase independence and reduce challenging behaviors.

- An organized schedule or reinforcement is important for young children with autism.

- To increase the chances of generalization, we might teach a new skill in a structured environment or in a one-on-one setting and then provide multiple opportunities for the child to practice the new skill throughout the day.

- Peer-mediated interventions, which help provide opportunities to interact with socially competent peers, are another evidence-based strategy for educating young children with ASD that can be used to teach a variety of social and communication skills.

- Milieu teaching has been used in a number of studies to develop communication and social skills in young children with ASD.

- Challenging behaviors of young children with ASD represent a serious impediment to healthy social, emotional, and intellectual development. Therefore, there is a great need for strategies that are effective at promoting positive behavior development.

- It is important to understand the "why" of a behavior so that we can determine the proper response.

- We can collaborate with families to implement interventions designed to address disruptive behaviors in young children with ASD, such as positive behavior supports. Understanding the function of a challenging behavior is a key component of PBS.

WHAT WOULD YOU DO?

Look back at the case study about Vincent presented at the beginning of the chapter. Based on what you have read in this chapter, what you have read in previous chapters, and your own experiences, how would you respond to the following questions?

1. What strategy would you suggest that Miss Jennifer try to help Vincent make a snack request or request preferred items during playtime?

2. How would you address Vincent's behaviors such as throwing toys and hitting others?

3. What strategies would you recommend to address his communication skills?

4. How would you work with the inclusive preschool teacher, Miss Jennifer, to develop behavior supports?

5. How would you respond to Vincent's mother, who would like to implement some strategies at home that would help with his behavior and communication skills?

CHAPTER REFLECTION QUESTIONS

1. Given what you have just read in this chapter, what was the most powerful insight you have acquired, and what are the implications for your teaching?

2. What are some early signs of ASD, and how do we approach diagnosis in the early years?

3. How do we best address challenging behaviors in early childhood settings?

4. Imagine that the local school district is recommending that all staff incorporate more visual supports in every classroom. What tips would you share about how to do this effectively?

5. What strategies would you suggest for a general-education preschool teacher who has several children with ASD in her classroom?

6. In what ways can you work with families and caregivers to implement some of the strategies from this chapter at home?

RECOMMENDED RESOURCES

Websites

- Autism Speaks. Study finds preschoolers with autism vary greatly in areas of progress. Available at https://www.autismspeaks.org/science/science-news/study-finds-preschoolers-autism-vary-greatly-areas-progress

- Early Childhood Development (U.S. Department of Health & Human Services). Autism awareness and acceptance in early childhood education. Available at http://www.acf.hhs.gov/ecd/child-health-development/asd

Articles/Publications

- Head Start Center for Inclusion. Checklist to guide inclusion practices. Retrieved from http://headstartinclusion.org/sites/default/files/teachers%20guide-MOC.pdf

- M-CHAT-R/F (Modified Checklist for Autism in Toddlers, Revised with Follow-Up). Retrieved from https://www.m-chat.org/mchat.php

- U.S. Department of Health & Human Services. Tips for early care and education providers. Retrieved from https://www.acf.hhs.gov/sites/default/files/ecd/508_tips_for_early_care_and_education_providers_april_2013.pdf

REFERENCES

Arky, B. (n.d.). *Treating sensory processing issues.* Child Mind Institute. Retrieved from https://childmind.org/article/treating-sensory-processing-issues

Autism Speaks. (n.d.). *Learn the signs of autism.* Retrieved from: https://www.autismspeaks.org/what-autism/learn-signs

Barton, E. E., Lawrence, K., & Deurloo, F. (2012). Individualizing interventions for young children with autism in preschool. *Journal of Autism and Developmental Disorders, 42,* 1205–1217.

Bearss, K., Johnson, C., Handen, B., Smith, T., & Scahill, L. (2013). A pilot study of parent training in young children with autism spectrum disorders and disruptive behavior. *Journal of Autism and Developmental Disorders, 43,* 829–840.

Case-Smith, J., Weaver, L. L., & Fristad, M. A. (2015). A systematic review of sensory processing interventions for children with autism spectrum disorders. *Autism, 19*(2), 133–148.

Christensen-Sandfort, R. J., & Whinnery, S. B. (2013). Impact of milieu teaching on communication skills of young children with autism spectrum disorder. *Topics in Early Childhood Special Education, 32*(4), 211–222. doi:10.1177/0271121411404930

Deris, A. R., & Di Carlo, C. F. (2013). Back to basics: Working with young children with autism in inclusive classrooms. *Support for Learning, 28*(3), 52–57.

Ganz, J. B., & Flores, M. M. (2010). Implementing visual cues for young children with autism spectrum disorders and their classmates. *Young Children, 65*(3), 78–83.

Ingersoll, B. (2011). The differential effect of three naturalistic language interventions on language use in children with autism. *Journal of Positive Behavioral Interventions, 13,* 109–118.

Johnson, C. P., & Myers, S. M. (2007). Identification and evaluation of children with autism spectrum disorders. *Pediatrics, 120*(5), 1183–1215.

Julien, H. M., & Reichle, J. (2015). A comparison of high and low dosages of a component of milieu teaching strategies for two preschool-age learners with autism spectrum disorder. *Language, Speech, and Hearing Services in Schools, 47*, 87–98.

Kaiser, A. P., & Roberts, M. Y. (2013). Parent-implemented enhanced milieu teaching with preschool children with intellectual disabilities. *Journal of Speech Language Hearing Research, 56*(1), 295–309.

Katz, E., & Girolametto, L. (2013). Peer-mediated intervention for preschoolers with ASD implemented in early childhood settings. *Topics in Early Childhood Special Education, 33*(3), 133–143.

Lane, J. D., Shepley, C., & Lieberman-Betz, R. (2016). Promoting expressive language in young children with or at-risk for autism spectrum disorder in a preschool classroom. *Journal of Autism and Developmental Disorders, 46*(10), 3216–3231. doi:10.1007/s10803-016-2917-z

Meadan, H., Ostrosky, M. M., Triplett, B., Michna, A., & Fettig, A. (2011). Using visual supports with young children with autism spectrum disorders. *TEACHING Exceptional Children, 43*, 28–35.

National Autism Association. (n.d.). Signs of autism. Retrieved from http://nationalautismassociation.org/resources/signs-of-autism

Nuner, J. E., & Griffith, A. C. S. (2011). Early signs of autism: How to support families and navigate referral procedures. *Dimensions of Early Childhood, 39*(1), 12–20.

O'Donnell, S., Deitz, J., Kartin, D., Nalty, T., & Dawson, G. (2012). Sensory processing, problem behavior, adaptive behavior, and cognition in preschool children with autism spectrum disorders. *American Journal of Occupational Therapy, 66*(5), 586–594. doi:10.5014/ajot.2012.004168

Robins, D. L., Casagrande, K., Barton, M., Chen, C., Dumont-Mathieu, T., & Fein, D. (2014). Validation of the Modified Checklist for Autism in Toddlers, revised with follow-up (M-CHAT-R/F). *Pediatrics, 133*(1), 37–45.

U.S. Department of Health & Human Services. (2013). *Tips for early care and educator providers: Simple concepts to embed in everyday routines.* Retrieved from https://www.acf.hhs.gov/sites/default/files/ecd/508_tips_for_early_care_and_education_providers_april_2013.pdf

Woods, J. J., & Lindeman, D. P. (2008). Gathering and giving information with families. *Infants and Young Children, 21*(4), 272–284.

Ziv, Y., Hadad, B. S., & Khateeb, Y. (2014). Social information processing in preschool children diagnosed with autism spectrum disorder. *Journal of Autism and Developmental Disorders, 44*, 846–859.

Transitioning to Adulthood

$\left(14\right)$

"While most students with ASD present challenging social and communication deficits, making it a challenge to find suitable work, they also show remarkable skills in different areas, and it therefore becomes important to identify the strengths of young people with ASD. We can then match those strengths to work and community environments where they can be successful."

CASE STUDY

Grant is a 16-year-old student with ASD in Mr. Helmsley's special education classroom. He has never held a paid employment position. Grant enjoys structure, following rules, and working consistently to accomplish his goals. Though Grant occasionally initiates conversation with others, he does not have friends, and he spends most of his time at home on his computer, reading the news on his Google page and listening to the police scanner. He loves to read about local crimes and criminal profiles whenever he can.

His favorite section of his small, local newspaper is the "crime reports" section. He enjoys reading "true detective" novels as well and considers himself skilled at finding out who committed the crime depicted in the novel. Grant's independent reading skills are at grade level, and he is skilled in typing and data entry. Grant created a spreadsheet of crimes he has read about, notes about the victims, and his suggestions about who is responsible.

Cooking is another area of interest for Grant. He enjoys finding recipes on the computer, asking his mom to purchase the ingredients, and preparing the meal for his family. He likes to wear his "chef's hat" while preparing the meal. Grant loves to watch cooking shows on cable television and sometimes imitates the TV personalities while he is cooking his own meal.

LEARNER OBJECTIVES

After reading this chapter, the learner should be able to do the following:

- Describe the symptoms of ASD that make the transition to adulthood particularly challenging for young adults.

- Discuss how symptoms of ASD can impact employment outcomes, positively or negatively.

- Discuss the responsibilities of school personnel to be involved in transition planning for adolescents with ASD.

- Explain how the symptoms of ASD can impact postsecondary education, and describe what school personnel can do to support the transition.

- Describe the daily independent living skills that should be considered when planning for transitioning to independent living.

- Discuss collaboration with families to ensure a successful transition to adulthood for our students with ASD.

In Mr. Helmsley's class, sometimes Grant rushes through his work so that he can read books or use the computer to learn about notable criminals or search for recipes he can cook at home. Watching YouTube cooking videos is another of Grant's favorite activities. When Mr. Helmsley tries to persuade and/or reinforce Grant to spend more time on his classwork (completing a math worksheet, for example), Grant becomes frustrated and sometimes tears his paper and throws his pencil in response. Even though he does not participate much in social interactions with his classmates, he does enjoy saying "hi" to everyone he encounters, and other people perceive him as "friendly."

Grant's mother would like to begin preparation for his transition to adulthood. She would like to begin addressing issues of future employment, possible postsecondary education, and daily community living so that he can achieve the highest level of independence possible.

....

INTRODUCTION

Increased attention has been given to the needs of students with ASD who are transitioning to adulthood. Because the symptoms of ASD fall along a spectrum, it affects each individual differently and to varying degrees of severity. Most individuals with ASD have difficulty making and keeping friends, trouble understanding the feelings or perspectives of others, and might not pick up on social cues or follow accepted social conventions—all of which place them at risk for being misunderstood by others (Adreon & Durocher, 2007) and for experiencing a difficult transition to adulthood and independence.

Symptoms of ASD can make the transition to adulthood a challenge. The communication patterns of individuals with ASD might include speaking in an overly formal manner, having a monotonous sounding voice, being unaware of how loudly or softly they are speaking, or inappropriate body language (i.e., standing too close to others when speaking) and can impact adult life (Adreon & Durocher, 2007). In addition, they may continue to talk at length about a topic of high interest, have difficulty taking the listener's needs into account in a conversation, and often interpret others' language in an overly literal way. Furthermore, they might have problems with comprehension, or interpreting and following multistep directions and discussions, and they tend not to use the slang expressions commonly used by their classmates (Adreon & Durocher, 2007). Further, their unique manner of speaking and use of body language may be misinterpreted by others as disinterest, frustration, or anger, causing others to avoid interacting with them (Adreon & Durocher, 2007).

Restricted and repetitive activities, interests, and behaviors can also make the transition to adulthood difficult for individuals with ASD. They might have body mannerisms that can be misunderstood by others, such as rocking back and forth, moving their hands in unusual ways, shuffling from one foot to the other, or drumming their fingers on a table. Their intense interest in one or two topics might set them apart from their peers, prevent them from engaging in social activities, or result in a lack of motivation for activities or course work not involving these topics (Andreon & Durocher, 2007). Inflexible adherence to routines or sameness may cause difficulty as well. (What if class was cancelled, a roommate rearranged the living space, or the semester schedule changed?) Adherence to rules is important for individuals with ASD as well. They may become agitated when others break the rules, or they may attempt to enforce the rules on their own.

Overall, the symptoms of ASD will likely have an impact on seeking and maintaining employment, pursuing postsecondary education, and living in the community. Therefore, planning for transition to adulthood is important. As educators, we are obligated to consider identifying postsecondary options, discussing when and how to disclose one's disability, teaching independent living skills, identifying meaningful work opportunities, and providing the appropriate supports and accommodations to smooth the transition process. One primary goal of public education in the United States is to equip students to transition successfully to adulthood. "Put simply, an essential component of secondary services and support must be on equipping adolescents and young adults with ASD to thrive in the schools, workplaces, and communities" (Carter, Harvey, Taylor, & Gotham, 2013, p. 888).

ISSUES IN TRANSITIONING TO ADULTHOOD

Researchers estimate that each year in the United States, approximately 50,000 adults with ASD turn 18 years old (Chen, Sung, & Pi, 2015). Therefore, demands for services such as postsecondary education, employment, residence, and community participation have increased in response to these individuals who are transitioning to adulthood (Chen et al., 2015). Moreover, as the numbers of children being identified with ASD increases steadily and as these children transition to adulthood, there is a greater need to identify meaningful work, postsecondary education, and community living and adaptive functioning outcomes for these individuals (Wehman et al., 2012).

EMPLOYMENT

Participation in employment is considered an essential component of adult life (Chen et al., 2015). "Being employed means earning one's own living, contributing to society, integrating into a social network, being seen as part of society, and being less reliant on taxpayer-funded programs" (Chen et al., 2015, p. 3015). Employment can promote personal dignity, it can help build self-esteem, and it can develop a sense of purpose in life (Chen et al., 2015, pp. 3015–3016). Yet the majority of individuals with ASD remain unemployed, underemployed, or underpaid following graduation from secondary school (Chen et al., 2015; Sung, Sanchez, Kuo, Wang, & Leahy, 2015; Taylor & Seltzer, 2011). In this section, we will discuss the difficulties in finding employment for individuals with ASD, and we will also discuss the many characteristics of ASD that can be considered strengths that potential employers could benefit from.

Employment is a desirable achievement for individuals with ASD who are transitioning to adulthood. However, employment issues remain a major concern for individuals with ASD (Chen et al., 2015; Sung et al., 2015). "Unemployment and underemployment are profound issues for these adults" (Chen et al., 2015, p. 3016). Research shows that only 55% of adults with ASD had been employed at least once in the first 6 years following high school (Chen et al., 2015).

Research on post–high school activities for adults with ASD paints a pessimistic picture of their employment (Taylor & Seltzer, 2011). Even those participants in Taylor and Seltzer's (2011) research who were able to find employment following formal education tended to have jobs that were poorly paid, or those who were employed tended to have jobs such as replacing dirty glasses with clean ones in a hotel. The discouraging employment outcomes of individuals with ASD do "not represent a lack of abilities on the part of the youths with ASD, but instead the inadequacy of the current service system to accommodate the needs of youths with ASD . . . as they are transitioning to adulthood" (Taylor & Seltzer, 2011, p. 572).

Wilczynski, Trammell, and Clarke (2013) pointed out the primary problem for individuals with ASD in gaining employment. They said that every job requires at least some of the skills that are a primary deficit of ASD. "Consider, what employment positions do not require communication and social interaction? Which employers seek staff with a rigid adherence to sameness and one's own routines?" (Wilczynski et al., 2013, p. 876).

While most students with ASD present challenging social and communication deficits, making it a challenge to find suitable work, they also show remarkable skills in different areas, and it therefore becomes important to identify the strengths of young people with ASD. We can then match those strengths to work and community environments where they can be successful (Wehman et al., 2012). It is important for school-based supports to be in place that improve the likelihood that employment positions are secured and maintained. Supports should be offered to students with ASD while they are in school that result in workforce placement when a student leaves formal education (Wilczynski et al., 2013).

BENEFITS OF HIRING INDIVIDUALS WITH ASD

Many characteristics of ASD can be considered strengths when considering employment. For example, individuals with ASD may be excellent employees because of their focus on details, and because they enjoy routines or repetitive tasks. Understanding this can help educators make a case with potential employers by illustrating these strengths. We can be of assistance by finding employers who appreciate our students' uniqueness.

For individuals with ASD, the heightened focus comes naturally. Such intensity can be an asset to employers because it helps them focus on the task at hand. Focus and commitment also make individuals with ASD "model" employees because they tend to work hard, even when no one is watching. Individuals with ASD can bring tremendous creativity to anything they encounter. Take a look at the artwork featured in each chapter of this textbook—all drawn by individuals with ASD, for example. Several of the artists featured in this book are working artists who are able to sell their artwork and have a consistent income.

Individuals with ASD have incredible imaginations and creativity that helps them look for new ways to solve problems. Because individuals usually have intense interests, the best jobs are those that allow them to be involved regularly with these interests. For example, we heard about an individual who was skilled at memorizing the schedule of every subway car and every route. That gentleman would therefore make an ideal subway station information officer, who could provide details to travelers who might not know such details. An individual with ASD who loves working in his area of extensive knowledge can be very focused and productive.

Jobs that require an intense amount of detail can be perfect for an individual with ASD. Consider software testing, for example, or coding or programming, or data entry, or statistical analysis, or anything detail oriented, which require a lot of precision, attention, and repetition. Individuals with ASD can possess exceptional and unique skills that enable them to thrive in many detail-oriented roles. As we learn to recognize their strengths and abilities and to promote those strengths to potential employers, we can be a tremendous help to individuals with ASD and their families.

POSTSECONDARY EDUCATION

Most statistics tell us that only about one-third of youth with ASD attend college (Autism Speaks, n.d.). Researchers explain that young adults with ASD may not benefit from education to the same extent as their peers without disabilities, they are least likely to participate in postsecondary education, and they experience poor postschool outcomes (Taylor, Henninger, & Mailick, 2015). Adults with ASD are substantially underrepresented in postsecondary education (Taylor et al., 2015). It is important to understand why individuals with ASD might be at a higher risk of disengagement from these activities (Taylor et al., 2015).

Challenges with communication, social interactions, and behavior may make the transition from high school to life after high school particularly challenging. And sometimes, this transition leaves many individuals with ASD without any support (Roberts, 2010) or without the support they are accustomed to receiving in the K–12 school years. There are also expectations of increased independence, more demands for self-directed learning, time management, less structured settings, and new peer groups and social situations that can make transitioning to postsecondary education difficult (Mitchell & Beresford, 2014). In addition, less developed social skills may compromise their ability to integrate into a new setting, develop social networks, and manage new expectations of independence (Mitchell & Beresford, 2014).

There are many differences between high school and college that young adults with ASD and their families should be aware of. For example, in high school, teachers may check and grade completed homework, remind students of upcoming assignments, make themselves available before and after class, have training in specific teaching methods, present material in ways that help students with ASD understand the text, and so forth. In college, professors may assume homework is completed, may not remind students of upcoming or incomplete assignments, may expect students to ask for assistance when they need it, may expect students to think independently, and may expect students to read the syllabus and class materials independently. The most significant factor in the transition from high school to college may be the fact that students will be expected to live independently and have the ability to advocate for themselves and take care of their own needs.

Families may not be aware of the significant changes that await their child upon transition to postsecondary education. Although laws require public higher education settings to provide reasonable modifications and accommodations, and some universities provide programming and supports specifically geared toward students with ASD, there may be a significant reduction in educational services and supports following the transition into adulthood. Familial supports might not be in place as they were in high school, as students may be living away from home for the first time. Young adults may no longer have siblings or family members to rely on to pave the way to making friends or being accepted into social groups. Sometimes, isolation and potentially depression plagues students with ASD who are new to postsecondary education.

T.I.P. – Theory Into Practice 14.1

STOP AND THINK: TRANSITION TO ADULTHOOD

Thinking about the transition to adulthood can be a difficult time for families.

1. What do you imagine that a family might be concerned about related to the transition for their child?

2. What do you imagine that a family would be excited about related to the transition for their child?

3. Imagine that you will have a conversation next week with a family of one of your students with ASD who is nearing the transition period. How might you approach this conversation?

4. How might you involve the family in planning for the transition?

Taylor and Seltzer (2011) reported encouraging figures from their research. Nearly 50% of the youth with ASD without an intellectual disability in their study were pursuing a postsecondary educational degree. For many individuals with ASD, attending and completing postsecondary education is a viable option (Roberts, 2010). Supporting that success may require extensive planning and ongoing support. Educators should know what supports the student requires for optimal transition and success from high school to postsecondary education.

DAILY LIVING AND ADAPTIVE FUNCTIONING

Transition into adulthood can be a very challenging time for individuals with ASD. In particular, the social challenges inherent in ASD can interfere with the process of building relationships, functioning well occupationally, and participating and integrating into the community (Kandalaft, Didehbani, Krawczyk, Allen, & Chapman, 2013). Social cognition, which includes the thought processes of accurately integrating, interpreting, and responding to social cues, can present new challenges for individuals with ASD as they transition into adulthood.

Skills necessary for age-appropriate independent living for young adults with ASD may need to be addressed as we consider transitioning to adulthood. In studies of individuals with ASD who were ready for transitioning into adulthood, with and without intellectual disabilities, adaptive functioning has been found to be an area of relative weaknesses (Matthews et al., 2015). *Adaptive functioning* refers to the ability to handle everyday tasks, such as managing a home and personal care, managing money, using the telephone, using public or private transportation, staying safe and healthy, following schedules and routines, and working. Additionally, adaptive functioning includes social skills, such as how one behaves around others, how you feel about yourself, how you solve problems, how you follow rules and obey laws, and how you make up your own mind or whether other people influence you unduly.

Daily living skills are an important area that should be addressed as we work toward transitioning to adulthood for students with ASD. Many of these skills can be addressed in the IEP's transition plan. Preparation in life skills is critical to ensure that young adults with ASD are prepared for the transition to adulthood (Organization for Autism Research [OAR], 2012). Potential living arrangements include supervised group home living, adult foster care, supervised apartment living, and independent living. Other life skills include personal care, time management, and dealing with relationships.

Additional skills include knowing how to speak on the telephone and access important numbers. How to clean and maintain a home, such as understanding how to use cleaning products and tools, is also important to address. It is critical to understand how to manage one's money, such as using a checking account, budgeting for weekly or monthly expenses, and knowing how credit cards work.

We also want our students with ASD to know how to use public transportation appropriately for increased independence. Knowing how to utilize the bus schedule, orientation to a map, or driving safety are also important considerations (OAR, 2012). Getting appropriate exercise, understanding nutrition, using cooking skills, keeping appointments, and time management are important areas to address to increase a young adult's independence and transition to adulthood (OAR, 2012).

T.I.P. – Theory Into Practice 14.2

COMMUNITY LIVING

1. Imagine that you have been asked to write a blog about transitioning to community living for young adults with ASD.

2. What key points will you make in the blog?

TRANSITION PLANNING

The Individuals with Disabilities Education Improvement Act (IDEA, 2004) ensures that children receive needed services in relation to their strengths, challenges, and interests. IDEA requirements are facilitated through the IEP process. And no later than age 16, the IEP must include transition planning services that are focused on instruction and services for employment, education, and other postsecondary living skills. There are also vocational rehabilitation services available in each state that can evaluate an individual's strengths and provide assistance in preparing for, finding, and keeping a job.

Transition planning is the coordinated set of activities designed to move students from school to post–high school settings successfully (Roberts, 2010). Up-to-date assessment should be performed, as a starting point, and that information should be used to develop the training, education, and supports that can facilitate a successful transition, academically and socially (Roberts, 2010). The transition plan will identify the services to be provided, specify the timelines and persons responsible for implementing the services, state the intended outcomes, and provide a plan for monitoring and following up on the implementation of activities (Roberts, 2010). The transition plan should also take into account the individual's personal goals and aspirations and individual strengths, learning styles, self-advocacy skills, and time management skills. "Successful postsecondary education transition requires preparation and planning that, for the educator, begin with knowing the adolescent" (Roberts, 2010, p. 159).

The Organization for Autism Research (OAR) indicates that a good transition plan should include long- and short-term goals, it should identify necessary supports, and it should be specific to the interests, abilities, and desires of the student. The plan may include vocational training, employment goals and a timeline for achieving them, goals that support independent living, community participation goals, postsecondary education goals, and coordination with state and private service agencies and providers (OAR, 2012).

An important part of the planning process involves assessing the student's personal interests. We want to know the topics and activities that are of particular interest to the young adult, what topics or activities the student has difficulty tolerating, current academic or related strengths and talents, and to what extent the current skill set matches potential demands of desirable activities or environments (OAR, 2012; Roberts, 2010). This helps to see connections between current interests and talents and what the student can do in the future. "Tailoring transition planning to your child's personal interests will help keep him focused and engaged, while suggesting clear and meaningful next steps toward achieving his goals" (OAR, 2012, p. 11).

Determining interests. There are a variety of assessments and person-centered tools that can be used to assist in determining the specific interests of a young person with ASD. These interests can be useful in matching individuals to potential work or living settings. A good way to approach finding the right job for an individual with ASD is to first list personal strengths and interests, and then search the job market to see what positions are available that match up closely with those strengths and interests (Autism Speaks, 2013).

We should be aware of the student's strengths or capabilities and weaknesses or challenges (OAR, 2012). This information can help us understand how these areas may be of benefit to students as they transition beyond high school, what areas might become a strength, how we can help the young adult best capitalize on a specific strength, and the extent to which identified challenges might impact the student's potential in the workplace or other areas of adult life (OAR, 2012).

Resources for Determining Interests	
The following resources offer comprehensive interest assessments for individuals with ASD. Several of these also offer a list of jobs that may be of interest to the individual based on his or her responses.	
Informal Interest Inventories	
Autism Speaks	What job is right for you? https://www.autismspeaks.org/sites/default/files/docs/etk_what_job_is_right_for_you.pdf
Autism Online	Interest Inventory Activity http://www.autismonline.com/pdfs/m3AO-AC.pdf
	(Continued)

(Continued)

Resources for Determining Interests	
The following resources offer comprehensive interest assessments for individuals with ASD. Several of these also offer a list of jobs that may be of interest to the individual based on his or her responses.	
Informal Interest Inventories	
Do2learn	http://do2learn.com/JobTIPS/DeterminingInterests/ InterestsQuiz/Overview.html
Institute for Community Inclusion	http://www.communityinclusion.org/article.php?article_ id=54&type=topic&id=11
Occupation Net	Preferences for work environments and outcomes. https://www .onetonline.org/find/descriptor/browse/Interests
Formal Interest Inventories	
Prework Multiple Stimulus Assessment Lattimore, L. P., Parsons, M. B., & Reid, D. H. (2002). A prework assessment of task preferences among adults with autism beginning a supported job. *Journal of Applied Behavior Analysis*, *35*, 85–88.	
Autism Work Skill Questionnaire Gal, E., Meir, A. B., & Katz, N. (2013). Development and reliability of the autism work skills questionnaire (AWSQ). *American Journal of Occupational Therapy*, *67*, 4–5.	

T.I.P. – Theory Into Practice 14.3

WHAT'S YOUR INTEREST?

1. Visit the website do2learn, and take the "Interests Quiz" at http://do2learn .com/JobTIPS/DeterminingInterests/ InterestsQuiz/Overview.html

2. Evaluate your results. Do you think this quiz represented your interests and matched you to an appropriate job?

3. Consider sharing the results and your reflections about taking the quiz with your classmates.

SUPPORTING TRANSITIONING TO ADULTHOOD

The goal of schools should be to support students in obtaining the highest degree of independence (Wilczynski et al., 2013). That means preparing young adults in how to gain and keep employment, how to navigate their postsecondary education, and how to live in the community with independence. Individuals with ASD have historically been at a significantly high risk of not continuing on to postsecondary education or securing employment following high school graduation (Sung et al., 2015), and so, we must fulfill our responsibilities to aid this transition to adulthood.

EMPLOYMENT

Given that the statistics for employment of individuals with ASD in their transition to adulthood appear less than optimal, examining related services that could promote successful transition outcomes is important. Schools play a critical role in easing the transition to adulthood by developing and/or collaborating with programs that are designed to meet the employment needs of individuals with ASD (Wilczynski et al., 2013). Transition planning for individuals with ASD should begin 3 to 4 years prior to exiting the school system, perhaps as young as 14 years of age (Sung et al., 2015).

While school personnel do not hold the sole responsibility for improving employment outcomes for individuals with ASD, they should be involved in collaborating with organizations, employment agencies, and vocational rehabilitation agencies that provide vocational training to increase the likelihood of employment (Wilczynski et al., 2013). Therefore, let us consider the services that are related to the successful employment outcomes for individuals with ASD in the research literature.

Chen et al. (2015) looked at employment outcomes for individuals with ASD based on a large national database and the types of rehabilitation services they received to determine which services positively contributed to their employment status. There were 23 types of rehabilitative services listed in their research. Of those 23 services, three emerged as the strongest predictors of successful employment outcomes—counseling and guidance, job placement assistance, and on-the-job support. In fact, among the youth ages 18 to 25, those who received on-the-job support services were over 4 times more likely to be employed than those in the under-18 or the over-25 age groups. All groups showed similar patterns with respect to counseling and guidance and job placement assistance (Chen et al., 2015).

On-the-job support was described as services provided to an individual in their place of employment, such as job coaching, follow-up, and job retention services. Implications of the Chen et al. (2015) research are evident. First, it is essential to develop individualized vocational assistance for individuals with ASD "to facilitate and support their smooth transition from adolescence to adulthood and/or from school to work" (p. 3027). Second, Chen et al. (2015) recommended that job-related services, such as job placement and on-the-job support should be more incorporated into an IEP for transition-aged individuals.

Wilczynski et al. (2013) recommended several categories of support that schools could provide to increase the likelihood that individuals with ASD gain suitable employment when they leave school. They recommended that schools help provide support in the job search process; a skills assessment; how to complete an application and prepare for an interview (i.e., role-playing or videotaped mock interviews); identification of potential work challenges; training on how to manage workplace conditions; and on-the-job support and coaching (Wilczynski et al., 2013). Similarly, participants in Sung et al. (2015) benefited from receiving counseling, job search assistance, and behavioral skills training. Clients also benefited from receiving assistance in preparing résumés, identifying appropriate job opportunities, and developing interview skills (Sung et al., 2015).

Wehman et al. (2012) identified and researched the Project SEARCH program, which provides a school-to-work transition model for young people with significant disabilities. The program combined real-life work experience, training in employability and independent living skills, and placement assistance with partnering organizations. The "hallmark" of the Project SEARCH model is workplace immersion, where "students spend their entire day at the workplace for a full school year, facilitating a seamless integration of classroom instruction and on-the-job training and support that cannot be achieved with occasional visits to the workplace or simulated work environments" (Wehman et al., 2012, p. 145). Wehman et al. (2012) implemented Project SEARCH with a group of youth with ASD and studied the outcomes.

Project SEARCH is a business-led collaborative partnership between schools and local large businesses such as hospitals, bank centers, or government centers (Wehman et al., 2012). In the model, students rotate through three internships throughout the school year. The internships are based on student aspirations for employment. For example, if a student expresses an interest in data processing, that student might rotate through internships that teach how to create donor files, how to create a database of doctors in a hospital, and how to input invoice numbers into a spreadsheet in the accounts payable office. Internships should represent marketable skills, and they should help the host business achieve the mission but not distract from the business (Wehman et al., 2012). Students are interviewed, and in their program, they receive intensive instruction based on their unique social, behavioral, and learning characteristics. For more details on Project SEARCH, see the Wehman et al. (2012) article listed in recommended resources at the end of this chapter.

It is also important to consider whether the student will disclose that he or she has ASD. Remember that disclosure is a personal choice, and there is no law obligating anyone to disclose that he or she has a disability, but to be eligible for accommodations, some level of disclosure may be necessary. There are also various social skills demanded in certain jobs that will help the young adult with ASD function well. One should be able to present oneself well, with appropriate clothing, cleanliness and hygiene, and grooming, and have basic interpersonal skills. Some areas of social competence that are important to consider are general manners, table manners, awareness of others' personal space, recognizing the need for assistance and obtaining assistance when appropriate, what to do on his or her break, and the like (OAR, 2012).

T.I.P. – Theory Into Practice 14.4

EMPLOYMENT: PROJECT SEARCH

1. Access the research report presented by Wehman et al. (2012) listed in the "Recommended Resources" section of this chapter.

2. In groups of your peers or other school personnel, discuss the implications of implementing such a project in your school.

POSTSECONDARY EDUCATION

Transition to postsecondary education can be a goal for many young adults with ASD. If so, then the transition plan should include preparatory work for proficiency tests and assessments (i.e., SATs). Once a particular program or school is identified, you may want to determine what services it may offer to help young people with ASD. Many universities have a department that specializes in ensuring compliance with federal legal requirements (OAR, 2012).

Deciding what type and size of college to attend and where the student is going to live are important considerations. Several things should be taken into account when making these choices, including the decision to pursue vocational or technical school, community college, or 4-year university and the proximity of these campuses to home. The size of the school should also be a consideration—sometimes, navigating a large campus can be daunting, yet larger schools often have programs to support individuals with ASD. Technical or trade schools may allow the student to focus on his or her concentrated area of interest or skill. In addition, support providers should give serious consideration to the best type living arrangement for the student. Should the student live on or off campus, have roommates, have to take public or private transportation to campus, and so on?

One thing to give specific attention to is self-advocacy. No longer will the young adult's school be held responsible for advocacy, and instead, the burden falls to the student, rather than school personnel or parents. "In fact, self-advocacy skills are considered so critical to your child's success in college that many such institutions do not even have a mechanism by which you, as a parent, may advocate on their behalf" (OAR, 2012, p. 36).

Skills needed in postsecondary education include the ability to organize assignments, manage time, set priorities, and break down projects into steps. Independent living skills also important are doing laundry, money management, cleaning one's dorm room or living quarters, problem solving, living with a roommate, and so forth (OAR, 2012).

Participants in Mitchell and Beresford's research described a number of supports they felt necessary to ensure a successful postsecondary experience. Participants acknowledged that the transfer from high school entailed some degree of administration (a role that their parents had assumed in their school years). They felt that someone organizing meetings and liaising with the college or university regarding their support needs was necessary. Participants also expressed that the process of decision-making, moving to college, finding out important information, and settling in raised anxieties and concerns and that having someone to talk to about these concerns was highly valued (Mitchell & Beresford, 2014). Overall, the young adults in Mitchell and Beresford's (2014) research said they welcomed the involvement of practitioners in helping them make the transition.

INDEPENDENT LIVING SKILLS

When we think of the young adult transitioning into new environments, it is important to give consideration to the students' daily living skills. Are there sensory issues that could impact daily living, such as sensitivity to noise and smells, lighting, or taste? It may impact the environment in which the young adult can work or attend school successfully. Common issues such as attending to personal hygiene, dressing properly, waking up to an alarm clock, getting to work or class on time, shopping, understanding how to navigate lunch time, finding the public restroom when needed, and acquiring transportation—all of these issues should be taken into account when planning for transition to adulthood.

It is also important to give consideration to the individual's problem-solving and decision-making skills (Adreon & Durocher, 2007). Budgeting, managing bank accounts, shopping, organizational capacity, using phones and e-mail, and managing any necessary medication should also be carefully considered as we plan for transitioning to adulthood. We should also not overlook the importance of disclosure when necessary, to employers or fellow workers, to college professors or peers, or to neighbors.

Adjusting to the social demands of life beyond high school should be under consideration. Young adults with ASD run the risk of social isolation due to their difficulty forming relationships, and due to their naïveté, others might exploit them (Adreon & Durocher, 2007). Consider planning where and to whom the young adult with ASD can go when he or she feels stressed, has questions, or feels overwhelmed or confused by social demands. We must take into account any supports needed to handle any of these tasks in planning for the transition to adulthood.

Interventions should focus on building social and communication skills that can improve the quality of interactions with others (Carter et al., 2013). This involves providing explicit instruction in conversational skills, turn-taking, initiating interactions, cooperating, and the like. Instruction should target specific skills needed to promote success when connecting with others in classroom, workplace, and community settings (Carter et al., 2013). "Connecting adolescents with ASD to community experiences that will launch them seamlessly and successfully toward adulthood is a central task of secondary and transition education" (Carter et al., 2013, p. 895). Our efforts to support meaningful community participation "can have a long-term impact on both the proximal outcomes and long-term trajectories of these important members of our schools and communities" (Carter et al., 2013, p. 895).

Kandalaft et al. (2013) implemented an intervention designed to assist with the transition to adulthood through the development of social cognition skills. They implemented virtual reality using Second Life, a three-dimensional virtual world software program. The intervention included avatars, representing the user in a virtual world, to navigate environments, including an office building, a fast-food restaurant, an apartment, a coffee house, an outlet store, a school, and a park. This intervention provided opportunities to engage in, practice, and attain feedback on relevant young adult social scenarios, such as interacting with a friend, initiating conversation, meeting strangers, negotiating with a salesperson, participating in a job interview, managing conflict with coworkers, and going on a date (Kandalaft et al., 2013).

Participants who navigated the virtual reality social situations in Kandalaft et al.'s (2013) research reported that the intervention provided "years of social training in just a few sessions" (p. 41) and that many people could benefit from the intervention. They said that using the computer intervention assisted with boosting their overall confidence and drawing them into social situations, and it gave them a greater willingness to experience social opportunities (Kandalaft et al., 2013).

Inclusion Tips
SUPPORTING TRANSITION TO ADULTHOOD

1. Provide opportunities to interact with same-age peers to help with building and sustaining friendships. Interactions during academic periods, lunch, or homeroom are good opportunities that can be worked into the regular school day.

2. As much as possible, build real-life situations into lessons, such as simulated workplace tasks, money management, shopping, and home management.

3. Make time to help students develop a resume, search for suitable employment, and prepare for job interviews. Consider holding mock interviews for practice.

4. Build lessons into the curriculum that help develop social skills, such as initiating or sustaining a conversation, interpreting body language, and so forth.

FAMILY INVOLVEMENT IN TRANSITION

For students with ASD, leaving high school and entering the adult world is a process that requires preparation and planning, as well as family support, to ensure that this transition is a successful one. Families of young adults with ASD face a difficult time when they think of their child transitioning to adulthood. Their child must learn to navigate transitions such as getting a job and/or pursuing postsecondary education and potentially new living situations and daily routines. Their child may be moving from public school services to the adult services system or a loss of formal support systems. The challenges that young adults face with social interactions and communication can further compound these issues for the family. In this section, we will highlight current research on best practices for supporting our students and their families during this major life transition.

Families of children with ASD can experience stress associated with transitional planning (Smith & Anderson, 2014). They may share their young adult's excitement about the future while also feeling uncertain about the challenges their child might encounter. And they may be unaware of how to navigate the transitional process to ensure it is a successful one. Smith and Anderson (2014) suggested that families of children with ASD feel less comfortable with the transition process, and they experience higher levels of anxiety prior to high school exit as they anticipate what will happen in the future. They may be concerned about postsecondary education—the level of coursework, potential problems in social arenas, their student's preparedness, and the college's ability to provide appropriate supports (Smith & Anderson, 2014). The needs of families can be multifaceted and complex. "As such, successful programming to support families as they support their students through the transition process likely will need to include approaches that are intensive, comprehensive, and multidisciplinary" (Smith & Anderson, 2014, p. 117).

Smith and Anderson (2014) provided a thorough summary of best practices that support families of students with ASD in the transition process. The researchers took a well-established intervention approach that was originally developed for families of individuals with psychiatric conditions and adapted it for families of young adults with ASD. Their comprehensive program involves education on a variety of topics related to transition planning and guided practice in problem solving around difficulties and stress (Smith & Anderson, 2014). The families in their research were eager for such supports, and the outcomes were favorable.

Schools can assist families by providing meaningful opportunities to inform and involve them in supporting the young adult with ASD as they transition to adulthood. Some suggested activities include holding family workshops, sharing insights with parents about how their child learns and assisting them in using strategies that work best for their student, hosting youth self-advocacy-building workshops, and hosting a community family support group, for example. Schools can host workshops for young adults to assist in résumé writing, searching for a job, or interview skills. Develop connections with local employers, and host a job fair for students and their families. Host family workshops to teach and discuss how to navigate postsecondary education. Form liaisons with local businesses to hold mock interviews or even potential employment opportunities. Steer families to local agencies and websites that provide support in the transition to adulthood. Above all, seek to understand the family perspective in the transition process, and work toward providing necessary supports to ensure a successful transition.

SUMMARY STATEMENTS

- Symptoms of ASD can make the transition to adulthood a challenge.

- Employment is a desirable achievement for individuals with ASD who are transitioning to adulthood. However, unemployment and underemployment are profound issues for these adults.

- Transition planning for individuals with ASD should begin 3 to 4 years prior to exiting the school system, perhaps as young as 14 years of age.

- Deciding the type and size of college to attend and living arrangements, as well as self-advocacy skills, organization, time management, and sources of support, are some important considerations when planning for a transition to postsecondary education.

- Daily living skills, such as sensitivities, personal hygiene, time management, problem solving, decision-making, and use of transportation should be considered when planning for the transition to adulthood.

- Families of children with ASD can experience stress associated with transitional planning. They may share their young adult's excitement about the future while also feeling uncertain about the challenges their child might encounter. And they may be unaware of how to navigate the transitional process to ensure it is a successful one.

WHAT WOULD YOU DO?

Look back at the case study about Grant presented at the beginning of the chapter. Based on what you have read in this chapter, what you have read in previous chapters, and your own experiences, how would you respond to the following questions?

1. What kind of business would you suggest for Grant to collaborate with for an internship project? What kinds of job skills would be a good match for Grant?

2. What are some ways that Grant's teacher could modify assignments or adjust the content that could capitalize on his particular interests of crime solving and cooking?

3. What behavior management strategies would you suggest for Grant (i.e., when he tears up his math worksheet and throws his pencil)?

4. Would you recommend trade/ vocational school or university for

(Continued)

(Continued)

Grant, and why? In what ways would you prepare Grant for transition to postsecondary education, if it is an appropriate option for him?

5. How would you respond to Grant's mother, who would like to prepare him to enter the workforce and live independently?

CHAPTER REFLECTION QUESTIONS

1. Given what you have just read in this chapter, what was the most powerful insight you have acquired, and what are the implications for your teaching?

2. How can the symptoms of ASD impact employment for our students?

3. How do we best address the transition to postsecondary education for our students with ASD?

4. Imagine that the local school district is recommending that all staff incorporate activities to aid in transition to employment for adolescents with ASD. What tips would you share about how to do this effectively?

5. What strategies would you suggest for a general-education teacher who has several students with ASD who are ready to transition to adulthood?

6. In what ways can you work with families and caregivers to implement some of the strategies from this chapter at home?

RECOMMENDED RESOURCES

Websites

- Autism Speaks. *Why a transition plan?* Available at https://www.autismspeaks.org/family-services/tool-kits/transition-tool-kit/why-transition-plan

- Autism Transition Handbook. Available at http://www.autismhandbook.org/index.php?title=Transition_Planning_during_the_School_Years

- Sarris, M. (2014). Coming of age: Autism and the transition to adulthood. *Interactive Autism Network.* Available at https://iancommunity.org/ssc/autism-transition-to-adulthood

Articles/Publications

- Organization for Autism Research. (2012). *Life journey through autism: Navigating the special education system.* Arlington, VA: Author.

- Wehman, P., Schall, C., McDonough, J., Molinelli, A., Riehle, E., Ham, W., & Thiss, W. R. (2012). Project SEARCH for youth with autism spectrum disorders: Increasing competitive employment on transition from high school. *Journal of Positive Behavioral Interventions, 15*(3), 144–155.

- Autism Speaks. (2013). *What job is right for you?* Retrieved from https://www.autismspeaks.org/sites/default/files/docs/etk_what_job_is_right_for_you.pdf

REFERENCES

Adreon, D., & Durocher, J. S. (2007). Evaluating the college transition needs of individuals with high-functioning autism spectrum disorders. *Intervention in School and Clinic, 42*(5), 271–279.

Autism Speaks. (n.d.). Postsecondary educational opportunities guide. Retrieved from https://www.autismspeaks.org/family-services/toolkits/postsecondary

Autism Speaks. (2013). *What job is right for you?* Retrieved from https://www.autismspeaks.org/sites/default/files/docs/etk_what_job_is_right_for_you.pdf

Carter, E. W., Harvey, M. N., Taylor, J. L., & Gotham, K. (2013). Connecting youth and young adults with autism spectrum disorders to community life. *Psychology in the Schools, 50*(9), 888–898.

Chen, J. L., Sung, C., & Pi, S. (2015). Vocational rehabilitation service patterns and outcomes for individuals with autism of different ages. *Journal of Autism and Developmental Disorders, 45*, 3015–3029.

Individuals with Disabilities Education Act (IDEA), 20 U.S.C. § 1400 (2004).

Kandalaft, M. R., Didehbani, N., Krawczyk, D. C., Allen, T. T., & Chapman, S. B. (2013). Virtual reality social cognition training for adults with high-functioning autism. *Journal of Autism and Developmental Disorders, 43*, 34–44.

Matthews, N. L., Smith, C. J., Pollard, E., Ober-Reynolds, S., Kirwan, J., & Malligo, A. (2015). Adaptive functioning in autism spectrum disorder during the transition to adulthood. *Journal of Autism and Developmental Disorders, 45*, 2349–2360.

Mitchell, W., & Beresford, B. (2014). Young people with high-functioning autism and Asperger's syndrome planning for and anticipating the move to college: What supports a positive transition? *British Journal of Special Education, 41*(2), 151–171.

Organization for Autism Research (OAR). (2012). *Life journey through autism: Navigating the special education system.* Arlington, VA: Author.

Roberts, K. D. (2010). Topic areas to consider when planning transition from high school to post-secondary education for students with autism spectrum disorders. *Focus on Autism and Developmental Disabilities, 25*(3), 158–162.

Smith, L. E., & Anderson, K. A. (2014). The roles and needs of families of adolescents with ASD. *Remedial and Special Education, 35*(2), 114–122.

Sung, C., Sanchez, J., Kuo, H. J., Wang, C. C., & Leahy, M. J. (2015). Gender differences in vocational rehabilitation service predictors of successful competitive employment for transition-aged individuals with autism. *Journal of Autism and Developmental Disorders, 45*, 3204–3218.

Taylor, J. L., Henninger, N. A., & Mailick, M. R. (2015). Longitudinal patterns of employment and postsecondary education for adults with autism and average-range IQ. *Autism, 19*(7), 785–793.

Taylor, J. L., & Seltzer, M. M. (2011). Employment and post-secondary educational activities for young adults with autism spectrum disorders during the transition to adulthood. *Journal of Autism and Developmental Disorders, 41*, 566–576.

Wehman, P., Schall, C., McDonough, J., Molinelli, A., Riehle, E., Ham, W., & Thiss, W. R. (2012). Project SEARCH for youth with autism spectrum disorders: Increasing competitive employment on transition from high school. *Journal of Positive Behavioral Interventions, 15*(3), 144–155.

Wilczynski, S. M., Trammell, B., & Clarke, L. S. (2013). Improving employment outcomes among adolescents and adults on the autism spectrum. *Psychology in the Schools, 50*(9), 876–887.

Glossary

ABC model of behavior (antecedent, behavior, consequence): A model for analyzing behavior to determine the antecedent (the cue, signal, or condition that influences a behavior), the behavior (an observable act that a person does), and the consequence (the outcome and/or feedback that occurs immediately following the behavior.

Accommodations: Strategies to help individuals learn the **same** material as their classmates, without modifying the curriculum (i.e., an audio recording of the text, extra time on a test, etc.).

Adaptations: Changes to the curriculum that allow individuals with disabilities to participate in inclusive environments by compensating for the learner's weaknesses.

Adaptive behavior: The collection of skills that people learn to function in their daily lives, including conceptual skills (literacy, numeracy, and self-direction), social skills (interpersonal skills, following rules, obeying laws, self-esteem, etc.) and practical skills (personal care, money use, safety, health care, using travel/transportation, schedules/routines, etc.).

Adaptive functioning: The ability of a person to interact with others and care for oneself.

ADOS: The Autism Diagnostic Observation Schedule, which is an instrument for diagnosing and assessing the communication, social interaction, and play behaviors for individuals suspected of having autism.

Anecdotal records: Informal notes that observers make about a behavior event.

Antecedent: Something that comes before a behavior and may trigger that behavior.

Applied behavior analysis: The process of systematically applying interventions based on the principles of learning theory to improve behaviors to a meaningful degree; the use of techniques and principles to bring about meaningful and positive change in behavior.

Assessment: An evaluation of the nature, quality, or ability of someone or something; documenting and using data to measure what students know and can do.

Assistive technology: Any piece of equipment, item, software program, or product that is used to increase the functional capabilities of persons with disabilities.

Auditory processing: The ability to recognize and process what other people are saying; taking in information verbally; making meaning of sounds; decoding. Auditory processing disorder is unrelated to hearing.

Augmentative and alternative communication (AAC): Includes all forms of communication (other than oral speech) used to express thoughts, needs, wants, and ideas; provides a means of communication for those who cannot speak.

Behavior support plan: A plan that assists an individual in building positive behaviors that replace or reduce challenging behaviors; outlines the steps to be used to promote the individual's success and participation in daily activities and routines.

Central coherence: The ability to understand context, or see the big picture; the ability to focus on both details, as well as the wholes; a person with weak central coherence appears to have a heightened focus on details rather than wholes.

Chaining: A behavior chain is a series of related behaviors, each of which provides a cue for the next; chaining involves the reinforcement of successive elements of a behavior chain.

Childhood Autism Rating Scale: A behavior rating scale intended to help diagnose autism; a trained clinician rates items indicative of ASD.

Cognitive assessment: An assessment of the cognitive function or mental processing of individuals with ASD.

Cognitive flexibility: The brain's ability to transition from thinking about one concept to another or to think about multiple concepts simultaneously.

Collaboration: The process of two or more people working together to realize or achieve a common purpose.

Common Core State Standards: Guidelines for what every student should know and be able to do in math and

English language arts from kindergarten through 12th grade, designed to ensure students are prepared for college and the work force; the Common Core focuses on developing critical-thinking, problem-solving, and analytical skills.

Concept diagrams: A graphical organizer that assists students in clarifying relationships between central concepts.

Consequences: Something that follows a behavior that makes it more or less likely to occur again in the future.

Didactic interventions: Didactic interventions present information directly from the teacher to the student, in which the teacher selects the topic of instruction, controls instructional stimuli, asks for a response from the child, evaluates the child's responses, and provides reinforcement for correct responses and feedback for incorrect ones; usually more rigid in nature than naturalistic approaches to teaching.

Disability: A legal term that indicates a physical or mental impairment that substantially limits one or more major life activity.

Early regression: The loss of social and communication skills in early stages of development (typically in the second year of life); an early history of typical development for 12–24 months, which is followed by a loss.

Executive functioning: A set of processes that all have to do with managing oneself and one's resources in order to achieve a goal; mental control and self-regulation.

Expressive language: The output of language; how one expresses his or her needs and wants.

Family-centered practices: A set of beliefs and practices that recognizes the family's values and beliefs as important components of educational decision-making; requires collaboration among children, families, professionals, and educators to best support the educational needs of the child; recognizing that all families have a range of strengths, beliefs, emotions, and goals for their child.

Fine motor skills: Small movements, such as picking up small objects and holding a spoon that use the small muscles of the fingers, toes, wrists, lips, and tongue.

Functional behavioral assessment (FBA): An approach for determining why a child behaves in a particular way; uses a variety of techniques to understand what is behind inappropriate behaviors; basic idea is that the child's behavior serves a purpose.

Functional skills: Those skills a student needs in order to live independently; includes life skills, community living skills, social skills.

Generalization: Refers to the transfer of what is learned in one setting or situation to another setting or situation.

Gestural prompts: Providing a cue to use a behavior or skills though the use of gestures (i.e., pointing or touching an object).

Gilliam Autism Rating Scale: A widely used norm-referenced instrument that assists teachers and clinicians in identifying and diagnosing autism in individuals aged 3–22 years and in estimating the severity of the child's disorder.

Gross motor skills: Bigger movements, such as rolling over and sitting, that use the large muscles in the arms, legs, torso, and feet.

Guided reading: An instructional approach that involves a teacher working with a small group of students of similar ability, providing reading instruction with skillful scaffolding.

Hypersensitivity: Oversensitive; extremely acute sensitivity to environmental stimuli; receiving too much information via the senses so the brain becomes overloaded; too much information can cause stress, anxiety, and sometimes physical pain.

Hyposensitivity: Undersensitive; a lower-than-expected sensitivity to stimuli; to stimulate their senses, individuals might wave their hands around or rock back and forth or make noises.

Incidental teaching: Involves creating a learning environment in which students' interests are easily fostered and nurtured, which maximizes learning opportunities through typical activities.

Inclusive classroom: A classroom in which students with and without disabilities learn together.

Individual work systems: A structured system, often done with visual cues, that explain to students the work that needs to be done, how much work should be done, how to know when they are finished, and what to do next.

Individualized education program (IEP): A legal document that outlines the child's learning needs, the services the school will provide, and how progress will be measured.

Joint attention: The shared focus of two individuals on an object or event; the ability to coordinate one's own attention between an object and another person to indicate a need or to share interest.

Least restrictive environment: The requirement that children with disabilities should spend as much time as possible with peers who do not receive special education services, to the maximum extent that is appropriate for the child.

M-CHAT-R/F: The Modified Checklist for Autism in Toddlers, Revised, with Follow-Up; a parent-reported screening tool to assess risk for autism spectrum disorder in toddlers between 16 and 30 months of age.

Maladaptive/maladjusted behavior: Behaviors that do not allow an individual to adjust well to certain situations; typically disruptive and dysfunctional; typically used as a means to reduce anxiety but are not effective in this regard; maladaptive behaviors associated with autism are rituals (repeated behaviors such as compulsively washing hands), self harm, tantrums, aggressive behaviors, and behaviors such as rocking, pacing, or scratching; behaviors that are detrimental to the individual.

Mand-modeling: Involves the teacher or caregiver modeling and/or manding (requesting) a response from the child; if the child makes the correct response, the teacher or caregiver then praises the child.

Milieu teaching: An intervention in which individuals are taught language skills and behaviors within the natural environment (the milieu).

Modifications: Changes what a student is taught or expected to learn; modifications to the curriculum might be a shorter or easier reading assignment, only 10 words on a spelling test, or different testing materials; children who receive modifications are not expected to learn the same material as their classmates.

Motor delays: Delays in body movements, such as learning to sit up, crawl, or walk, as compared with speech delays.

Naturalistic interventions: A collection of practices used across settings and within routines and activities that occur through the day.

Negative punishment: Removal of a reinforcer in response (preferred) to an unwanted behavior; reduces the likelihood of the behavior occurring again by removing the preferred stimulus.

Negative reinforcement: Removal of an aversive stimulus after a particular behavior is exhibited; increases the likelihood of the behavior occurring again due to the removal/avoiding the negative consequence.

Nonverbal communication skills: Communication between two people without words, through the use of behaviors such as such as hand gestures, eye contact, facial expressions, touch, physical distance, and so forth.

Operant behavior: Behavior that "operates" on the environment or is controlled by the individual; done because it produces some type of consequence.

Peer-mediated interventions: Interventions in which peers are trained to provide necessary tutoring through interaction, modeling, or reinforcement.

Picture exchange communication system (PECS): An augmentative/alternative communication method that teaches an individual to give or point to a picture of a desired item or event to a person who honors the exchange as a request.

Pivotal response treatment: An intervention based on applied behavior analysis that is implemented in the natural environment (e.g., during regularly scheduled activities such as play time, meals, school, outings, etc.); based on four pivotal areas of development, which are motivation, responding to multiple cues, self-initiations, and self-management.

Positional prompts: Putting the correct response closest to the learner (e.g., teacher shows the learner three items—a toy truck, a ball, and an apple—then asks the learner to point to which item you can eat and places the apple closest to the learner).

Positive behavior supports (PBS): A process for understanding why an individual engages in a particular behavior and strategies for preventing the occurrence of the problem behavior while teaching new skills.

Positive punishment: Presenting a negative consequence after an undesired behavior is exhibited, making the behavior less likely to happen in the future.

Positive reinforcement: Presenting a reward following a desired behavior, making the behavior more likely to happen in the future.

Pragmatic intervention: An intervention that focuses on initiation and spontaneity in communication, which follows the child's focus of attention and motivations.

Pragmatic language: The social language skills we use in daily interactions with others, including what we say, how we say it, our body language, and whether it is appropriate to the given situation.

Prompting: A cue or hint that induces a person to perform a behavior that might not otherwise occur.

Receptive language: The understanding of language input, including words and gestures.

Reinforcer: Something that increases the likelihood of a specific behavior or response occurring again.

Respondent behavior: Behavior that occurs in response to a stimulus.

Self-regulated strategy development (SRSD): A strategy used to improve writing behaviors; an instructional approach designed to help students learn, use, and adopt the strategies used by skilled writers; encourages students to monitor, evaluate, and revise their writing, which reinforces self-regulation skills and independent learning.

Self-regulation: The ability to monitor and control your own behavior; ability to focus attention, control emotions, and manage one's thinking, behavior, and feelings.

Sensory input: Stimuli that is perceived by our senses, like smell, sight, touch, taste, or hearing.

Sensory overload: Occurs when one or more of the body's senses experiences overstimulation from the environment.

Shaping: Technique whereby behavior is modified by stepwise reinforcement of behaviors that produce progressively closer approximations of the final desired behavior; instead of waiting for the individual to exhibit a desired behavior, any behavior leading to the target behavior is rewarded until finally the target behavior is reached.

SMART goals: Goals that are specific, measurable, achievable, results-focused, and time-bound.

Social cognition: How people process, store, and apply information about other people and social situations; understanding social interactions; gathering information about and understanding social rules.

Social communication impairments: Inappropriate use of language and/or gestures in social contexts.

Social communication questionnaire (SCQ): One tool used to screen an individual for ASD, completed by caregivers and evaluated by a trained professional.

Social engagement: The degree of one's participation in a community or society; the ability to work constructively in social groups; the interaction between people.

Social reciprocity: The back-and-forth flow of social interaction; how the behavior of one person influences and is influenced by the behavior of another and vice versa.

Social scripts: A narrative that provides instruction for a specific social situation (e.g., a script instructing one how to order a meal at a restaurant and saying "thank you" when the meal arrives).

Social Stories: A text or story describing a specific social situation, describing who is involved, what happens, when the event takes place, and how it happens; a sequence of visuals that explain and illustrate social concepts.

Stereotypic behaviors: Repetitive or ritualistic movements or utterances.

Systematic instructions: A method of teaching that includes presenting material in small steps, pausing to check for understanding, and student practice after each step.

Task analysis: The analysis of how a task is accomplished, including a detailed description of activities involved in the task; breaking down complex tasks into a sequence of smaller steps or actions.

Transitional planning: A section of a high school student's IEP that outlines strengths, abilities, and goals for life after high school.

Treatment and Education of Autistic and related Communication-handicapped CHildren (TEACCH): A system of diagnostic evaluations, parent training and support, and interventions that address the learning characteristics of individuals with ASD, including their strengths and challenges, to promote meaningful engagement in activities, flexibility, independence, and self-efficacy.

Verbal prompts: Verbal hints, clues, or directions that provide a cue to use a desired behavior.

Video modeling: A visual teaching method that occurs by watching a video of someone modeling a targeted behavior or skills and then imitating the behavior or skill watched.

Video self-modeling (VSM): A visual teaching method using a video recording as a model, whereby the student views a video recording of themselves performing the behavior or skill successfully.

Vineland Adaptive Behavior Scales: An assessment tool for evaluating adaptive behaviors, including the ability to cope with environmental changes, to learn new everyday skills and to demonstrate independence; evaluates communication, daily living skills, socialization, motor skills, and maladaptive behavior.

Visual cues: Visual prompts or hints to exhibit a desired behavior.

Visual schedules: The use of pictures to communicate a series of activities or steps of a specific activity; used to help children understand and manage daily events.

Visual scripts: Written and pictorial examples of phrases or sentences that provide cues for verbal interactions.

Vocal stereotypy: Nonfunctional speech, such as singing, babbling, repetitive grunts, squeals, or phrases that are unrelated to the present situation.

Work systems: Instructional strategies that use visual supports to increase independent functioning; a visually organized space where learners can independently practice skills that define the tasks the learners are expected to do, how much work is to be completed, how the learner knows when he or she is finished, and what do to when he or she is finished.

Working memory: The cognitive function responsible for keeping information, manipulating it, and using it in one's thinking; the ability to remember and use relevant information during an activity (e.g., remembering the teacher's instructions, recalling the rules of a game, or recalling the steps of a recipe while cooking).

Index

impairments in social, 6–8
in inclusive classrooms, 190–191
joint attention, 180–181
picture exchange communication system
    (PECS), 184–186
pivotal response treatment for, 189
school-family collaboration differences in, 47–52
script training for, 190
social, 179–180
technical aids for, 186–187
video modeling for, 189–190
Consequences of behaviors, 106–108
Consequence strategies, 127–130
Context of behaviors, 106
Cramer, S. F., 51
Cue cards, 150
Culture:
    awareness of, 29–31
    linguistic diversity and, 45–47
Current life contexts, 52

Daily living, skills for independent, 269–270
Dake, L., 188
Data gathering, in assessment, 61–62
Davison, K., 34
deFur, S., 29
Delayed development, 5–6
Delay procedure, in milieu teaching, 255
Depression, 12
Deris, A. R., 249
Descriptive sentences, in social stories, 163
Determining interests, 271–272
Diagnostic and Statistical Manual, Fifth Edition
    (*DSM-5*, APA), 6–7
Diagnostic assessment, 62–64
Di Carlo, C. F., 249
Didactic methods, communications skills taught by, 181
Dillon, G., 33, 35
Direction of communication, 48–50
Disability, cultural interpretations of, 29–30
Discrete-trial teaching, 91–93
DSM-5 (*Diagnostic and Statistical Manual,*
    Fifth Edition, APA), 6–7

Early interventions. *See* Interventions, early
Echolalia, 12, 178
Educational decision making, family involvement in,
    21, 77–78

Edwards, R. P., 162
Emerson, E., 34
Emotional control, 223
Emotional vulnerability, 12
Empathetic listening, 23
Employment issues, 265–267, 273–275
Environmental influences in ASD, 4
Environmental supports, 137–157
    ASD-necessitated modifications, 139–141
    case study on, 137–138
    classroom physical structure as, 141–144
    family involvement in, 152–154
    overview, 138–139
    TEACCH (Treatment and Education of Autistic
        and related Communication-handicapped
        CHildren) as, 144–145
    visual supports as, 146–152
    See also Positive behavior supports (PBS)
Evidence-based practices, 71–73
Executive function:
    cognitive flexibility in, 225–227
    planning and organization in, 229–230
    response inhibition in, 224–225
    role of, 222–224
    self-regulation in, 228–229
    working memory in, 227–228

Families, 19–40
    academic skills and, 214
    applied behavior analysis with, 95–96
    assessment and, 75–77
    case study on, 19
    children, respect for, 22
    communicating with, 23–26
    communication skills and, 191–192
    cultural awareness, 29–31
    early intervention involvement by, 248, 257–259
    educational decision making with, 21, 77–78
    environmental supports and, 152–154
    functional behavioral assessments (FBAs)
        and, 112–114
    functional skills teaching with, 239
    goal and intervention development with, 26–27, 247
    partnering with, 20–21
    perspective centered on, 22–23
    positive behavior supports (PBS) and, 131–132
    social skills development and, 172–173
    stress of, 31–35

Individuals with Disabilities Education Improvement
    Act (IDEA) of 2004, 14–15, 71, 270
Individuals with Disabilities Education Improvement
    Act (IDEA) of 2006, 20
Inequality, perceptions of, 52–53
Ingersoll, B., 183
Initiative, taking, in parent-school partnerships, 25
Instructional planning. *See* Assessment, instructional
    planning and
Interests, determining, 271–272
Interventions:
    assessment linked to, 65
    behavior intervention plans, 109–112
    delivered by peers, 236
    evaluating positive behavior supports in, 130
    meeting IEP goals by, 71–72
    Project ImPACT, 192
Interventions, early, 243–262
    case study on, 243–244
    classroom conditions for, 247–248
    communication skills development in, 254
    family involvement in, 257–259
    goal development in, 246–247
    instructional approaches to, 252–254
    milieu teaching in, 255–257
    modeling in, 251–252
    naturalistic teaching in, 252
    overview, 244–245
    reinforcement in, 251
    screening for autism, 245–246
    sensory stimulation and, 249
    visual supports in, 250
    work systems in, 250–251
Iossifov. I., 4

Jain, A., 4–5
Johnson, C., 258
Joint attention, 180–181
Jordan, Dixie, 100–101
Journal of the American Medical Association, 4
Julien, H. M., 254
Jung, A. W., 46

Kamps, D., 231
Kandalaft, M. R., 277
Katz, E., 253
King, Bryan, 4–5
Koegel, R. L., 189

Krantz, P. J., 172
Kucharczyk, S., 219

Language:
    assessment of, 63–64
    diversity in, 45–47
    skills in, 12–13
    See also Communication skills
Learning theory, 182
Least restrictive environment (LRE), 73
Ledbetter-Cho, K., 190
Life contexts, current, 52
Light, sensitivity to, 142
Lindeman, D. P., 247
Linguistic diversity, 45–47
Listening, empathetic, 23
Lorimer, P. A., 162
LRE (least restrictive environment), 73

Maladaptive behaviors, as source of family
    stress, 32–33
Malmberg, D. B., 168
Mand-modeling, 255–256
Mathematics, teaching, 211–212
McClannahan, L. E., 172
M-CHAT-R/F (Modified Checklist for Autism in
    Toddlers, Revised with Follow-Up), 244–245
Meadan, H., 139
Melchior, K., 5
Memory, working, 223, 227–228
Menninger, Karl, A., 19
Messages, primary, 50
Michna, A., 139
Milieu teaching, 255–257
Mitchell, W., 276
Modeling:
    early intervention use of, 251–252
    milieu teaching use of, 255–256
Modified Checklist for Autism in Toddlers, Revised
    with Follow-Up (M-CHAT-R/F), 244–245
Moon, T. R., 137
Motor skills, 8, 11–12
Mount, N., 33, 35
Multistep sequence of events, planning for, 222
Myles, B. S., 162

National Health Interview Survey, 2
National Institute of Mental Health (NIMH), 12

Trust, families and, 27–28
Turnbull, A. P., 22, 77, 121

Universal support, in PBS, 122–123
University of North Carolina, 144
University of Washington, 4
U.S. Department of Health and Human Services, 253

Vaccination controversy, ASD and, 4–5
VDE (Virginia Department of Education), 107–108
Video modeling:
　activity transitioning assisted by, 150
　advantages of, 168
　communication skills, 189–190
　developing, 169
　family involvement with, 172–173
　functional skills taught by, 235
Video self-modeling, 235, 239
Vineland Adaptive Behavior Scales, 64
Virginia Department of Education (VDE), 107–108

Visual supports:
　academic skills taught by, 203–204
　classroom, 143–144, 151–152
　early intervention use of, 250
　functional skills taught by, 233–234
　home, 153–154
　schedules as, 146–149, 152–153
　transitions helped by, 150–151
Vocal stereotypy, 8
Voice output communication aids (VOCAs), 186–187

Ware, J. N., 170, 173
Wechsler Intelligence Scale, 64
Wehman, P., 274
Whinnery, S. B., 254
Wilczynski, S. M., 162, 266, 274
Woods, J. J., 247
Working memory, 223, 227–228
Work systems, 145, 239, 250–251
Writing, teaching, 208–211

Young children (ages 3–5). *See* Interventions, early